Red Groove

Acknowledgments

My thanks go to the following jazz lovers and colleagues who had much to do with the production of this book: Mike Gavin, Martin Davidson, Bill Trythall, Ann and Roger Cotterrell, David Fraser, Iain Murray, Stuart Bailey, Kerstan Mackness, Hazel Miller, Kevin Johnson, Steven Joerg; and *Morning Star* stalwarts Ivan Beavis, Cliff Cocker and Dawn Power.

Thanks too to Five Leaves Publications, in particular Ross Bradshaw and Pippa Hennessey.

Red Groove

Jazz writing
from the *Morning Star*

Chris Searle

Five Leaves Publications
in association with the *Morning Star*

Red Groove
by Chris Searle

Published in 2013
by Five Leaves Publications,
PO Box 8786, Nottingham NG1 9AW

www.fiveleaves.co.uk
in association with the Morning Star
www.morningstaronline.co.uk

The reviews in this book first appeared,
sometimes in a slightly different form,
in Chris Searle's weekly jazz column
in the *Morning Star* and are reprinted by permission

ISBN: 978-1907869495

All royalties for *Red Groove* will be paid
to the *Morning Star* Fighting Fund
(tinyurl.com/mstarfightingfund)

Five Leaves acknowledge
financial support from
Arts Council England

Typeset and designed by
Four Sheets Design and Print

Printed by Imprint Digital in Exeter

Contents

Section 2: Live Reviews

Preface

What Chris Searle does is to place jazz musicians in the real world: where they come from, and what impact their environment, both local and global, might have had on their work. It shows how what creative musicians do is in part a way of negotiating the obstacle course of an often patronising, sometimes downright hostile zeitgeist. But Chris always looks for the silver lining, and finds it in a delightfully detailed and imaginative evocation of innumerable moments of recorded and live magic.

A totally unpredicted music and extraordinary historical phenomenon unfolds. (And what a back-story it has: how African-Americans emerged from a life of forced and unpaid labour 'beneath the underdog', fuelling white America's first taste of widespread opulence, to precipitating the United States' first, and I would say only, truly original art form.)

In one of the series of portraits in *Red Groove*, the young British saxophonist Soweto Kinch is quoted as saying about his 2010 record *The New Emancipation*: "It challenges the comfort and complacency of our modern world, when the same conditions that enslaved and immiserated people 150 years ago are still powerfully in effect today. Yet above all it's about celebrating the endurance and resilience of the human spirit."

Much the same could be said about this book itself. There's rigorous scholarship here, yes, but essentially *Red Groove* is a dazzling celebration, motivated by a sense of respect, gratitude and love.

Robert Wyatt
Louth

Introduction

I have been writing a weekly jazz column for the *Morning Star* for a decade and a half, so when I began to compile a selection of them for this present book, I had over seven hundred to choose from. It hasn't been an easy task to exclude so many words on such marvellous music, but I hope that what remains tells something of jazz's century of storytelling and beautiful musicianship. The reviews are in a largely chronological order, according to their recording or performance dates.

To me, at the heart of jazz is a music of unity, freedom and sonic invention, strongly focussed on the real world on which its sounds have been a constant commentary.

When I say 'world' I mean it, for jazz, a music of intense hybridity and syncretism born in the Mississippi Delta in a combustive flux of cultures in New Orleans, has moved everywhere in the world. So this global collection of writings includes jazz virtuosi who go as far beyond the music's birthplace as it is possible to go: from Bengal to Toronto, from Benin to Iraq, from Cuba to Tunisia, from Indian and Chinese provenances to Argentina and Brazil to Palestine and Chicago, from Cape Verde to Cape Town to Sicily and Norway. And because I am an Englishman and grew up as a jazz lover in London fifty years ago, there is much of my own country's jazz within these writings.

And when I write of the 'real world' I hear jazz signalling great human migrations, the struggles for justice and peace, a hatred of war, racism and inequality, an assertion of proud womanhood, a love for humanity and humanity's striving for the betterment of the world. All that is deep inside the passion, artistry and beauty of the sounds of jazz, and the real narrative of a whole century's events bursts from its notes.

My thanks go equally to the powerful music-makers who have invented the cause of these columns, and to the readers, always critical, who have taken the time and empathy to read them, in offices, on buses and trains, building sites and in factories, cafés, workplaces and homes in many parts of Britain where the *Morning Star* is regularly read. I'm grateful to the newspaper's journalists who have always dealt with my weekly handwritten pages with patience and professional skill. And to Robert Wyatt for his preface.

I first met Robert and his partner Alfie Benge more than thirty years ago when we were working to organise 'Art Against Racism and Fascism' with other artists, musicians, actors, comedians and writers in London. We have often met since then, frequently at jazz concerts, the last time being at an astonishing Ornette Coleman concert at, of all places, the Royal Festival Hall. I had been sitting in the stalls during the first half of the performance and was walking from the hall during the interval when I heard someone calling from above, way over my head. I looked up and saw Robert, stretching over the Royal Box balcony. "Hey Chris, come up here!" he shouted. "What, up there?" I answered. "Yes man, we've got a place for you." The RFH management had found the best of spots for Robert's wheelchair, so up I went and put my *Morning Star* backside on a seat next to him and Alfie, where many a royal posterior had parked itself since 1951. I listened to the veteran jazz revolutionary Ornette and his Moroccan fellow players and took my notes (the review is included towards the end of the book). So thanks, Robert, for providing this *Morning Star* reviewer with such a transcendent view of the proceedings, and for an intimation of a day when all privilege in the arts and life will dissolve to the accompaniment of the jazz sound, dancing feet, ever-active brain cells, hearkening ears and the whirling imagination.

And to all my readers, as ever: happy grooving!

Chris Searle

Section 1: Album Reviews

Weeping the Blues

Johnny Dodds

King of the Blues Clarinet

(Upbeat)

The blues dripped from his reed with every note that he blew and, along with his horn partner Louis Armstrong in Hot Five and Hot Seven Chicago recording sessions, he was one of the first sustained soloists in jazz.

Born in New Orleans in 1892, Dodds began learning the clarinet when he was seventeen, and was virtually self-taught. He joined Kid Ory's band in 1912, leaving in 1917 to play with Fate Marable's riverboat orchestra. The 1920s found him in Chicago where he played with legendary New Orleans bandleaders like Freddie Keppard and Joe "King" Oliver, making a living like the millions of others who had also made the great migration northwards to escape southern poverty and Jim Crow racism. The Upbeat *King of the Blues Clarinet* album follows Dodd's jazz journey from 1923 and his early tracks with Oliver in Richmond, Indiana, to his final session in Chicago in 1940. In between times in the 30s — when New Orleans jazz lost much of its popularity — Dodds managed a Chicago apartment building and a cab company, but the blues still lingered in his clarinet and never left him.

From first to last his most regular confrère was his brother Warren "Baby" Dodds, the first of the great jazz drummers. The 1923 Oliver sides have Dodds chirping above Baby's woodblocks in *Mandy Lee Blues*, and in the earliest ever version of *Dippermouth Blues* his stop-time chorus precedes Oliver's sublimely muted solo. He whines appealingly through the Hot Five's *Lonesome Blues* before Armstrong's archetypal vocal.

In 1926 in Chicago he teamed up again with Ory and cornettist George Mitchell in the New Orleans Wanderers for a memorable session. Hear the earthy notes teem from his horn in *Perdido Street Blues*, and in *Gatemouth* his sound kicks and dances in parade memories. In the same year he produced *Stockyards Strut* — a reminder of new Chicago workplaces — with Freddie Keppard, another migrant Crescent City cornet giant, and also recorded with the bigger band of King Oliver's Dixie Syncopators. Brought in especially for the ballad *Someday Sweetheart*, his solo still weeps the blues in a burgeoning new era.

There's a trio rendition of *Oh! Lizzie* with pianist Lil Armstrong and guitarist Bud Scott. Dodds is at his spikiest here, his notes prancing on the edge of the melody. The two Armstrong Hot Seven sides *Willie the Weeper* and *Wild Man Blues* put the two great New Orleans virtuosi together again in unified power and beauty, with Baby crashing his cymbals belligerently in the former, and in the latter the duo follow each other in successive pausing and breaking solos, each emulating and inspiring his colleagues with every unique and pulsating breath, creating one of the truly epochal jazz performances.

In the late 20s Dodds made a series of recordings with washboard bands led by Jimmy Bertrand and Jimmy Blythe. Full of zest, verve and humour, tracks like the lively *My Baby* and the spoofing *Oriental Man* show another dimension to Dodds's blues-soaked sound, while on *Southbound Rag* the trio rambles with guitarist Blind Blake and Bertrand plays a very basic pre-vibes performance on xylophone.

It's back to the Southern blues for his accompaniment to singer Sippie Wallace on the vaunting *I'm a Mighty Tight Woman*, and 1928's *Bull Fiddle Blues* sets Dodds alongside another fine cornetist Natty Dominique. There's also a deeply felt trio version of the spiritual *Steal Away*, showing how much tradition and history blew out of his horn.

The 30s were lean years for Dodds and, a decade on, the session with his Chicago Boys included the New York-born swing trumpeter Charlie Shavers, signalling a new epoch in which the Dodds New Orleans clarinet was out of vogue. Yet as the tracks *29th and Dearborn* and *Blues Galore* show, his sound was still a formidable force not easily doused or quelled — even when set beside the sophisticated guitar of Teddy Bunn or the entirely new smooth timbre of Shavers's horn. And when Dodds re-enters with a long, bleeding note to begin his solo on the former after Shavers finishes his, it is like two jazz worlds in strange but beautiful juxtaposition.

Gravier Street Blues of 1940 — the album's final track, cut in Chicago with Baby, Dominique, trombonist Preston Jackson and the sublime blues guitarist Lonnie Johnson two months before Dodds died — takes us right back to his origins in New Orleans. And we are walking down its streets with him again all the way, the blues pulse throbbing.

19 December 2011

Chemist or Jazzman?

Fletcher Henderson

A Study in Frustration: The Fletcher Henderson Story

(Essential Jazz Classics)

Fletcher Henderson was a true exploring pioneer of jazz, the founder of the music's big band tradition who assembled some of its first great instrumentalists together in a unit which played especially written arrangements, while encouraging all its virtuosi to set themselves loose and free with their solo genius.

He was born to black middle-class parents in Cuthbert, Georgia, in 1897. Luckily for jazz, his mother was a piano teacher, but Fletcher's ambition was within chemistry rather than music. He gained a chemistry degree from Atlanta University and migrated to New York to find work. But the liberal North had no place for a black chemist, so Henderson turned to his mother-taught skills and drifted into bandleading with a libertarian impulse. By 1924 he was heading a stomping band at the luxurious and exclusive Roseland Ballroom for its all-white clientèle.

His fellow musicians were the prime players of the era. Louis Armstrong joined him in 1924, followed through the years by other brilliant trumpeters like Red Allen, Rex Stewart and Roy Eldridge, trombonists Charlie Green, Dickie Wells and Benny Morton and saxophonists like Coleman Hawkins, Ben Webster, Benny Carter and Chu Berry. It was a shimmering galaxy of horns, unmatched even by Ellington's greatest line-ups, yet Henderson's bands never achieved the Duke's consistency or success. Henderson was a notoriously uninterested manager and businessman. The record producer and impresario John Hammond called him "casual to the point of irresponsibility."

After the stock market slump in 1929, he sold two hundred of his arrangements to the rising white "King of Swing", Benny Goodman, in order to survive. Goodman's subsequent fortune and fame was largely due to Henderson's original black musical genius.

Hammond's selection of sixty-four of Henderson's greatest sides, first issued as a four-record combined package in 1961, *A Study in Frustration*, directly reflected the racist obstructions and ignorance that he confronted all his life, while expressing his huge achievement of black sonic artistry, verve and beauty. I remember that I had three of the four LPs, but I never found the fourth, so the three-CD reissue with another ten bonus tracks is precious indeed and full of marvellous music.

Critics used to say that the Henderson band on record never challenged their matchless live appearances, but listen, for example, to the astonishing verve and drive of the March 1931 cut of *Sugar Hill Stomp*, which had already stomped in a previous life as King Oliver's *Dippermouth Blues*. Claude Jones's muted trombone growls in, Stewart's cornet sings, Morton roars a stoptime chorus and Hawkins swings and rumbles out a rampaging solo before the ensemble bring the tune home.

Or how about *Hot and Anxious*, composed by Fletcher's pianist brother Horace? It's only after some worrisome unified hornwork and a true muted oracle from Stewart that the band take up the theme which you quickly realise is the tune that Glenn Miller was to borrow for the famed *In The Mood* more than a decade later straight out of the Henderson family folio. There are some more sublime Stewart and Hawkins choruses in *Blue Moments* of 1932 and, from the same session, Fats Waller's *Honeysuckle Rose* rocks with the gruff slidework of JC Higginbotham and the huge tenor engine of Hawkins. Red Allen replaces Stewart for the pounding *Yeah Man* of 1933, which has a spiky Russell Procope clarinet solo, and Hawkins's tune *Queer Notions* ebbs and flows with its composer's tidal sound.

By 1936 Roy Eldridge had joined the trumpet section, and he soars above the ensemble motion in *Blue Lou* with newcomer in the tenor saxophone chair, the mighty Chu Berry, also cutting loose. *Wild Party* is exactly that with Buster Bailey's rampant liquid clarinet playing host as the ensemble boils over. The reed section jumps joyously all through *Rug Cutter's Swing* and Ben Webster and his tenor emerge from its midst to stamp his signal husky timbre on the proceedings. Allen burns in *Hotter than 'Ell*, chased by a breathless Webster. I've often wondered how much straight autobiography lies in *Jangled Nerves*, with the furious neurosis of its ensemble, and Horace's *Riffin'* of 1936 closes the essential collection with Eldridge searing, passionate and cutting the studio air with his importunate brass zeal.

It is tempting to view Henderson's brilliant life in jazz as a chemist's life frustrated by racism, with music simply a compensation. But, oh, what he gave, and what they took from him too.

19th October 2011

Struggle and Solidarity

Duke Ellington Orchestra

The First Carnegie Hall Concert, January 23 1943

(Prestige)

It was January 23 1943, a week before the German 64th army surrendered to the Soviets in the Stalingrad snows after months of a murderous Nazi invasion and siege, dramatically turning the course of the war. In New York, at the prestigious Carnegie Hall — usually reserved for exclusive classical music concerts — the Duke Ellington Orchestra played a fund-raising concert for Russian War Relief, the first time that the venue had ever been used for a black orchestral jazz concert.

The struggle against fascism was being waged on two continents — in Europe, militarily against Nazism, in America, culturally against the Ku Klux Klan and Jim Crow racism, with the latter openly supporting and raising resources for the former. The Ellington concert marked a unique 20th-century moment and jazz was its international fanfare and signal.

Ellington's orchestra was widely acclaimed by 1943, with a combined personnel that included a matchless battalion of horns. Johnny Hodges was on alto saxophone alongside the rumbling fury of Ben Webster's tenor and Harry Carney's baritone. The trombone section was diversely inspired, with the muted delights of Jamaican Garveyite Joe "Tricky Sam" Nanton, the Latin edge of the orchestra's only non-African-American member, the Puerto Rican Juan Tizol, and the creamy slides of Lawrence Brown. Rex Stewart's half-valve trumpet sounds, Ray Nance and Harold Baker's lucid, burnished solos rose up from the brass chairs too, with Nance frequently switching to his violin.

As the apex of their performance the orchestra played for the first time in public Ellington's pioneering suite of black history and struggle in the US — *Black, Brown and Beige*, a musical forerunner of the Civil Rights movement that followed in the postwar years. Like most revolutionary moments in jazz history, when the orchestra played this suite the responses of the predominantly white critics ranged between lukewarm and hostile. There hadn't been anything like it ever before, neither in jazz itself and certainly not at the Carnegie Hall — a 45-minute "jazz symphony" in three movements which Ellington called "a tone parallel to the history of the American negro," with themes narrating worksongs and the beauteous spiritual theme of *Come Sunday* played by Hodges at his most warm-toned and sublime, which became the climactic sequence of the first movement.

The second movement, *Brown*, emphasised what Ellington called "the West Indian influence" and the integral part played by African-Americans in their country's military campaigns, a truth being played out again at the time in the US struggles against European and Japanese fascism. Vocalist Betty Roche sang earthily that "the blues don't know nobody as a friend" with some beautiful deep and low tenor sax from Webster. But the Soviet people in Stalingrad knew, even if that friendship stretched as far as Harlem and had its voice in jazz.

Beige is the third movement and, as Ellington stresses in his announcement, much of its theme is about the black struggle and aspiration to educate, with Baker and Brown in strong mettle and Stewart's final reprise of the *Come Sunday* theme a chorus of glory.

Black, Brown and Beige was only a part of the concert captured on this double CD. The rest is a succession of classic Ellington performances that show the brilliance of the orchestra's ensemble power and the individual virtuosity of its soloists.

Hear the stomping, rumbustious Webster on *Cotton Tail*, or Nance's serpentine violin strands on Tizol's *Bakiff* with Sonny Greer's booming drums and the composer's own valve trombone motif. Or, one after the other, there is *Jack the Bear* with Junior Raglin slapping his bass like fury under Carney's delving baritone, *Blue Belles of Harlem* with Duke's piano to the fore, Hodges' luscious rhapsody on *Day Dream* and Stewart's mini-concerto *Boy Meets Horn*, where his "squeezed tone" notes find a unique high point. Brown's slides saunter through *Rose of the Rio Grande*, Nance's mute howls out in *Black and Tan Fantasy* and Nanton's growling notes find a perfect pitch at the end of *Portrait of Bert Williams*. Ellington's tribute to the black singer Florence Mills, originally called *Black Beauty*, crackles with Baker's lucid, pure-toned horn.

Hear this precious concert from a time in history where two peoples so profoundly needed each other and their solidarity message rang out in live jazz. It stays in your ears forever.

July 20th 2011

Hunting Notes Together

Roy Eldridge, Dizzy Gillespie, Harry Edison and the Oscar Peterson Quartet

Tour De Force

(Fresh Sound)

Here are three of the truly great jazz trumpeters hunting notes together, led along the trail by one of the most brilliant swinging pianists of jazz, and kept close to the earth by the bass *nonpareil* of the era.

I once met Roy Eldridge in a pub in St Martin's Lane in the mid-1970s and bought him, a black American from Pittsburgh, a very English pint. He said he enjoyed it, which I found surprising. It also surprised and shocked me to hear that this powerful horn artist, while he was the star soloist with the otherwise white Artie Shaw Orchestra in the mid-40s, could only enter the very theatres that displayed his name in lights through the back doors. Yet he was so affable and friendly to me, a strange and admiring white Englishman. A couple of hours later, as he tore into his notes around the corner at Ronnie Scott's, I discovered the intensity which came out in his every breath.

Dizzy Gillespie came from Cheraw, South Carolina. He was a jazz revolutionary and exporter of jazz around the world with his Afro-Cuban Orchestra and musical humour, who always acknowledged Eldridge as his model and mentor. A trumpeter of prodigious technique and high note glory, he provoked absolute excitation, especially when he played with Charlie "Bird" Parker, with him one of the prime founders of bop.

And thirdly Harry Edison, from Columbus, Ohio, who came out of Count Basie's great Kansas City band of the late 30s. Nicknamed "Sweets" by his fellow tenor Lester Young, he blew with incisive power in the ensembles, while his glory with the Harmon mute and his ability, like Basie himself, to create beauty and swing from a minimum of notes made him unique.

In the late 80s I heard Edison at the Leadmill in Sheffield with a local rhythm section. In between numbers and surging solos, this hornman in his mid-seventies used his announcements to roundly curse both Reagan, and the size of his alimony bills.

In 1955 the threesome came together in a New York studio with Oscar Peterson of Montreal, bassist Ray Brown of Pittsburgh, New York swing drummer Buddy Rich and the Texan guitarist Herb Ellis. These were musicians who all knew each other well as long-time associates of "Jazz at the Philarmonic" concerts and tours, but it never stopped them striving or blunted the sharpness of their performances. The *Tour De Force* album, despite its renown on vinyl, has never been reissued before now as a CD, and as soon as Peterson runs up his keys for the opener *Steeplechase* there is the promise of something special.

Eldridge is first out of the traps, his notes bursting with his characteristic subliminal breathiness and urgency, the raw emotion boiling inside his sound while incessant rhythm swings all around him. Gillespie is next up, and while there is less heat, the note selection and execution is faultless with the poised sound an epitome of the balance of sheer technical dexterity and unleashed emotion. Then in comes Sweets, and, although the rhythmic intensity hardly allows it, he finds a more laid-back and almost relaxed time and timbre, dancing on the beat with assured skill and grace.

Such three-horn sessions were often set up to be competitive, gladiatorial and mutually hostile — but not with these three. As they exchange phrases, step aside for each other and weld their successive short breaks into one holistic, shared musical message, the horns of plenty are also horns of co-operation and unity. Peterson steps in at last for a short but romping interval, and the horns fade into silence.

The conventional ballad medley follows with Eldridge blowing *I'm Through with Love* segueing into Gillespie and a delicate, touching version of *The Nearness of You*, with Ray Brown's leaping bass in ascendancy. Eldridge follows his melodic muse for *Moonlight in Vermont*, and Gillespie returns for a brief run through *Summertime.*

But this is all as a breathcatcher for the final title number. *Tour De Force* was always a Gillespie anthem, composed to display his huge bravura. But it is Edison who opens the solo brass proceedings here, fusing his economy of notes with an impassioned delivery. Roy steps in, his underlying huskiness of tone pressing against the boundaries of his sound, with Peterson chinking his accompaniment. Then it is all Gillespie, soaring upwards, plunging downwards, stretching everywhere until his confrères join him in a joyous conversation of comrade horns.

This brass trio was to join up again two decades down the line as the "Trumpet Giants," with other maestros including Freddie Hubbard and Clark Terry. But this meeting will more than do as a scintillating taster of the jazz trumpet played with a varied and diverse brilliance by three unique masters of brass on one excellent day in New York.

December 8th 2010

Hawkin' the Horn

Coleman Hawkins and Ray Bryant
Complete Recordings
(Solar Records)

Coleman Hawkins, the father of the tenor saxophone in jazz, born in St Joseph, Missouri, in 1901, was one of my first jazz heroes. When I first heard his unique sound it seemed like an engine of beauty and untrammelled power, like one of those overwhelming Britannia-class steam locomotives that used to roar between Liverpool Street and Norwich in the 50s — mighty and unstoppable with a huge musical force.

His solo choruses surged forward from the beginnings of recorded jazz history in 1921 when he made his first records with Mamie Smith's Jazz Hounds. In 1924 he became the featured and pioneering tenor soloist in Fletcher Henderson's Orchestra in New York. And the rest was musical history, both in the US and in Europe, where he spent much of the 30s.

Hawkins stayed at the crest of jazz performance until his death in 1969. Yet despite his astonishing talent and legendary status as a jazz inventor, jazz never made him a fortune as he stayed a hard-working jobbing musician all through his life. The story goes that his final gig on his last tour of Britain in the early 60s took place in the not-so-esteemed venue of the saloon bar of the Leysdown Hotel on the Isle of Sheppey, in the holiday camp resort where my family used to go every July for our summer break. For sure, a long, long way from the Big Apple's Roseland Ballroom where the Henderson Orchestra had its 20s and 30s heyday.

During the late 50s, Hawkins teamed up with the young Philadelphia-born pianist Ray Bryant to cut a succession of fine albums. Bryant was only twenty-six when the first of these, *The Coleman Hawkins All-Stars At Newport*, was recorded in 1957.

So it was an amalgam of two far-apart jazz generations taking the stage at the Newport Jazz Festival, with the rest of the band composed of veterans like the Pittsburgh trumpet giant Roy Eldridge, the great Basie drummer and pioneer of the hi-hat Jo Jones, the effervescent Maryland altoist Pete Brown and bassist Al McKibbon, who also plunged his strings into bop. Hawkins takes a rampant solo in *I Can't Believe that You're In Love With Me* and shows his brilliance as a balladeer all through *Moonglow*. The head version of *Sweet Georgia Brown* sprints through some breathless Brown choruses, a typically impassioned Eldridge solo, Hawkins in full and fiery throttle and

Bryant unleashing some pacey keyboard runs in complete empathy with his powerful band members.

In February 1958 Hawkins and Bryant came together again with the Virginian guitarist Tiny Grimes for the sextet album *Blues Groove*. The blues swings of Grimes's chinking strings dominate the rhythm of the groovy and earnest track, the eighteen minutes of *Marchin' Along*. Hawk chugs his way through bar after bar with a huge build-up of emotive strength, his horn throbbing with power while Bryant's blues choruses are lucid and telling. There's the delight of the previously absent-from-CD *Tiny Bean* too, which has some fine Charlie Christian-like guitar from Grimes, and Hawkins chomping into his reed.

In November 1958 the twosome joined with the Detroit ace guitarist Kenny Burrell to record the album *Soul* with bassist Wendell Marshall and Osie Johnson on drums. Burrell's presence lent a closer-to-bop ambience to the proceedings, although in the opener, *Soul Blues*, Hawkins weeps out his notes and Burrell's fleet phrases catch the same mood. The same intensity pervades *I Hadn't Anyone Till You* with a skipping Bryant solo, and *Groovin'* is just that — upbeat and bouncing, while the pure melodic beauty of the English ballad *Greensleeves* doesn't seem out of context at all. Hawk rounds the session off with his own tune, *Sweetnin'*, with romping fast-flowing solos from all members.

Grimes returned for *Hawk Eyes!*, a 1959 album with the stellar swing trumpeter Charlie Shavers. The title tune features some twanging Grimes in stop-time rhythm, Hawkins eating up his notes, Bryant's customary two-handed eloquence and a hair-raising chorus from the often overlooked Shavers. The very bluesy *C'mon In* has some earthy, down-home piano from Bryant and sweet-toned Shavers with a pulsating entry from Hawk, whose engine is fiercely revved up all the way through *Through For the Night*.

The final album of this marvellous 3-CD package is *Stasch*, first released in February 1959, with three extra horns — Detroit baritonist Pepper Adams, Jerome Richardson on alto and flute and the bop trumpeter Idrees Sulieman. There's a much fuller-ensemble sound. On the Kansas City classic *Roll Em Pete*, Hawk unleashes a huge sound from the midst of the reeds, followed by a KC-fired Bryant solo. Wonderful music, great value and the eternal sound of the incomparable Hawkins striding through jazz history.

April 14th 2011

Wilson the Keys

Teddy Wilson Trio with Jo Jones

Complete Recordings

(Essential Jazz Classics)

Pianist Teddy Wilson was born in Austin, Texas, in 1912. Not for nothing was he known as the Marxist Mozart. Benny Goodman said of him: "My pleasure in playing with Teddy Wilson equalled the pleasure I got out of playing Mozart," and his phenomenal swing artistry made him a musician admired and emulated by many of the great musicians of his era.

His father was an English professor at the all-black Tuskegee Institute, where his mother was the chief librarian. Perhaps their influence helped to propel him forward, for during the heyday of the hugely popular swing orchestras in the 30s — when Wilson was still in his twenties — he campaigned and organised relentlessly for the Popular Front in jazz, promoting and supporting musical fundraising for anti-lynching and trade union struggles at home and for the Spanish republicans and Ethiopian people in their resistance to the Italian fascist invasion abroad. By 1943 he was chairing an artists' committee in the campaign to elect black Communist candidate Benjamin Davis to the New York City Council, and was alongside some of the era's greatest jazz musicians as organiser and performer for benefits for Russian war relief.

As a musician, Wilson broke through huge racist barriers. In 1936 he became the first black jazz musician to play with the Benny Goodman Orchestra and was a permanent member of Goodman's trio and quartet. As a young bandleader he led many of the renowned small group sessions of the late 30s with Billie Holiday, Lester Young, Buck Clayton and many of the stellar musicians of the Count Basie and Duke Ellington orchestras.

One of these was Basie's prodigious Chicago drummer Jo Jones, born in 1911, a pioneer among swing drummers who shifted the timekeeping function of the drums from the bass drum to the hi-hat cymbal, creating a whole new buoyancy in the Basie band alongside his partners, pianist Basie, guitarist Freddie Green and bassist Walter Page. "The Basie rhythm section was just like the wind," said fellow drummer Eddie Locke. "It was so smooth."

In January 1955 Wilson and Jones reunited with another swing veteran, bassist Milt Hinton, for a trio session put out on the Verve label, *For Quiet Lovers*, composed of American songbook titles that were second nature to them all, although the opener *Blues For the Oldest Profession* has a much more down-home and earthy feel than the titles that follow. They are the opening tracks of this three-CD package featuring Wilson and Jones on all tracks. A precious reissue indeed.

The sense of constant swinging movement from the first notes of *It Had To Be You*, through *Three Little Words*, *Get Out Of Town* and *When Your Lover Has Gone* relive the Billie Holiday epoch without Billie, but still with the texture and subliminal floating airiness of musicians who create a miraculous lift with note after note, phrase after phrase.

Jones makes the music fly with his astonishing brushwork, and Hinton — unlike the delving, almost subterranean echoing sound of many great jazz bassists — creates a depth of beat which somehow jumps and leaps beside Jones's sweeping brushes and Wilson's precision and purity of tuneful beauty. Listen to them at work on the lightning of *Who's Sorry Now*, which soars Wilson's keys out into the New York skies.

The second session of March 1956 brings in another bass master, Gene Ramey from Louisville, Kentucky, for a continued songbook feast. Jones's brushes shimmer on *Stompin' At the Savoy* as Wilson veers away for his customarily sure-piloted improvisation — *All of Me* and *On the Sunny Side of the Street* crystallise the sheer optimism of the ensemble with brief solo breaks by Ramey and Jones on the former, and a stomping *Limehouse Blues* gets behind the surface chinoiserie and rocks down the Commercial Road and through cosmopolitan East London's streets.

September 1956 brought another trio session with Al Lucas on bass and a further crop of standards. *I Want To Be Happy* is rapid and feather-light, *Laura* radiates sheer melodism but the summation is *When You're Smiling*, where Billie Holiday's sublime 1938 recording with Wilson's band, including Jones, haunts every note. As a bonus this reissue gives us a 1954 trio session without a bass but with the pioneer alto saxophonist Benny Carter stepping squarely in. Carter's angular, quasi-geometric phrases are a foil to Wilson's light keyboard touch and almost levitational swing, and Jones's understated rhythmic pulse. Hear them, three true jazz giants combining their unified genius on *The Birth of the Blues* or the plaintive cry of *When Your Lover Has Gone.*

There are many ways of brilliance and beauty in this threesome, and in Wilson's endless swing there were many ways of struggle too.

September 14th 2011

New Orleans Birdman

George Lewis

In Hi-Fi

(Upbeat)

The great post-bop alto saxophonist Eric Dolphy once said that hearing George Lewis's clarinet breaking out of a New Orleans ensemble was like hearing a burst of birdsong, so pure and close to nature was its tone, so clear and joyous was its timbre. The reissue of the session *In Hi-Fi*, recorded in San Francisco in 1956, gives another opportunity to hear the ex-stevedore's tumbling liquid phrases, his serpentine notes.

I can remember when I bought an EP with four of these tracks while I was discovering jazz in the late 1950s. What excitation rang from them. Lewis's lucid message, trumpeter Thomas Jefferson's vocalised and Armstrong-like power, trombonist Bob Thomas rumbling beneath the other two horns, pianist Alton Purnell jiving his keys, "Slow Drag" Pavageau's relentless bass beat and Joe Watkins' rattling drums. They were men in superb unison, manifesting the common, beautiful unity of the Delta City sound, taped in a faraway West Coast studio looking out to the Pacific Ocean.

By 1956, the New Orleans jazz revival was more than a decade old and Lewis had become one of its prime ambassadors. In 1957, he was to consolidate this with a European tour and a famous recorded concert with the Ken Colyer band at Manchester's Free Trade Hall. But, here, by the 'Frisco Bay, he is part of a revitalised front line and a rocking rhythm section galvanised by Purnell's jumping piano rhythm and Pavageau's bass heartbeat.

All of the musicians show their power and intent during the opener *The Original Dixieland One-Step*. Lewis is chirping like fury, Jefferson's lead is full of brass muscle and Thomas's slides radiate wit and creative surge, with Purnell's comping delights never better recorded as he storms along his keyboard. Lewis has a beautifully restrained low-register solo after Watkins's spirited vocal on *Four or Five Times* and Jefferson shows his command of the mutes. On Armstrong's *Struttin' With Some Barbecue*, the Chicago-born trumpeter inspires his New Orleans line-up into ensemble fire.

But my favourite from this session has always been the rumbustious *Don't Give Up the Ship*, prompted by a short Jefferson fanfare, then it is the Crescent City swing all the way. Lewis is fast, flickering and felicitous in his choruses, Thomas's solo goes well beyond tailgate and Purnell's piano pulsates with verve — a classic track.

Ghosts of New Orleans funeral parades and "second line" salutations arise from *Didn't He Ramble*, with Lewis's flying notes soaring over the levees while Thomas's slides rumble along the earth. The session's final track is a ten-minute-long version of *Tishomingo Blues*. Pavageau's twanging bass sets it all up, Watkins offers an elegaic vocal and then Lewis and Thomas share an evocative horn colloquy, the high and low of their voices in soulful contrast.

A precious opportunity to hear the bird-man's clarinet in a sparser quartet setting is offered on the final six tracks of the album, recorded across the bay in Oakland in 1956-7. Lewis has an empathetic brass partner in trumpeter PT Stanton, plus banjo and bass, and the sheer purity of his sound radiates all through the fizzing opener *Should I?* The much slower *Mecca Flat Blues* follows and Lewis reflects on many of the phrases in the tune he wrote about the New Orleans street where he was born, *Burgundy Street Blues*. Lewis is rhapsodic all through *Till We Meet Again*, plays an exquisitely melodic woodwind song for his chorus in *The Glory of Love*, saunters ruefully through *Good Morning Blues* and warbles and trills as he flies through *Smiles*, as if the sky is his true element.

This is as fine an introductory album to Lewis's lyrical beauty as you will hear — the bird of New Orleans waxing in full flight.

18th March 2009

Intertwined Paths

Thelonious Monk and John Coltrane

At Carnegie Hall
(Blue Note)

During the latter months of 1957, one of the most compelling partnerships in the history of jazz was performing every night at the Five Spot in New York. Monk and Coltrane. Two huge musical imaginations, two jazz originals, each with a unique and epochal consciousness combining their inventive genius.

For Coltrane, it was a critical period. In mid-April, he had departed from the Miles Davis Quintet and was wrestling hard with a heroin addiction. During that summer of 1957, he began to cast off his habit and practised with an even more dedicated frenzy. He later wrote that he had experienced "a spiritual awakening which was to lead me to a richer, fuller, more productive life" and that his catalyst had been Monk and their nightly combinations.

Until now, only one album existed of this collaboration which hastened Coltrane's metamorphosis, an amateur recording released by Blue Note in 1993 called *Live at the Five Spot: Discovery*, taped by Coltrane's wife Naima on a conventional portable tape recorder.

Now, another jazz treasure is exposed — a tape buried in the vaults of the Library of Congress.

The quartet was composed of Monk, Coltrane, bassist Ahmed Abdul-Malik — born Sam Gill in New York, of Sudanese parents — and drummer Shadow Wilson, an ex-Basieite who had a sizeable reputation as a big band drummer. The occasion was a fundraising Thanksgiving concert, a benefit for the Morningside Community Center which was an oasis for local, mainly black, dispossessed Harlem youth and which offered a day nursery, a "mental hygiene" clinic and the prospect of summer camp escape. On stage, too, were Dizzy Gillespie, Ray Charles, Billie Holiday, Sonny Rollins, Zoot Sims and Chet Baker — quite a line-up.

"My time with Monk brought me into association with a supreme architect of music," Coltrane later told *Downbeat* magazine. The pianist was also struggling to relaunch himself after having been deprived of playing in public since 1951, when he was falsely arrested for narcotics possession. Thus, this Carnegie Hall event found a pairing of musical genius fully ready for a revelation of jazz artistry.

Listen to it, for example, on *Sweet and Lovely*, where the tempo suddenly speeds up and Coltrane flies through several ecstatic choruses. *Blue Monk* follows, and the buoyancy of Malik and Wilson launches a sky lift for the biting improvisation and airy phraseology of Coltrane as he takes off into his own saxophonic stratosphere, while Monk chinks out his comping prompts and then moulds his own angular journeys through the Carnegie rafters.

The quartet played two sets that evening — an early show and a late show. The first performance begins with a solo Monk stepping through *Monk's Mood*, before Coltrane joins him, assured, blowing with finesse and grace. As the four men carve into *Evidence*, with Wilson's drums at full throttle and Malik pounding his bass, the brilliance of the quartet's playing makes the listener think southwards to the Carolina birthplaces of Monk and Coltrane.

It had been the birth of the Civil Rights movement the previous year in Montgomery, with the brave mass boycott of the segregated buses and King's defiant words, "Freedom comes only through persistent revolt, through persistent agitation, through persistently rising up against the system of evil." This is what these implacable jazz artists were also doing on this 1957 night in New York, through the brilliance of their musical invention.

When you listen to performances like the two versions of *Epistrophy, Nutty or Bye-Ya*, you begin to understand how their sound and structure were fused with the mass activity in the homelands of these musical discoverers and how their collective freedoms were inseparable.

16th August 2006

Blues for an Awakening Africa

Wilton "Bogey" Gaynair
Africa Calling
(Candid)

Jazz and migration are ever compulsive bedfellows. The huge movement of peoples from the southern rural share-cropping states to the northern cities of the US, from the 1920s to the 50s, brought brilliant and transforming musicians to cities such as Chicago and New York.

Something similar happened during the post-war Caribbean migrations, also south to north, but this time the destination was Britain, epicentre of empire. Brilliant jazz musicians accompanied the men and women from Guyana to Trinidad to Jamaica, arriving on the *Empire Windrush* in June 1948 and subsequent vessels.

There were calypsonians, of course, but also luminous jazz hornmen such as trumpeter from Barbados, Harry Beckett; from Jamaica, altoist Joe Harriott and trumpeter Dizzy Reece; Shake Keane, trumpeter and poet from St Vincent; and, slightly later than the others in 1955, tenor saxophonist of Kingston, Jamaica, Wilton "Bogey" Gaynair.

Gaynair, born in 1927, was an accomplished jazzman well before he arrived in Britain. Sensing that work was not going to be either regular or satisfying in London, he headed for mainland Europe, where he made a good living. In 1959, while visiting London, he made a superb quartet album for the Tempo label called *Blue Bogey* and, on his return in 1960, he cut the tunes for *Africa Calling*, with Terry Shannon playing piano, Bill Eyden on drums, and bassist Jeff Clyne, with trumpeter Shake Keane sitting in on three tracks.

But the album stayed unissued. Bogey left for Germany to join the Kurt Edelhagen Orchestra, and the huge jazz achievement of *Africa Calling* remained on the stacks unlistened to and un-appreciated, a jewel of its era never allowed to shine — until now, with Gaynair, Keane and Eyden dead and only Clyne still musically active.

Forty-six years later, the music still sounds as fresh and epochal as the hot June night when it was created, in the early hours of the morning in the Portland Place studio that is now the Colombian embassy. Gaynair had a sound unlike any of his British tenor contemporaries such as Tubby Hayes, Ronnie Scott or Jimmy Skidmore. Partly because of an adenoidal gruffness not unlike Monk sideman Charlie Rouse, and partly through a certain Caribbean edge — Sonny Rollins, with his Virgin Island roots, has it too — and a detachment from the London jazz scene.

The opener exemplifies this. It's a Gaynair original, inspired by his home city, *Kingston By Pass*. Shannon, who doesn't stop swinging all through the album, comes in strong and Bogey joins him with superb confidence, speaking his own reed language and spinning off phrases with eloquent aplomb.

Ghana's independent statehood in 1957 created a number of jazz tributes. Gaynair's was *Blue Ghana*. Keane joins him on the opening ensemble theme, then Bogey's solo burns with a Coleman Hawkins-like power and surge, until Keane enters with some searing notes and Shannon's bluesy chorus holds the tempo before Eyden and Clyne add their own solo solidarity.

The album's only ballad and non-Gaynair composition is *The Way You Look Tonight*, which Bogey attacks with a fierce and rousing energy. *Just for Jan* brings in the ebullient Keane again with a flying, audacious chorus before Bogey enters, saxophone motor in full-throttle force. *Rianyag* — Bogey's surname in reverse — is more reflective and self-examining, but compelling too, sucking in the listener by Gaynair's sheer force of unique sound.

But the climax is *Africa Calling*, in which two African-Caribbean horn men and their British jazz comrades reach out to a continent whose nations, inexorably, one by one, were throwing off their colonial bondage.

It is music completely of its time, marking an era and a continental struggle, alive now for us again. Imagine that early morning before dawn in 1960 in Keane's stretching notes and Bogey's unleashed ancestral love and passion for an awakening Africa. You can hear jazz becoming history and prophecy, its sound telling and real.

July 26th 2006

Twins of Swing

Buck Clayton with Humphrey Lyttelton and his band

Le Vrai Buck Clayton
(Lake)

Thirty years ago, Number 77 Charing Cross Road — Doug Dobell's record shop — was like a meeting-hall of jazz. Downstairs in the basement, the secondhand department was run by an extraordinarily generous and genial man called John Kendall. You might see great visiting jazzmen such as Red Allen or Ben Webster staggering down the steep stairs. Or you might meet dockers' leader Jack Dash breezing down to see what vinyl jewels Kendall had put aside for him. It was jazz's gold mine.

Upstairs, Dobell sold his new LP issues, some of them waxed on his own label 77 Records. He produced some unlikely classics, many of them still unissued on CD. Now, Lake Records have found one of Dobell's marvels from the mid-1960s, a double album of the Kansas City, ex-Basie-ite trumpeter Buck Clayton playing with the Humphrey Lyttelton band. It was a meeting which produced two of the truly momentous sessions of British recorded jazz, where Clayton's beautiful sounds inspired his British bandmates to produce music as fine as anything across the Atlantic.

Clayton was a note-perfect, lyrical horn man whose notes, crystalline as they were, were born in the blues. He was Billie Holiday's favourite trumpeter, and they sang and blew together — often with Lester Young's tenor — on many precious late 1930s sessions.

By 1966, Clayton was 55 and still blowing superbly and Lyttelton was 45 and at his peak, blowing alongside a US jazz hero — so much so, that I have always had great difficulty telling the two men apart on these tracks. And when they solo side by side, exchanging phrases as they do, for example, on *The Wrestler's Tricks*, the result is doubly felicitous.

These tracks were recorded on two Clayton tours in 1964 and 1966, and Humph had two different bands. The 1964 session includes some wonderful work by the then young tenorist Tony Coe, with his slurring Paul Gonsalves-emulating, serpentine solos on *Talk of the Town* or *Blue in the Afternoon*. And hear him slither out his notes on Clayton's classic *The Hucklebuck*. Also on hand were baritonist Joe Temperley — now a veteran member of Wynton Marsalis's Lincoln Center Orchestra — and pianist Eddie Harvey, who excel in their respective choruses on *Red Barrel Blues*.

By May 1966, Clayton was back and Humph still had Harvey with him, plus a new set of personnel. Dave Green, who was to become Britain's *nonpareil* bass man, anchored the rhythm. Chris Pyne came in on trombone and tenorist Kathy Stobart replaced Coe. There is the same informal, relaxed sound, and the two trumpeters played together again as if they had never been apart — black US citizen from Parsons, Kansas, and white Brit from Eton who played free concerts for the *Daily Worker*. A strange enough pairing, definitely and uniquely of its times.

The second session even outdoes the first, starting off in true KC style with Jay McShann's *Say Forward, I'll March*, taking in a spirited *Jumpin' the Blues* and hopping an ocean for Buck's own evocative *An Evening in Soho*. Again, the two trumpeters play with so much empathy that they frequently become one united horn.

There's no cold war in the version of *Russian Lullaby*, just a beautifully poised performance with open horn and piano, a drum roll followed by some swinging ensemble, a solo by Buck, then back comes the ensemble, and out. The trumpets share some vocalisation on *Talkback*, before Stobart enters for an earthy chorus and Pyne shows some dexterous slides.

Humph wrote *Blue Mist* for Buck, and it carries a Basie spirit, portrayed in muted horns and a languid beat, until the horns suddenly open and London sun pours through their sound. In *Poor Butterfly*, the other horns lay out and Clayton and Stobart play together in a moving melodic rhapsody. All the band members thrive with a succession of inspired solos on *The Swingin' Birds*, as if paying tribute to Clayton, a messenger from the heartland of jazz, giving and receiving.

September 27th 2006

Saturnian Blues

Sun Ra and his Arkestra

Jazz in Silhouette/Sound, Sun, Pleasure

(Gambit)

Sun Ra featuring Pharaoh Sanders and Black Harold

(ESP)

Sun Ra and his Cosmo Discipline Arkestra

A Night in East Berlin

(Leo Records)

His earthling name was Herman "Sonny" Blount and he was born in 1914 in what he averred was a "magic city" — Birmingham, Alabama, which was to become a key venue of the 50s Civil Rights movement. He always claimed that he was but a sojourner on Earth, a visitor from his true home which was Saturn. As he declared from his 1966 album *Nothing Is...* while the rebellion for justice raged in the southern states of his adopted nation, "We can't go nowhere here. I guess we can go somewhere there."

His interplanetary spaceship was his "Arkestra," a summation of frequently changing brilliant musicians who were both grounded and launched into jazz glory by the long-serving presence of three master hornmen who spent the majority of their musical lives in the Arkestra.

There was altoist Marshall Allen from Louisville, Kentucky, who played with Sun Ra from 1956 until the maestro's death in 1993, Chicagoan baritonist Pat Patrick who was with him for the same duration but who also between-times played with Ellington, Monk and Coltrane, and the sublime tenorist John Gilmore. Born in Summit, Mississippi, in 1931, Gilmore's family moved to Philadelphia, Coltrane's home town. He had a profound influence on the developing 'Trane, played for brief stints in Art Blakey's Jazz Messengers and was one of the great underestimated saxophone geniuses of jazz.

Jazz In Silhouette (1958) and *Sound, Sun, Pleasure* (1953-60) were two of Sun Ra's earliest releases on the Saturn label, now happily combined and reissued on a Gambit CD.

During 1946-47 Sun Ra worked as a pianist and arranger with the great 30s orchestral leader Fletcher Henderson, and his orchestrating skills were well-honed — listen to the pounding ensembles of *Velvet*, for example — as well as his dexterity in encouraging his prime soloists to fully unleash their beauty and eloquence. Listen to Gilmore's romping solo on *Saturn* or the way he and Patrick bite into *Velvet*.

Patrick's cavernous baritone opens up *Enlightenment* with trumpeter Hobart Dotson's echoing horn. *Ancient Aiethiopia* digs into the African earth and flies aloft too with the flutes of Allen, Patrick and James Spaulding, while Patrick's depth of deftness rumbles through *Horoscope* before Gilmore's massive saxophone engine bursts in. *Blues at Midnight* is the track of tracks, though. It opens with Sun Ra's pounding piano, but not for long. Gilmore tears through the stars, Patrick's huge sound is full of the earth yet still unearthly, and Julian Priester's growling trombone is fiercely tender. Allen swings through a juicy alto chorus with the leader comping furiously before Patrick returns with the plunging breath of a giant and Dotson peals out his piercing galactic message — jazz of the spheres, indeed!

In December 1964 Gilmore was touring with Blakey, and Sun Ra, short of a tenor, enlisted Ferrell "Pharoah" Sanders from Little Rock, Arkansas, to replace him. Sanders had been working as a cook in a restaurant downstairs from the venue where the Arkestra was performing. His characteristic roaring, guttural sound is powerfully audible on the *Live at Judson Hall* session, finally released in its totality on the ESP label.

Cosmic Interjunction, a sumptuous duet between Sun Ra and bassist Ronnie Boykins is followed by *The Other World*, featuring the furious drumming of Cliff Jarvis and Jimmy Johnson. The flute of Black Harold (Harold Murray) rises from *The Now Tomorrow*, and Sanders's universal rasp pours out *The World Shadow*, spurred by the leader's relentless piano chimes, while the shakers, pipes, shells and mass percussion fill out the foreground, played by musicians "costumed in turbans, wool hats and gold and silver lamé tunics."

During the latter years of Sun Ra's long career, many of the Arkestra's concerts were informally recorded and later issued on the Leo label. Two of these form the *Night in East Berlin / My Brother the Wind No 9* album, taped in 1986 and 1988 respectively. On the former session, enthused and possibly partially bemused Berliners were treated to the full-on ensemble of *Mystic Prophecy*, with the wild and free bass clarinet and alto rhapsodies of Eloe Omoe and Allen, and the warmer tones of Gilmore's vocalised tenor and Sun Ra's piano taking the Arkestra home.

Ellington's *Prelude To a Kiss* features the leader's synthesiser and Allen's cutting alto, then suddenly we are into Gilmore and Sun Ra's exclamatory chanting: "We travel the spaceways / From planet to planet". The long climactic moment is Gilmore's frenzied free tenor provoked by Sun Ra's electronic keyboard flourishes at the end of *The Shadow World*. Then with a single strike of the drum the music is silenced, there is a pause, and the volleys of German applause are heard. It is both a fitting testimony and an apt tribute.

October 20th 2010

Elm Park Riposte

Ken Colyer's Jazzmen, Skiffle Group and Omega Brass Band

Lonesome Road

(Lake)

A few weeks ago I watched the BBC news reporting the grotesque story of the British National Party's decision to "allow" black people to join its racist ranks. It was with a deep shock of recognition that I saw the venue where this decision had been formalised at an official BNP meeting. It was in the hall next to the Elm Park Hotel, on the borders of Dagenham and Hornchurch in the East London where I grew up and where as a youth, fifty years ago, I had been doorman every Friday and Sunday night at the St Louis Jazz Club. In the late 1950s a school friend's dad opened the club which hosted the prime British New Orleans bands, and since I was the weightiest and tallest of his mates I was invited to be unpaid doorman and cloakroom attendant.

That hall swung and grooved like an east London Bourbon Street twice a week. Now on TV I saw the doorway where I used to tear the tickets and the inside of the hall where the dancers jived and the bandsmen played *Dippermouth Blues*, *Muskrat Ramble* or *Bourbon Street Parade* — and where occasionally a black US guest musician would be announced such as the bluesman and one-man-bandsman Jesse Fuller, who danced and sang one night to the heated applause of local jazz lovers.

Now the stage was jammed with British fascists. As I watched the news I felt sick, angry and distant and I wondered how many other older men and women who remembered the venue felt the same. Later that evening I dug out the latest reissue CD of the Ken Colyer band, always my favourite outfit at the St Louis.

Colyer was a white man with a trumpet and an unfettered love for the black music of the Crescent City. Hailing from the lily-white coastal town of Great Yarmouth, he joined the Merchant Navy and jumped ship with his horn at the much greater port of New Orleans. There he lived and played with the pioneer black jazzmen in a city where the racial divide was still barbarous. He venerated these musicians and found glory in their achievement, but he didn't sit docilely in their shadow.

After his return to London in 1953 he gradually developed an ensemble with an emphatically and peculiarly English New Orleans sound which was entirely recognisable and dependent upon his own unassailable brass lead. His tunes' final choruses were often played through an always-present Derby mute, and the powerful musicianship of his bandsmen — juicy clarinettist Ian Wheeler, Leeds trombonist Mac Duncan, bassist Ron Ward, banjoist Johnny Bastable and the *nonpareil* of British New Orleans drummers Colin Bowden — all provided the relentless rhythm.

With these men he marched to Aldermaston. He invited the legendary New Orleans clarinettist George Lewis to join his band for British and European tours, and kept the flame of black music burning through the cities and suburbs of England before, during and after the so-called "trad fad" of the early 60s and the skiffle craze of a few years before. The whole era is chronicled in this evocative and powerful record.

The Omega Brass Band is the marching band that accompanied the peace marchers to Aldermaston. The record contains eight of their tramping and joyous performances with tuba, bass drum and Bowden's snares in full throttle plus Colyer leading eight horns. *Panama* really digs deep and *Over In Glory Land* and *Bugle Boy March* with their spirited ensemble and relentless beat must have revived even the most flagging marchers.

Unlike Lonnie Donegan, Colyer never made the hit parade with his skiffle group, but the intervals at their gigs were always eagerly anticipated with Colyer turning to a strummed guitar and Bowden picking up his wash-board and thimbles. Colyer didn't sing so much as tunefully warble, but there is a weird authenticity to hardship stories like *Ham 'n' Eggs* or *Ella Speed*. Bluesman Leroy Carr's *Midnight Hour Blues* and *Go Down, Sunshine* are from a very English Harold Macmillan-era blues and bring back a whole late-50s world. But the real soul of Colyer's music, which so respectfully emulated his black and creole heroes as he blew night after night in places like the Elm Park Hotel all over Britain, is revealed in huge measure in his band performances on numbers like *Bye and Bye* with Colyer's forceful brass lead, Wheeler's liquid beauty all through *Gatemouth* or Duncan's growling tailgate slides on George Lewis's *Dauphine Street Blues*.

Half a century on they are a clear, principled riposte to the racist lies and vicious divisiveness of the BNP fascists. The message of their echoes still blows from the walls and floorboards of the Elm Park Hotel, never to be silenced.

March 24th 2010

Raw Power of a Bass Giant

Charles Mingus / Eric Dolphy Sextet

Complete Live in Amsterdam

(Jazz Collectors JC429)

In April 1964 the Charles Mingus Sextet toured Europe. It was one of Mingus's most powerful bands with a stellar line-up of the leader on bass, his old buddie Dannie Richmond on drums and the eclectic piano master from Worcester, Massachusetts, Jaki Byard. The three momentous horns were west coaster Eric Dolphy on alto, the Chicago tenorist Clifford Jordan and the sweet-toned trumpeter from Trenton, New Jersey, Johnny Coles, who collapsed and almost died from a burst stomach ulcer after the Paris concert of April 17.

But on April 10 in Amsterdam they were a complete amalgam, and their momentous concert at the Concertgebouw was recorded. The whole two-hour performance is now available, full of precious jazz moments — beginning with Byard's tribute to two of his most luminous predecessors Art Tatum and Fats Waller, *A.T.F.W.* As he charges up and down his keys in a stomping dance, then pausing, reflecting and hurtling forwards again, he brings jazz history into times that were making their own history as much of the concert's later music would testify.

The next tune is *Parkeriana*, Mingus's nod to his great contemporary Charlie Parker. There's almost twenty-two minutes of it, beginning with dramatic choruses by the Bird's most brilliant alto successor, Dolphy. During Mingus's introduction to the performance he salutes Parker as a "genius". He adds: "We're trying to make him live a little here." Parker had died nine years before and his death heralded the slogan "Bird Lives!". Using themes associated with him, starting with *Ow*, the horns soar, Richmond's combustive drums add fire and Mingus's beat digs into the silty Amsterdam earth.

After the tour Dolphy was to go his own way in Europe, fatally as it transpired, for he was to die in a diabetic coma in Berlin in June at the age of 36. So the band's *So Long Eric* was more than a valediction. After the concert Dolphy was to say in an interview: "When you hear music after it's over, after it's over, it's gone in the air, you can never capture it again, so it's pure creation." So it makes you want to praise the carrier of the travelling tape recorder who caught Mingus's opening cavernous phrases, Coles's beautifully fragile choruses, Byard's ever-inventive solo lines, Jordan's deep song and Dolphy's reciprocal farewell, full of characteristic bursts and cadences. "He's leaving the band because America's so beautiful and free," adds Mingus wryly at the end.

Orange Was the Colour of Her Dress completes the concert's first half, and includes the underrated Coles in full flight, some plucked glory from Mingus, and Dolphy massaging with an ominous beauty on bass clarinet.

In the second half, Ellington's *Sophisticated Lady* gives Mingus a prime solo opportunity, accompanied only by a far-sounding Byard, and the bassist's huge love for Ellington is given full and sublime expression.

The year 1964 was the apex of the Civil Rights movement in the southern US states. Seven months before this concert a murderous blast had blown apart the Sixteenth Street Baptist Church in Birmingham, Alabama, killing four choir girls. The outrage had created an even more focused resistance among the campaigners. The concert ended with two extended performances, both in direct support of the struggle.

The first, *Meditations On Integration* — or alternatively, *Meditation On a Pair of Wire Cutters* — reflected the lives of the millions of prisoners of racism in the US. Each of the soloists seems to be telling a story of Jim Crow and how to crack it, with Mingus sawing on his bowed bass and Dolphy blowing his flute. To end, there are thirty-one minutes of *Fables of Faubus*, Mingus's burlesque of Governor Orval Faubus of Arkansas, who in September 1957 had stood in the doorway of Central High School in Little Rock with members of the national guard to block the entry of nine black children.

Mingus's satire is rich with dark humour but also carries the huge conviction of Martin Luther King's declaration of July 1964: "There will be no tranquillity or cessation of demonstrations until every vestige of racial injustice is eliminated from American society."

And how these particular Americans play in accord with those words — Coles' high-reaching trumpet, Byard mischievously bracing *Yankee Doodle Dandy* with the black anthem *Lift Every Voice And Sing*, Jordan's defiant horn and Richmond's crashing drums, Dolphy's spidery and tenacious bass clarinet and the ubiquitous Mingus, his bass heartbeat thumping everywhere as he lampoons *When Johnny Comes Marching Home*, his fingers stoking up the dream of racial justice.

This is an epochal record, history carried and made in music.

August 4th 2010

Under Soho Skies

Ronnie Scott and his American Friends

Secret Love

(Candid)

You would see him suddenly appear from behind the wooden pillar of his Soho club stage in Frith Street, his tenor saxophone strapped around his neck, clutching a microphone. With a few terrible jokes — so old that you could recite them with him — about members of the audience or his own club chef, he would welcome his listeners, announce his own support-act numbers or introduce a black jazz star from across the ocean.

This was Ronnie Scott, born and raised in Bow, East London, a child of an immigrant Jewish family brought up by an uncle who was a veteran of the Battle of Cable Street. And that fire and militancy never left him or his music. He was responsible — more than any other promoter or musician of his generation — for exposing British audiences to the black glory of US jazz, while thousands of other black men and women in the rabid South of their own country were challenging and defeating the age-old viciousness of US racism and its murderous protagonists.

He could play too, and how! "He's as good a saxophone player as I've played with," proclaimed the superb hornman Sonny Stitt, one of his partners on this album. Yet reticent and hyper self-critical, he regularly consigned himself to a secondary role warming up his club's listeners to the great musicians who would follow him. More often than not, he proved himself to be close to their equal.

I can remember how his rampaging horn preceded Illinois Jacquet's rumbustious tenor, the trumpets of Roy Eldridge or Dizzy Gillespie or the volcanic drums of Art Blakey or Elvin Jones. He never disappointed, was never a mere second best — he blew as if he were absolutely a part of their world, part of their sonic universe, and the sounds of the marvellous compendium album *Secret Love* are ample evidence of this.

The album shows an amalgam of British and US jazz genius, for accompanying Scott at his club's first premises in Gerrard Street in 1964 are the Boston-born Stitt; the founder of bop trombone from Indianapolis, JJ Johnson; trumpeters Donald Byrd from Detroit and Naptown's Freddie Hubbard; plus the greatest of British jazz piano contenders, south London-born Stan Tracey, who during the halcyon era of these sessions was Ronnie's regular house pianist. These recordings are a part of the precious Jazz Archive of Les Tomkins, who in 1963 was invited by Ronnie to record the great visiting US citizens on his own relatively unsophisticated equipment. Thank history that he did, for it means that we can listen back in pride and wonder to such unique jazz performances with Ronnie's horn at their centre.

And how he romps into the opening choruses of twenty-six minutes of the familiar title tune with Tracey, Malcolm Cecil on bass and Jackie Dougan's drums pelting behind him. When Stitt eventually enters with his smoother but no less inventive sound, you realise that there are two star reedmen blowing with all their jazz-making power.

Two months later Byrd was on Ronnie's stage with the two of them scorching out Miles Davis's *Blues by Five*. Ronnie gets a quasi-acerbic tone in his opening solo and Byrd takes up the mood with a final caustic repartee. Monk's *Well You Needn't* is more playful, with plenty of horn wit from both protagonists and Tracey stepping between them for some disarming choruses.

When JJ Johnson invited Ronnie to share the stage in September 1964, the rapid-fire exchanges ignited by Tony Crombie's fierce drumming must have rocked the earth beneath the Soho drains, all through a resplendent *Bye Bye Blackbird* with JJ's lightning slides making sprinting phrases of surprise and delight. Ronnie wasn't slouching either, bursting into flaming clusters of beautiful invention.

But the apogee of the album is Hubbard's tribute to the post-Windrush generation of young Caribbean British, his own composition *WI*, with Ronnie and Tracey as his formidable partners. West Indian communities in South and West London and many other British urban settings were fighting their own struggles against British racism, and Hubbard recognised this with power, insight and eloquence, with the rhythmic foundations of Tracey, Rick Laird on bass and Allan Ganley's throbbing drums. Scott called Hubbard "the greatest of the new trumpet players," and as he carves out his dramatic and fanfarish choruses, you can certainly hear why.

Then enters Ronnie himself — this is one Londoner from an immigrant family at the heart of tackling racism, in praise of thousands of others. It is moving, full of emotional meaning and a musical dedication across oceans of great artistry. Long live Hubbard's internationalism, Ronnie's East London sound and Tomkins' priceless work.

March 30th 2011

Within Sacred Walls

The Michael Garrick Sextet
Jazz Praises at St Paul's
(Jazz Academy)

Spiritual inspiration has frequently been one of the grounding forces of jazz. From funerals in New Orleans and the hymnal marches which preceded them, through Ellington's sacred concerts, from Coltrane's soaring passion of *A Love Supreme* to Charles Gayle's free jazz fervour in albums like *Kingdom Come*, *Consecration* or *Touchin' on Trane* and Abdullah Ibrahim's South African Islamic visions, the spiritual surge combined with the hunger for justice has driven jazz genius of every era and idiom.

An original perspective on this religious motivation for jazz was set down as part of the sleeve notes to his 1968 recording *Jazz Praises at St Paul's* by pianist Michael Garrick. "Religion has to do with the soul," he wrote. "So does jazz. Only after a very long time is it at all possible to begin to see through religion, with its paraphernalia, its power structures, its bequeathment of identity to its real foundation, the human condition. At best, it can offer a non-coercive focus on our life experience. So can jazz."

A powerful secular reading of the relationship between jazz and religion, and not one that you would usually associate with the devotional music played in the huge Christian cavern of St Paul's Cathedral. But Garrick's *Jazz Praises* is a much more layered work. During the 1960s, it was played at Oxford Street's 100 Club as well as in St Paul's, and was broadcast both on radio and television.

Garrick assembled some of the leading British jazz players of the day to perform the work as a sextet, including saxophonists Art Themen and Jim Philip, brass man Ian Carr, drummer John Marshall and Jamaican bassist Coleridge Goode. Garrick gained special permission from the Dean to perform the *Praises* in St Paul's, and the organist let him into the cathedral at night, through the eerie crypt, to practise on the huge organ, which had never previously been used as a jazz instrument. The extraordinary truth is that Garrick composed music for a number of biblical, liturgical, Book of Common Prayer and Anglican Psalter texts. He had no grounding in ecclesiastical tradition or church experience. Thus, he arrived at the music from a secular perspective while finding himself within the epicentre of religious experience and hierarchy.

The first notes of the opening *Anthem*, played by solo organ, make a huge cavernous sound that's full of echo — all picked up by the single microphone suspended across the chancel straight above the musicians, feeding into a stereo tape machine bought especially for the performance. So true was its sound that you can actually hear the silence behind the horn men and the amateur choir from St Michael the Archangel in Aldershot.

The mysterious spectral sound of human voices on *Kyrie* reminds me of the soundtrack of Eisenstein's film *Ivan the Terrible*, with its menace and obscurantist power, until Philip's flute and Carr's flugelhorn enter to sever through the chorale with their clarity and incisiveness, as if born of reason. *Behold a Pale Horse*, with its revelatory and eschatological suppressed thunder, sounds like Vietnam agonies, with Marshall's powerful drumming and Carr's expressive notes contesting with the soaring choir.

Garrick's serene organ chorus opens *The Beatitudes*. "Blessed are the peacemakers" has a potent new meaning after the two tracks that came before, and Goode's bowed bass has an irresistible strength. Carr and Themen exchange phrases in a dialogue of life and beauty, creating a colloquy of democratic music in the centre of British ecclesiastical power and rule. It is an exquisite passage. Perhaps it is such moments that provoked Garrick to write in his notes that "these pieces were written for a time which seems yet to come."

Although these sounds were made within cathedral walls, they are never trapped by them. They escape and find freedom, as do their subliminal messages.

December 14th 2005

Emblem of Hope

The Jimmy Woods Sextet

Conflict

(Original Jazz Classics)

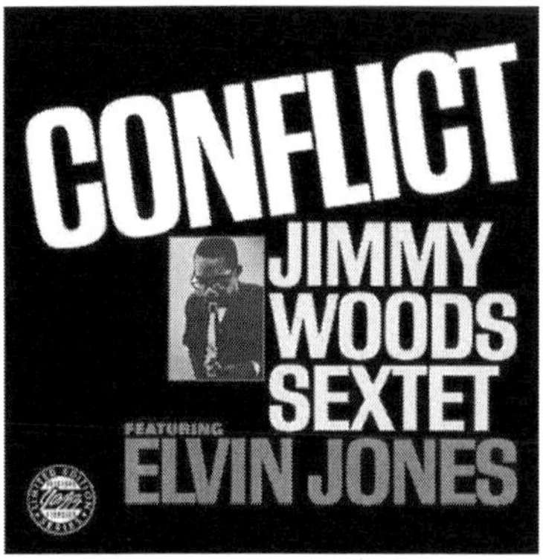

For certain, 1963 was a tumultuous year in the US. At the August march on Washington, Martin Luther King proclaimed his dream and, in June, President Kennedy federalised Alabama's National Guard to protect two black students seeking to enrol at the state university. In June, the Civil Rights organiser Medgar Evers was shot down outside his home in Jackson, Mississippi, and there were mass protest demonstrations against racism in Birmingham, Alabama, where campaigners faced snapping police dogs and the high-pressure hoses of city firefighters. "I want to see the dogs work. Look at those niggers run!" screamed police chief Bull Connor. On September 15, four black children were murdered by a bomb in a Birmingham church. Two months later, Kennedy was assassinated in Dallas.

Such events prompted the St Louis-born alto saxophonist Jimmy Woods to describe this same year in which his album *Conflict* was born as "a time of almost war." Woods had spent four years in the USAF before being demobbed in 1956. He moved to California, where he played with leaders like Horace Tapscott and Chico Hamilton. He made his first album, *Awakening*, in 1962. The outstanding and prophetic *Conflict* was to be his second and last. He became one of the "disappeared" of jazz, his unique alto sound a momentary epiphany of the era.

For *Conflict*, Woods assembled a remarkable line-up. On drums was the explosive Elvin Jones of the John Coltrane Quartet. The pianist was the enigmatic Chicago genius Andrew Hill, shortly to make a series of brilliant albums for Blue Note. The undersung Harold Land from Houston played tenor, and another sidelined hornman Carmell Jones was the trumpeter. Relentless time was kept by George Tucker on bass.

Woods is the composer of all six original tracks, and they join in a suite-like shape, adding more to the album's achievement. From Hill's first ironically jaunty notes of the title track, written to reflect the "creative energies of people on the march in a time of conflict," you feel the tensions of the US. Land's opening burst of notes, Carmell's tangy chorus, a sprayed solo from Hill and Woods's own final whirling statement are all a commentary on the times, summarised by Elvin's concluding thunder.

The more optimistic *Coming Home* suggests that there is a place of return and all members contribute with heart and will. The highly charged tune *Aim*, with Woods in particular offering a soaring contribution, suggests that this music is an emblem of hope, the notes of continuous movement and strengthening, a commentary in sound of surrounding struggles and dreams.

Woods's composition *Paz y Muerte* — Peace and Death — is his musical drawing of "the ultimate alternatives" for which his people campaign within the US nightmare of Birmingham, Little Rock, Montgomery or Selma. Tucker comes through with a bouncing bass solo before Elvin booms to the fore, his muscled percussion sounding powerful and unstoppable. But it is with the balladic *Look to Your Heart* that Woods truly leaves a piece of jazz writing and playing that are both memorable and racked with beauty. He plays with some of Ornette's singing sound, birdlike and melodious, but with a subliminal strength that suggests that these wings will return in their millions to claim what is theirs.

This reissue of *Conflict* has three extra takes. After forty years of obscurity, the session resonates with both history and a robust commentary of modern times. it makes you wonder what happened to Jimmy Woods. He'd be nearly seventy now. How would his musical brain envision the new conflicts of a Bush-led US? As you listen, you also imagine.

November 5th 2003

A Drummer's Drummer

Phil Seamen

The Late Great Phil Seamen

(SWP Records)

During the early 70s I asked my friend, the doyen of the British free jazz drummers John Stevens, which drummer he admired the most. Without hesitation he turned to me and said: "It has to be Phil Seamen." I was taken aback. I thought he would say Roach, Blakey or Philly Joe Jones or one of the US masters from the avant garde.

Seamen (1926–72) was a native of Burton-on-Trent. Primarily from the bop generation, he was also a veteran of British swing bands and an avid student of the African drums. He exalted the beat but kept a distance from free jazz despite one or two forays with the Splinters band, playing beside Stevens. Seamen was a drummer's drummer. The Paris-based father of bop drums Kenny Clarke said to him: "You're the first man on drums I've heard swing since I've been here." Louis Bellson, one of Ellington's great drummers, said: "It really was a thrill to watch and hear Phil play" and Philly Joe himself, who lived with Seamen when he was in London, said of British jazz drummers: "Phil was about the best." The jazz-rocker Ginger Baker of Cream said: "There were few drummers in the world that could come close to Phil Seamen."

Seamen was part of the transatlantic post-war jazz generation scourged by addiction. A concoction of heroin, alcohol and barbiturates forestalled many opportunities during his drumming life and eventually killed him in his flat in Old Paradise Street in Lambeth when he was at the peak of his artistry.

The Late Great Phil Seamen, a composite album of some of his most dynamic recorded work, is more than timely. From his thunderous sound behind the US bluesman Jimmy Witherspoon at a live date in 1966 to the last track with Tony Coe in 1971, Seamen's rhythmic drive and inventiveness are ever-present. The tracks on this album show why he was so esteemed and give ample space to his contemporaries. Harold McNair's scathing alto on *Tangerine*, with Seamen powerhousing behind him, Stan Tracey's *Free*, with Tracey on vibes and Seamen projecting Africa playing five tuned tom-toms with hot mallets alongside him, and two tracks by the Joe Harriott Quintet, with Shake Keane on trumpet, Harriott's alto, Coleridge Goode's bass and Pat Smythe's piano — a stellar fivesome with Seamen's combustive power at its centre, particularly on *Tonal*.

As a big band drummer Seamen laid down an irrepressible foundation. The distant 1954 recording of *Kick Off* by the Jack Parnell Orchestra features the drum duo of Parnell and Seamen, and the Victor Feldman Big Band track *Big Top* of a year later has Seamen grounding powerful solo work by, among others, Feldman's vibes, Harry Klein on baritone and Derek Humble's alto.

He is there with Jamaican trumpeter Dizzy Reece and Tubby Hayes playing baritone on music from the 1958 film *Nowhere To Go* and on the same soundtrack strikes a nifty cowbell next to Reece's tom-tom on *The Escape*. His solo drum track *Question and Answer* of 1961 is full of creative surprise and unexpected changes of beat. There are two tracks from one of Tracey's early trio LPs. One, a personal treasure, is *Little Klunk*. On the Monkish *Boo-Bah*, Seamen is unostentatious, but he responds wittily and eloquently to Tracey's provocations with vibes and piano.

Seamen was an essential member of Kenny Graham's Afro-Cubists. And *Haitian Ritual*, while covered in exotica, gives Seamen full rein with his skilled cymbalism. And hear him at full pelt and solo power on *Seamen's Mission* of 1954 by the Ronnie Scott Orchestra — he lets go and rises all through the track.

In Jamaican Joe Harriott and Vincentian Shake Keane he found two genius confrères — and how they gel on Harriott's number *Formation* of 1960. And his accompaniment to the Canterbury-born reedman Tony Coe in *Reza* of 1971 at Ronnie Scott's, alongside pianist Brian Lemon and arch-bassist Dave Green, seethes with creative fire, the signature of a wounded but brilliant British jazzman whose drums pounded with artistry and inspiration.

February 16th 2010

The Elemental Drums

Art Blakey and the Jazz Messengers

Live in Zurich 1958

(Solar)

What was it like, sitting in 1975 at the front table of Ronnie Scott's, only five yards away from a rampaging Art Blakey at his full and thunderous drum fury? There was something wildly elemental about it, that's for sure — a combination of unleashed and full sonic power and a brilliant musical artist at the peak of his creative virtuosity. And how the decibels pounded and stormed.

Blakey was born in Pittsburgh in 1919. Expelled from school at fourteen for standing up for the greatness of African civilisation and rejecting his teachers' racist version of cannibalism and grass skirts, he was plunged into the steelworks before turning to the drums, where he swung out with some of the great dance bands of the era, led by Fletcher Henderson, Lucky Millinder and Andy Kirk, before settling with the stellar Billy Eckstine Orchestra in 1944.

Blakey gradually moved from swing to bop as he was exposed to young contenders like Miles Davis, Fats Navarro, Charlie Parker and Clifford Brown. In the process of this transition he travelled to West Africa in the late 40s, learning about its music and converting to Islam. In 1955 he formed the Jazz Messengers with Horace Silver, Kenny Dorham and Hank Mobley, taking its leadership when Silver left in 1956. For the rest of his life, until his death in 1990, Blakey continued to lead the archetypal hard-bop band, giving apprenticeships to some of the great horns of jazz, from trumpeters like Lee Morgan, Freddie Hubbard, Wynton Marsalis and Terence Blanchard and an array of saxophonists from Jackie McLean and Wayne Shorter to Mobley, Johnny Griffin, Billy Harper and Bobby Watson.

The 1958 line-up was one of the most powerful formations. Philadelphia trumpeter Morgan, just twenty at the time, partnered 29-year-old Philly tenorist and outstanding musical director and composer Benny Golson. Bassist Jymie Merritt (born 1926) was also a Philly boy, as was the 23-year-old pianist Bobby Timmons, full of gospel and funky fire.

This fine previously unreleased double album consists of the tunes the Messengers played at a concert at the Volkshaus, Zurich, on a European tour in December 1958.

The session begins with a blast of Blakey, then moves into Parker's bop classic *Now's the Time*. The drums surge beneath Golson's tenor chorus and Morgan's crackling horn, and Merritt's pumping bass heartbeat throbs inside Timmons's pulsating keys. On to the Miles Davis tune, *The Theme*, which is sparked off by some felicitous Morgan, soaring and sprinting simultaneously. The familiar Timmons original, *Moanin'*, comes blueswalking in with room for spectacular solos from all members, with Morgan in particular belying his age and Golson's down-home tenor rocking the thresholds.

Blakey was a frequent, brilliant and empathetic drum partner to the equally percussive Thelonious Monk, and the pianist's tune *Evidence* — "We named it *Justice*," says Blakey in his introduction — sets Morgan's notes on fire. Golson rocks defiantly and Blakey's crashing drums bring the great protests of Civil Rights in Montgomery and Atlanta straight to mind. Justice was calling, all right.

The atmospherics of *Whisper Not* introduce the first of four Golson compositions. Morgan's horn dances over Merritt's throbbing twang, Golson lends a mysterious aura and Timmons's blues-sodden chorus heaves with dark feeling. Morgan takes the emotive lead on Golson's tenderly melodic tribute to Clifford Brown, *I Remember Clifford*, and clips into *Just By Myself* with zest and verve before its composer comes galloping in on the saddle of Blakey's relentless drums. Twelve minutes of Golson's intriguing *Along Came Betty* follow, with Morgan's spluttering chorus, Golson giving his protagonist an elegant gait with Timmons close on her tracks.

An interval for standards follows, first with Timmons, Merritt and *My Funny Valentine*, with the piano's high notes falling over the Volkshaus stage like droplets of rain, and then the full complement of Messengers essaying *Come Rain or Come Shine* with a fluent, serpentine Golson followed by a skyward-leaping Morgan. The final track, Dizzy Gillespie's *A Night In Tunisia*, maybe never explicitly anticipated that nation's upsurge in January 2011, but the prolonged Messengers' version, featuring Blakey's volcanic drums, is certainly a prelude to it, some six decades before Tunisians unleashed their freedom sounds across their land. A jazz prophecy, but who knew it then?

December 6th 2011

Into the Heart's Blood

Bud Powell

Live at the Blue Note Café, Paris 1961

(ESP)

The Parisian customers who sipped their coffees at the Blue Note Café that night in 1961 were not half lucky, when the Bud Powell Quartet tore out their music with such invention and beauty. And luckier still for us that the session was recorded and now reissued by the ESP label, still with a superb piano-side sound.

Powell had come to live in France as a refuge from the constant harassment and suffering that he lived through in the USA. Beaten over the head by police in Philadelphia in 1945, taken to a New York hospital for electric shock "treatment" in 1951, and his prodigious hands battered by Baltimore police against his driving wheel in 1958, Powell suffered from brutal headaches and mental breakdowns for the rest of his life.

Paris was his oasis, where he found opportunity for freedom and creative nourishment denied to him at home. And this album exemplifies this with huge abandon and virtuosity. In full control of his brilliance, he plays like a man liberated. Listening to it again, I remembered the enormous impact that the vinyl recording of the same session had on me more than four decades ago, with the pianist's punctuating grunts and snarls a bizarre yet captivating vocal accompaniment.

With Powell were the father of bop drumming, Kenny "Klook" Clarke, the French bassist Pierre Michelot and, on the first tracks, the West Coast white tenor saxophonist Zoot Sims. The previously unissued Zoot Sims tracks weren't on the vinyl album, so they were new to me. Sims seems a little hesitant at first on the twelve-and-a-half minutes of *Groovin' High*, but he soon settles and, with Clarke's buoyant encouragement and Michelot's relentless heartbeat, he begins to swing intuitively, prefacing Powell's own endless explorations.

In *Taking a Chance on Love*, you realise again the huge gift to jazz of Kenny Clarke, his listening ear and ever-active limbs responding to every phrase of Powell and Sims, his cymbals pulsating with life, his snares rattling with all its moods. And Michelot's solo sounds as if he is plucking some natural strands inside an empty tree trunk, so cavernous is his bass utterance. In *Bud's Blues*, we hear echoes of Sims's prime source of emulation, Lester Young, as he begins to float over the fertile earth of his confrères' unity. Then Powell comes in, the blues seeping from his hands as they dazzle along the keys, his life and tragedy pouring from every note.

The trio set begins with one of Powell's favourite ballads *There'll Never Be Another You*. He digs so deeply inside his notes that you marvel how, one after the other, they can still emerge with such crystalline power.

Then he plays three tunes by his great friend and mentor Thelonious Monk and two by the other bop creator Dizzy Gillespie. He strides into Monk with huge energy, thrust into action by Clarke's momentous uplift and Michelot's steadfast anchorage. *Round Midnight* is like a sound oracle, an anthem of the moon and stars, full of galactic piano drama, while *Monk's Mood* amply shows how sonorously Powell could play when he played slowly, when he was completely unhurried, as he so frequently was in the latter years of his musical life. Not funereal, not flagging, just beautifully slow.

Dizzy's *A Night in Tunisia* sounds as if the desert has been citified, as if Manhattan has been resettled on the edge of the Sahara, with so much urban excitation rushing from Powell's notes and Klook's thrashing drums. *Shaw Nuff* is a breathless sprint, the trio hurtling for four rapid-fire minutes.

I still love this record as I always have done, and I urge you to hear and share it. If there is one jazz piano album that you buy this year, make it this one. Bud Powell makes you dive into the very heart's blood of jazz.

February 6th 2008

Notes that Tell the Whole Truth

Hugh Masekela

Grrr

(Mercury)

Home is Where the Music Is

(Verve)

Walking through Sheffield city centre this morning, under Paul Waplington's giant brick mural of a steel worker, I passed the memorial to the sixty-nine South Africans massacred by the police while peacefully demonstrating at Sharpeville on March 21 1960.

When I arrived home, I played the reissue of Hugh Masekela's album *Grrr* (Mercury), with its moving trumpet testimony, *Sharpeville*, that tells the story with a naked pain. This was Masekela's second US album, waxed in 1965, six years after he had exiled himself from his home country to find solace in the land of jazz.

He was born in Witbank, some hundred miles from Johannesburg, in 1939. He came to the city as a boy and found music in the Trevor Huddleston band of Sophiatown. Soon, he was playing with pianist Dollar Brand — later to become Abdullah Ibrahim — and the alto saxophone genius Kippie Moeketsi in the Jazz Epistles.

Grrr brings jazz and the South African township vibrancy of Mbaganga rhythms together as one in a pounding syncretism. The accompanying musicians are unnamed but the distinctive sound of arranger Jonas Gwangwa's trombone is often heard, particularly in *Sharpeville*, where his mourning slides growl into resistance after Masekela's burnished and defiant chorus. Another momentous track is the tune associated with Miriam Makeba, *Ntjilo-Ntjilo*, played as an elegaic blues rhapsody. Masekela is assured and powerful, bending his notes, soaring then plunging into dramatic cadences before returning to the heights.

Home Is Where The Music Is (Verve), which was recorded seven years later in London, has the sound of a very different and developed proposition. Masekela has two brilliant compatriots with him, altoist

Dudu Pukwana from another exiled group, the pathfinding Blue Notes and the brilliant drummer who frequently played with Ibrahim, Makhaya Ntshoko. The Puerto Rican bassist Eddie Gomez is present, as is the New York-born pianist and ex-Jackie McLean sideman Larry Willis, who played on Masakela's 1965 album *The Lasting Impressions of Ooga Booga.*

The dramatic sleeve artwork by Dumile Feni carries the desperation of a people enduring and resisting the hideousness of apartheid, and the music radiates a similar urgency. *Grrr* is locked in brevity, just thirty-two minutes long, but this later album stretches with artistry and testimony for seventy-six minutes. As soon as Pukwana blows his insistent choruses on the opener, *Part of a Whole*, and Masekela follows, compounding the defiance, the listener knows the struggle in the homeland has moved on and the musicians in exile are making their sounds of solidarity.

Willis' lyrical introduction to *Minawa* and Gomez's twanging bass-strings prelude a horn ensemble and a lone Masekela brass soliloquy, with Ntshoko's drums piling up momentum before Pukwana's solo, liquid and gushing, flows like rising waters through the river-course gaps of veldt rocks. Gomez's compelling bass riff accompanies Masekela's rousing opening chorus of Makeba's *Uhome*, before Pukwana adds his chilling message. The capital of Lesotho, South Africa's land-locked and state-locked neighbour, Maseru is exultantly evoked, with Masekela rocking in elation above Willis's bounding keyboard. Pukwana joins in, festive and boiling with joy.

Moeketsi's salutary tune, *Blues for Huey*, begins with Ntshoko's pounding drums before the horns enter in unison and the solo drums thrash over the cone of Africa from this faraway London studio.

The album's prophetic climax comes in *Ingoo Pow-Pow (Children's Song)*. 1972 was four years before the Soweto schoolchildren marched for their future through their own streets and hundreds of them were mown down by the apartheid police. This children's song begins with a peal from Pukwana over throbbing drums, some gruff choric vocals, two wild horns and Masekela's final, fanfarish coda calling all to attention. What was to come? What suffering, loss, victory and ultimate homeward journey?

December 3rd
2008

Reverence and Revulsion

Albert Ayler

Prophecy / Bells

(ESP)

Albert Ayler's series of recordings for the ESP label in 1964 made a profound impact upon the prevailing jazz consciousness in the US and Europe. His unfettered, wild, howling rasp surged through the music, alienating many, engrossing many more, but it left its mark of either reverence or revulsion wherever it sounded.

Ayler learned his saxophone art as a boy altoist in his father's funeral band in Cleveland, Ohio, where he was born in 1936. He went on to accompany blues harmonica player Little Walter, spent 1958–61 in the US army playing in military bands and toured Denmark and Sweden with Cecil Taylor in 1962. But it was his 1963 New Year's Eve performance with the pianist at the New York Philharmonic Hall that staggered his audience and sent his bellowing echoes around the world of the jazz avant-garde.

All these experiences had been absorbed into Ayler's revolutionary sound by the time of his trio performance on *Prophecy* with bassist Gary Peacock and drummer Sunny Murray at the Cellar Cafe in New York City on June 14 1964. The unearthly tune titles — *Spirits*, *Wizard*, *Prophecy* and *Ghosts* — were one aspect, but the core of his sound was very much of this real world. His notes had the street sound of a busking musician, his horn still wailed out the funereal dirge-songs of his father's band, connecting to New Orleans marching bands and the praise-songs of his people's music well before the advent of recording.

The note-swirls and plunging breath cadences after Peacock's cavernous solo choruses on *Wizard* precede the opening phrases of *Ghosts*, with its child-like theme that is a preface to an extraordinary chorus of aural respirations. Sometimes you think you are hearing a distressed horn on a wild and lonely sea, sometimes the last howl of a titanic beast, but mostly it is an utterly human sound, guttural with life, a sound radiating by turns evisceration, pain and joy in an amalgam of living contradictions as in the very innards of jazz.

But as if *Prophecy* is not enough, this reissue album of two ESP classic performances then follows with the rampant twenty minutes of *Bells*. Here Ayler is joined by his trumpet-playing brother Donald, and the two audacious musical siblings share the stage of New York City's Town Hall on May Day 1965 with Murray again, altoist Charles Tyler and bassist Lewis Worrell.

Bells was first issued as a short-time, one-sided long-playing record with a blank flip-side. As part of an hour-long "two-fer" reissue, it is at last real value for money. The Ayler brothers are a ferocious twosome, with Donald's ear-splitting staccato phrases careering beside Albert's roaring vibrato. It was a jazz sound like no other, although when you listen to New Orleans parades, you begin to understand from where it emerged.

An astonishing aspect is the role of the brilliant Peacock, who with Murray's rattling drums holds down the rhythm with aplomb, while frequently surfacing with sudden bursts of deep solo fire. When you hear the same bassist still plucking with complex artistry as part of the Keith Jarrett Standards Trio, playing to thousands in the world's concert halls, contributing to the reinvention of the American Song Book, you marvel at the diversity and the extraordinary changing tableaux of jazz.

As the brothers Ayler play out their transformations of army fanfares and church gospel themes all through *Bells*, you also think about the last hours of Gary Peacock's old bandmate before his body was recovered from New York's East River in November 1973 at the age of 37.

Another jazz tragedy, another mystery, and his music, fused with joyousness, still rings with both.

July 23rd 2009

Breath of Genius

Roland Kirk

Pre-Rahsaan

(Prestige)

Of all the true geniuses of jazz, Rahsaan Roland Kirk (1936–1977) was to me the most heroic. Blinded at the age of two, he dedicated his life to music, mastering more than forty instruments through the forty-one years of his life, creating simultaneous combinations of performance that astonished all who beheld them.

He played three woodwind horns with the same breath. He modified the keys of his tenor saxophone with rubber bands and used his left hand to cover its range while also playing with his right hand the stritch and manzello, rare early saxophones used in 19th century Spanish marching bands, which he found one day in the cellar of a musical instrument shop with a pile of old horns which the owner called the "scraps."

Employing his own device of circular breathing, he managed to sound like a complete orchestral reed section. Yet there was nothing of gimmicky about his artistry, as a hearing of the two albums which compose *Pre-Rahsaan* will soon make evident. Kirk began to call himself "Rahsaan" in the wake of these recordings, which show very different dimensions of his brilliance. From New Orleans clarinet to rasping R'n'B tenor to the coolest of flutes, from the avant-garde to hard bop, he was simply the living breath of jazz, dedicated to Civil Rights for his people and an end to the "volunteered slavery" all around him.

The first album takes in the 1961 session with organist Jack McDuff, called *Kirk's Works*. Prime bop drummer Art Taylor was on hand, with ex-Ellingtonian bassist Joe Benjamin. The opener, *Three for Dizzy*, is an offering to the great trumpeter, consisting of all three horns, which played alongside McDuff's blues-laden notes, make a heavy, soulful pitch. When Kirk re-enters on solo tenor, his command of the horn is immediately apparent, as it is on the chirping flow of *Makin' Whoopee*, where he sets off with startling fluency and speed, changing to manzello halfway through his solo.

On *Funk Underneath*, it is all flutes, although, as you listen, you seem to hear a pair of them above Benjamin's walking basslines. McDuff's solo is full of the earth. *Kirk's Works* sounds as if there are diverse horns all around — as there are, of course, all coming from one man's breath. The soprano-like manzello solo is particularly fine.

The "section" sound is dominant on *Doin' the Sixty-Eight*, with some eloquent tenor and manzello and the peal of a siren whistle concluding the chorus. *Too Late Now* shows Kirk's melodism, his full tenor sound prefacing a leap to manzello and back again, while, on *Skater's Waltz*, he solos on the stritch, the familiar theme whirling across the ice with McDuff's buoyant chords.

If there was any pianist in jazz who could connect with Kirk with his own inventive genius and eclecticism, it was Jackie Byard, who was born in Worcester, Massachusetts in 1922. Byard played bop, all forms of post-bop and the avant-garde, while also being a postwar *nonpareil* of stride piano as well as balladry. So, to hear them at full pelt together with master bassist Richard Davis and prime drummer Alan Dawson on a session that previously comprised a Byard-led album and was first issued as *The Jackie Byard Experience* is a joy indeed.

Bud Powell's *Parisian Thoroughfare* leads off the session. It's a frenzied interpretation with Byard crashing down on his keys. Byard's solo, full of stride sounds and percussive echoes, is a piano anthem and Davis's bass echoes as if he is plucking in the deepest of tunnels, miles below the city's streets. *Hazy Eye* is a Byard-Davis duet, with both virtuosi playing with a startling stridency. Kirk is back, this time on a wailing clarinet for the spiritual *Shine On Me*. He returns playing a guttural tenor before Byard, testifying gospel-style, brings the congregation home. Their version of Monk's *Evidence* is astonishing, with Kirk's tenor sprinting through the familiar theme, belching out notes with unpursuable speed and Byard delivering a series of blistering cadences that would have had the composer dancing in glee. The ballad *Memories of You* is played as a piano-tenor duo, with Byard all over the keyboard and Kirk sonorous and gentle, his final note a universal breath.

Pre-Rahsaan is a superb CD set, exposing the artistry of more than one jazz genius and celebrating the music of Rahsaan Roland Kirk, whose mind and body poured with the music of life.

July 2nd 2008

A Sound at Boiling Point

Sonny Simmons

Staying on the Watch

(ESP)

A few months ago, who should come to my home city of Sheffield to play his avant-garde jazz rhapsodies but the 77-year-old alto saxophonist born in faraway Sicily Island, Louisiana, Sonny Simmons. His stage was downstairs in the gothic basement of a domed, all-but-derelict cinema where he sat in with local free improvisers, adding his pioneering, almost hierophantic sounds to the proceedings, his horn wailing and shuddering from its subterranean venue and flying up, gurgling out over the Pennines.

I was fiercely reminded of this spectral event when a CD reissue of one of Simmons's early recordings winged its way to my letterbox. Cut in August 1966 for the adventurous ESP label, *Staying on the Watch* pitches Simmons with his trumpeter wife of the time Barbara Donald, the ultra-versatile pianist from Atlanta, John Hicks, percussionist Marvin Pattillo, with Teddy Smith playing bass.

Simmons had recorded epochal album *The Cry!* with fellow altoist Prince Lasha in 1962, and in 1967 the two reedmen were to come together again to record their masterpiece *Firebirds*. Simmons also played with another great altoist, Eric Dolphy, and the momentous drummer of the John Coltrane Quartet, Elvin Jones. Two years after this 1966 session he played with trumpeter Bill Dixon's University of the Streets Orchestra in New York. For nearly twenty years between the mid-70s and the early 90s he endured personal crises and dropped away from jazz visibility, finally re-emerging in 1992 with astonishing power on the album *Ancient Ritual*, and continuing an extraordinary jazz life.

Metamorphosis, the opening track of *Staying on the Watch*, kicks off with an ensemble blast before Simmons's skittering solo, full of pace and turbulence, makes way for some fierce brass choruses from Donald.

Born in Minneapolis in 1942, Barbara Donald's primary instrument was the piano. Her classical training was seriously disturbed in the mid-50s when she first heard the bop tones and the drama of trumpeters like Clifford Brown, Miles Davis and Fats Navarro. She joined a rock band, moved to New York with them, then went to California, where she met Simmons at a club in San Diego.

It wasn't easy for a woman, a white woman too, to break into the avant-garde jazz scene, but her strength and talent were such that she managed it, and her brasswork all through *Staying on the Watch* is ample proof of her surging sound which rips open *Metamorphosis* with a caustic timbre and sense of sonic savagery.

Smith comes in for a sawing bowed solo before the young and prodigious Hicks, just twenty-five at the time, pounces ferally up and down his keys with Pattillo's spluttering snares urging him on. It's a frantic and compelling twelve minutes indeed, ended by Donald's brusque and harsh coda.

And very different from what follows, the musing mysterious beauty of Simmons's horn on *A Distant Voice*, accompanied by Smith's mournful bowed bass. Simmons's breathy and serpentine wails seem to spring from remote agonies, perhaps in Vietnam or South Africa, sounding out right across the world — a duo with universal reach.

There is a plunging cadence early in *City of David*, preceding some solo plucked bass, before Donald gets working on a boisterous run, muscular and sometimes soaring over Hicks's comping. Simmons begins his chorus in high register and his intensity never falters, piling note upon note, which Hicks continues with breakneck pace, hurtling through his choruses.

Simmons was the composer of the album's four tunes, but the closer *Interplanetary Travellers* sounds as if it could well have been the work of Sun Ra. There are full-on rapid riffs and sprinting solos, and all the musicians travel the spaceways with a frenzied objective to reach their far-flung destination. Simmons begins with an uncatchable haste, his lightning notes splattering everywhere, and Donald is not much less swift, accelerating even more audaciously as her chorus progresses. Smith's fingers scurry through his strings and then we arrive at Pattillo's long solo moment, reaching between his drums as if they too were neighbouring planets as the ensemble returns, its sound at boiling point.

This was 1966, and Simmons is still doing it. Look and listen out for him — as I found out in Sheffield, he arrives at the most surprising places.

July 8th 2011

Ark, the Feral Angels Swing

Noah Howard
The Black Ark
(Bo' Weavil)

Here's a jewel and a legend of a record — for decades a rarity, now at last reissued and still screaming at its listeners with a torrid and visceral eloquence.

The year was 1969, the place New York City. The war in Vietnam was still raging and the Civil Rights movement in the South had passed its apogee. Martin Luther King was dead and the Poor People's campaign over.

Black anger mounted at the mass incarceration of young black militants and George Jackson began writing the powerful prison letters that were to form his political message in *Soledad Brother.*

In New York, Noah Howard — a young alto saxophonist born in the cradle of jazz in New Orleans in 1943 who had arrived in the Big Apple to play his first gigs with free jazz pioneers like Marion Brown, Pharoah Sanders, Archie Shepp and Sun Ra — entered the Bell Sound Studio to record the session that produced *The Black Ark* with a group of virtually unknown jazz adventurers.

These were Arthur Doyle on tenor sax, trumpeter Earl Cross and pianist Leslie Waldron, Mohammed Ali at the drums, Juma on congas and bassist Norris Jones — shortly to be called Sirone, and who in 1971 was to join the pathfinding free trio the Revolutionary Ensemble.

The percussion flutters, Sirone's bass digs deep, Waldron stomps out his chords and the opener *Domiabra* begins. Howard's biting alto leaps out of the rhythm and makes its long piercing chorus before Cross's solo brass voice sounds with a fanfarish entry and a tumbling cadence. Doyle then delivers what must be the most feral chorus in the jazz canon.

Born in 1944 in the Alabama city of Birmingham — where the Civil Rights upsurge had expressed its apex of resistance against the brutal forces of police chief Bull Connor in 1963 and where almost every white church had refused entry to black worshippers — Doyle seems to be bringing that defiance with him to the heart of New York, untrammelled, unfinished, unblockable.

Sirone and Ali add their own testimonies, there is a burning ensemble passage and all is over. *Ole Negro* follows, played by a brigade of young black musical militants. The sound is born of a fierce and deep respect radiating first from Howard's caustic solo, then

Doyle's adenoidal song and the sheer fervour in Cross's blasted and ardent notes.

Waldron gets his keys marching, Sirone's bass dances through some stygian New York cavern and the stern theme returns and concludes. A sudden imaginative transmigration and it is Howard's Japanese sonic landscape, *Mount Fuji*, that follows. Fifteen and a half minutes long, it begins with an orientalist theme and a clashing of cymbals before Cross's corrosive solo, fiery and unrelenting, scorches the ambience.

Doyle continues, searing and incendiary, his sound full of wounded, pained notes before Howard, playing at the top extremes of his horn, compounds the agonised timbre — all youthful mountaineers of improvised sound searching for the summit of their music, in the US, in Japan. Waldron's chords are like gothic chimes and Sirone's bounding bass leaps up from the cold rocks. The final track, *Queen Anne*, begins as if it is going to be *You Go To My Head*, but soon veers away from any balladic illusion.

What its provenance is, who its title denotes, what aristocracy it is depicting or lampooning are all a mystery, but as Howard blows over Sirone's jauntily agile beats, something subterranean is stirring in this queen's realm. Doyle's haunting, guttural sound was described as "skronky" when it first emerged, and as it blows out at the track's denouement the word seems apt and expressive.

As for Howard, after some years of obscurity he made other fine albums, none more so than his *Message To South Africa*, recorded the week Steve Biko was murdered in 1977 while in detention, and cut with South African Blue Note pioneers pianist Chris McGregor and bassist Johnny Dyani.

Following his death in 2010, his music is still going, still blowing on that ark of beauty and insurgence.

October 5th 2011

Serpentine Horn

Paul Gonsalves

Humming Bird

(Deram)

It has happened many times in the story of British jazz. Set up a recording session or record a performance where a visiting US virtuoso plays with a group of British musicians and you frequently find that the latter play out of their skins.

It happened when Benny Carter played at Maida Vale in 1936 and when Fats Waller played with his Continental Rhythm in a London studio in 1938. When Ken Colyer blew with George Lewis in a 1957 Manchester concert and Buck Clayton locked horns with Humphrey Lyttelton in 1966. Or when Charlie Rouse went "playin' in the yard" with the Stan Tracey Quartet in 1987.

It is as if the British players go up several notches while in the inspiring company of authentic jazz genius — and it happened again when Paul Gonsalves played with a group of British stalwarts in London in 1970. Gonsalves, of course, was one of jazz's great tenorists — and this reviewer's absolute favourite. His quivering, serpentine yet full-bloodied sound was at the heart of the Duke Ellington orchestra from 1951 until 1973, when both he and the Duke died within weeks of each other.

The reedman's 27-chorus long solo while playing *Diminuendo and Crescendo in Blue* at the 1956 Newport Jazz Festival became a major factor in Ellington regaining favour with the world of jazz public after a period of relative neglect.

The Duke never forgot that. His last performance in London, at Finsbury Park's Rainbow Theatre in 1973, was the only time that I ever screamed from the audience for a soloist. It was Gonsalves's name that I shouted. The Duke heard my raucous tones and those of my friend next to me and responded. Gonsalves played *Happy Reunion* and I have never been so moved by a jazz performance.

Soft, shuddering and fragile, yet full of Gonsalves's unique saxophone glory, it was the final solo that he ever played to a London audience.

Now *Humming Bird*, recorded in 1970, is re-issued on CD for the first time. Gonsalves plays with some of Britain's hottest, including pianists Tracey and Alan Branscombe, Toronto-born expatriate trumpeter Kenny Wheeler and the *nonpareil* of British bassists Dave Green.

The title tune establishes the ethos with grace and beauty. Gonsalves plays some delicate, weaving choruses, Wheeler is lyrical and Tracey is characteristically percussive and earthy. A medley follows — there is a beautifully pitched *Body and Soul* from Wheeler and Gonsalves is warm, breathy and enveloping through *Talk of the Town*.

Gonsalves and Wheeler chase each other across the studio in four-bar exchanges in *All the Things You Are* and, in *Sticks*, all members resonate with Branscombe in particular catching keyboard fire. Tracey's own composition *XOX* begins with unaccompanied Gonsalves and Tracey at his most Monkish, before the tenorist's hurdling choruses with the brass riffing behind him.

In a Mellotone remembers Duke, a virtual whispering at first turns into a much more biting Gonsalves solo — the kind that he forged with the whole orchestra urging him on.

Finally, there is *Almost You*, where all members create a swinging groove with Wheeler then Gonsalves unleashing their free spirits and Branscombe leaping along the keys in some sunny chorus — before Gonsalves re-enters to add even more buoyancy and close a memorable London session.

November 9th 2005

'Trane Discovery

The John Coltrane Quartet

One Down, One Up: Live at the Half Note
(Impulse)

Any unearthed recording of the John Coltrane Quartet is going to provoke immense interest among jazz lovers and *One Down, One Up*, produced from forgotten tapes of two early hours radio broadcasts made in 1965 at the Half Note in New York City, will certainly do that.

This performance, now available on a double CD, was made just three months after the session which cut *A Love Supreme*, generally regarded as Coltrane's greatest masterpiece and one of the decisive moments in all jazz. It was during the same year which birthed *Sun Ship*, *Live in Seattle* and *Meditations*, some of his most powerful recordings.

One Down, One Up was also one of the final recordings made of Coltrane's most renowned quartet, with the orchestra-in-a-piano of McCoy Tyner, the combustive drums of Elvin Jones and the pounding bass of Jimmy Garrison.

The sleeve photographs reveal what a small venue the Half Note was, intimate and cramped with a capacity of only 130. Archie Shepp, a tenor saxophone comrade of Coltrane and a sizeable musical rebel himself, remembered: "They played until four o'clock in the morning and it was like being in church. I mean, Coltrane brought something which raised this music from secular music to religious world music."

It was Ravi Coltrane, John's tenor saxophone-playing son, who found these recordings in 1991 after they had been piled in a cupboard in the Coltrane house for twenty-five years. He immediately heard the timbre of their significance. "You really feel like he's in two places," he mused, "you can hear everything that came before and begin to hear where the music was going."

Garrison's bass punctuates the announcements and thuds forward into the title composition until Jones, Coltrane and finally Tyner enter almost simultaneously. Coltrane creates a colloquy on his saxophone — stating then answering, stating then answering, before he flies off into a twenty-seven-minute-long uninterrupted solo which forms the rest of the performance.

For chorus after chorus, the improvisation powers onward like a great locomotive tearing across mainland US from east to west, with Tyner's tireless comping, Jones' percussive fury and Garrison's subliminal bass providing a seemingly endless fuel. Coltrane's notes are now gutterally down, sawing at the basement of his sound, finding his power in an astonishing duet with Jones, then taking the struggle of ascent as if he is fighting for his life as he rises.

It is a truly narrative piece of music, combative in its story, with an ending of arrival and beginning.

The familiar melodic strains of *Afro-Blue* follow. Tyner, having waited so long through the previous tune, is first into solo opportunity here, spinning off sentences and paragraphs of notes from his keys with relentless abandon, with Garrison and Jones hugely united behind him. Coltrane eventually wades in playing soprano, raising the historical imagination of Africa, yet reflecting the then present reality, the struggles for decolonisation and the continental search for freedom. All that is there — submerged, boiling, volcanic in his overwhelming sound.

Six weeks later on May 7 1965, the quartet returned to the Half Note for another broadcast, which comprises the second record of the double CD. The live version of *Song of Praise* became as a final rehearsal for the studio recording of the same tune ten days later and is twice as long.

The pace quickens and Coltrane is soon roaring. Tyner follows with some rolling choruses with Jones forging thunder all around him. Coltrane returns improvising as if he has never left off, his notes surging everywhere.

You can only surmise what the lucky 130 felt, so close to such artistry and glory.

Finally, Coltrane blows his soprano through *My Favourite Things* — almost his signature tune since 1961. That such a wet and mawkish song could become a jazz anthem was and is a part of the transformative power of the music. In the breath of Coltrane, it was a golden sound, a signal of genius. Every version different, every note still a joyous surprise.

Lost no more. And a record to savour, to marvel at and to love.

November 2nd 2005

Two for the Duke

Ben Webster and Stan Tracey

Soho Nights Vol. 1

(Resteamed)

It might be thought that a combination of Ben Webster's tenor saxophone suspirations and Stan Tracey's angular, chiming piano notes could be a forbidding union. But in January 1968 they played together at Ronnie Scott's in Soho and created hugely powerful music — the visiting US horn giant and the local house pianist.

This wasn't for the first time. You can hear one of their 1964 dates at Ronnie's on a Storyville album called *The Punch*, but the *Soho Nights* session four years later is played by two jazzmen, one born in Kansas City in 1909, the other in south London in 1926, who had come to know each other's artistry well. They also shared an admiration for the genius of Duke Ellington. Webster had been Duke's virtuoso tenorist between 1940-3 and again in 1948-9 and played featured solos on tunes like *Cotton Tail* and *All Too Soon* countless times.

Ellington was also, along with Monk, Tracey's greatest inspiration. His albums of the Duke's music, *We Still Love You Madly* (1996-98) and *Duke Ellington: The Durham Connection* (1998) are among Tracey's finest achievements.

Completing the quartet on *Soho Nights* are drummer Tony Crombie and the arch-bassist of British jazz the brilliant Dave Green who, like Tracey, is still everywhere in the domestic jazz scene. During the later years of his jazz life when he lived in Europe, in his live performances Webster blew a succession of breathy ballads and Ellingtonian themes which were as close to him as blood and much loved by his audiences.

So after Ronnie's generous introduction it's straight into *Johnny Come Lately* by Duke's long-time musical partner Billy Strayhorn. Ben ambles, jumps, grunts, leaps and strolls through the familiar theme in turns, before Stan strides in, utterly at ease with the master hornman.

Then it is Ellington's own rhapsody to black emancipation in his country from the *Black, Brown and Beige* suite, *Come Sunday*. Webster sings through his horn, knowing breath is life, is freedom. And Tracey's white hands know this too and in his touch is also deliverance, a succession of phrases of absolute empathy — so much so that Webster exclaims spontaneously, "Yeah, the man" and returns with notes of sublime beauty, exhaling their message of millions of lives unchained.

I don't know what Webster knew about the origins of *Londonderry Air/Danny Boy*, which was sung in every pub in working-class London, but he plays it as if it were his own. So much so that there are two versions on the album. As he moves into the second verse the key rises, with Tracey's chords behind him. When he reaches the climactic line there is no assumed drama, just a calm and beautiful restraint.

The quartet moves directly into the ballad *For All We Know*, with words which always have a poignant meaning for a veteran jazz musician. Green's relentless bass is well heard on this track and Tracey sounds as attuned in his solo as he did for all those nights he played with such brilliance throughout the 70s in the jazz oasis of The Plough, Stockwell. The fact that he is playing with a legend of jazz does not faze him one iota.

How many times must Webster have romped out his *In a Mellotone* solo with Ellington? He does it again here with Tracey, still full of bite and movement. Then it is into *The Jeep Is Jumpin'*, a tune written for his alto saxophone confrère in the Ellington orchestra Johnny Hodges. Tracey is at his Monkish best, Crombie jumps too with some lively drum breaks in Webster's concluding solo and Green excites Ben too in a bouncing chorus in the depths. "Great man, yeah!" he shouts. A scintillating quartet performance.

What Am I Here For? is the final Ellingtonian contribution and the question is eloquently answered in the brilliance of the music. Webster stays fast to the strong melodic line for the first chorus, explores a little then gives Stan the creative edge he loves.

A precious reissue this, with Ellington the enormous invisible presence. One to buy, give and savour. An age gone, but now rescued after a mere four decades.

March 3rd 2010

Freddie's Burnished Beauty

Freddie Hubbard

Without a Song: Live in Europe 1969

(Blue Note)

When Freddie Hubbard died in December 2008, jazz lost one of its great trumpeters as well as one of its most defiant radicals.

He was born in Indianapolis in 1938, where as a young horn he played with other Naptown jazz prodigies Wes and Monk Montgomery. He moved to New York in 1958, shared a room with the great altoist Eric Dolphy and played on his pathmaking albums *Out to Lunch* and *Outward Bound*. His period between '61–'64 with Art Blakey's Jazz Messengers also produced a series of brilliant Blue Note albums, among them *Hub Cap*, *Here To Stay*, *Ready For Freddie*, *Hubtones* and *Breaking Point*.

In 1971 he recorded the audacious *Sing Me a Song Of Songmy*, an entirely innovative album of jazz and poetry condemning the US massacre at My Lai in Vietnam. Through the 70s he made a string of commercial albums for Columbia, but returned to blazing jazz sounds with his 1980s albums for Pablo, Blue Note and Atlantic. Serious problems with his lip provoked a downturn from his brilliance in the 90s and removed him from the forefront of jazz, but his 60s heyday and epochal albums with Ornette Coleman (*Free Jazz*, 1960), Oliver Nelson (*Blues And The Abstract Truth*, 1961), John Coltrane (*Ascension*, 1965) and Herbie Hancock (*Maiden Voyage*, 1965) produced some of the most significant sounds of their era.

So this 1969 Hubbard recording *Without a Song* found the great trumpeter at the apex of his power and artistry in a live setting, accompanied by three masters, the Detroit pianist Sir Roland Hanna (given a "knighthood" by the President of Liberia for donating $100,000 of his earnings to Liberian schools), the Michigan-born arch-bassist Ron Carter and old Brooklyn apartment-mate and ex-drummer with Cannonball Adderley and Horace Silver, the rampaging Louis Hayes. Of the seven tracks, five were recorded in England and two in Germany, with the title tune opener from a concert in the Royal Festival Hall.

Hubbard plays with a lucid melodism, with Hayes thrashing his snares. His horn chirrups like a south-bank bird in the midst of his opening chorus, Hanna saunters through his solo with some stop-time phrases and the rhythm section lays out for some sprightly postbop-like choruses before Hubbard's horn comes dancing back.

The Things We Did Last Summer was recorded the following December day at Bristol's Colston Hall. Slow and waltz-like, Carter's plunging bass tethers it to the earth. Hubbard, always a pure-toned balladeer, almost sings through his horn so expressive is his lyricism and Hanna's solo is totally empathetic.

During the 70s Hubbard was to make a series of albums for Pablo as one of the "Trumpet Kings" with Dizzy Gillespie, Harry Edison and Clark Terry. Gillespie's *A Night in Tunisia* comes from the Bristol concert, begun with some stomping choruses by Hanna before Hubbard's solo soars out over Hayes' thunderous drums. This performance must have sent the Clifton suspension bridge swinging over the Avon, with Hubbard's final coda, touching all parts of the trumpet's range, a dramatic climax.

Red Garland's *Blues By Five* follows, with Hubbard's sheer horn power and Hanna's rocking piano preceding Carter's walking basslines. On his return a ferocious Hubbard gives way to Hayes in full fury. *Body and Soul* is usually a tenor saxophone test-piece, but Hubbard makes it his own with breathy beauty and a burnished brilliance.

Perhaps Hubbard's own *Space Track* was commemorating satellite travel and moon landings, but its speed and sonic power makes it a vehicle for his prime brass artistry and shows us again what we have lost. Bless the travelling sound engineers who have given us this fine recording previously unreleased, a memoriam to one of music's great and most passionate hornmen.

November 3rd 2009

Urgent Response to the Times

Chris McGregor Group
Very Urgent
(Fledgling)

Their music was "very urgent" certainly, but so was the cause of their people's struggle. This was 1968. The Blue Notes had arrived from apartheid-cursed South Africa in 1964.

There were five of them: trumpeter Mongezi Feza, drummer Louis Moholo, bassist Johnny Dyani, pianist Chris McGregor and altoist Dudu Pukwana. By 1968 they had also enlisted another South African compatriot, the tenorist Ronnie Beer.

The influence that they had over their British free jazz peers was huge and dramatic. The London-based jazz musicians had never heard anything quite like them before.

The band played with a raw emotive power which reflected the cruelty and struggle in their misgoverned nation. Feza's stark, biting notes set his listeners' nerves on a dangerous edge. Pukwana's saxophone runs seemed to express a stubborn resistance. McGregor's keyboard recast his church upbringing and Monkian angles with an agonised, bursting sonic power. Dyani's resonant strings combined a deep, insurgent twang with Moholo's tempestuous drums.

Their music spoke of their emergent nation, its pain, its cry, its tenacity, its wilfulness, its resistance. And yet this album was waxed in a studio just off the trendiest and vainest street in London — King's Road, Chelsea, the antithesis of everything that the music stood for.

As the swinging Londoners sauntered by outside in their sack dresses, fur waistcoats and embroidered jeans, South Africans were removed from their homes, "endorsed out" of their communities, beaten up by savage police, and taught the hated Afrikaans language in broken-down schools, while their faraway fathers worked in deadly tunnels in gold and diamond mines. And the music of Chris, Johnny, Dudu, Ronnie, Louis and Mongezi told all these stories in every note they played.

The opener is Pukwana's starkly melodic *Marie My Dear*, a love-dirge blues, with the caw of Dudu's alto woven into the unity of the other two horns, creating a dark township narrative of hidden sorrow. It moves directly into the ominous prance of McGregor's *Travelling Somewhere*, featuring Mongezi's buzzing pocket trumpet sound glowering over Moholo's crashing drums and the sullen off-chimes of the piano. When Dudu enters with his carping notes echoed by Dyani's humid undertow, there is a bitter testimony being told.

Heart's Vibrations begins with a rampaging free ensemble and McGregor's pounding keys in the ascendant, met by the searing phrases of Dudu and Mongezi, crying out the notes of their lives carried with them from their homeland. Dyani takes a solo of such throbbing vibrations below Moholo's clicking sticks like giant night insects.

The Sounds Begin Again pits Feza's screeching horn beside McGregor's pummelling of the keys, while Beer's regurgitating tenor adds its voice. Collectively, it is an unleashed sound like nothing before in jazz, born from a tradition concealed from European and North American listeners until the advent of these musicians.

McGregor's piano fury is unabated and Dyani's wondrous solo seems to rise up from some deep subterranean source, as the theme recasts itself to that of *White Lies*, the title suddenly telling the truth of the sonic agony.

The final track is the traditional tune *Don't Stir the Beehive*, a cautionary slogan that was being disobeyed every second somewhere in the musicians' patrimony. McGregor flays the piano like a complex drum as the horns combine to cry out the tune, and then dissolve into separate and free narrative.

As you listen, you think about the reactions of those European listeners who first heard this music four decades ago. What would they have thought, how would they have interpreted this music's stories?

As for the storytellers, McGregor, Dyani, Pukwana and Feza are all gone. So bless their music, and the sound-witness that it brought to us across continents.

July 28th 2009

From RAF Band to Freedom: Two Free Jazz Pioneers

Spontaneous Music Ensemble

Withdrawal/Frameworks/Quintessence

(Emanem)

To emerge from the militarism and highly structured musical environs of the Royal Air Force in 1964 and then pioneer a transformation into a jazz setting which sought free improvisation without the conventional props of rhythm, melody or harmony was truly one of the most audacious leaps in the long history of music.

Yet this was the achievement of two young London ex-airmen, drummer John Stevens and altoist Trevor Watts, when they established the Spontaneous Music Ensemble in 1966. And as musical fortune would have it, their revolutionary union was matched by finding a brave recording engineer and producer who would record them and disseminate their astonishing sound. Enter Martin Davidson and his tenacious label, Emanem.

For the 1966-7 sessions on the *Withdrawal* album, created for a film soundtrack, Stevens and Watts assembled an ensemble of musicians who were to become beacons and prophets of the British free jazz movement — Toronto-born trumpeter and flugelhornist Kenny Wheeler, another Londoner and ex-RAF man Paul Rutherford on trombone, Bristolian Evan Parker on tenor and soprano saxophones and London bassist Barry Guy. Stevens knocks away on glockenspiel as well as drums and Watts adds his oboe.

Such a configuration of horns creates a mesmeric sound pattern and an insurgent dialogue of musical breath. English jazz had never heard the like, with Parker's stuttering wails, Wheeler's breathy, soaring phrases, Watts's bluesy interludes and Rutherford's growling interjections. Something new was being born in every note. On track five, Sheffielder Derek Bailey joins on amplified guitar and Watts plays vibes. Bailey's chinking notes add another sound dimension on *Sequence One*, where Rutherford's seismic slides create beautiful uproar with Wheeler's brass journeys and Stevens's snapping snares and pulsating cymbals.

A subliminal melodism flows from Watts's flute as *Sequence Two* begins and the percussion-emphatic *Puddles, Raindrops and Circles* features his oboe over bells, castanets, pole-drum and triangle. And as you hear the skittering ensemble on the final *Movement Three* and consider the sleeve photographs taken in the dungeon-like confines of the basement of a London bookshop, you think of the pioneering aspect of this music, which was as essential to the development of new ways for jazz as Armstrong's *Hot Five* or Charlie Parker's *Dial* sessions.

The CD *Frameworks*, comprising of 1968, 1971 and 1973 sessions, bring in the wordless voice of Norma Winstone and the prodigious but short-lived bassist Ron Herman. The 32-and-a-half-minute opener *Familie Sequence* has Watts on bass clarinet and Winstone in full ensemble with the horns of Wheeler and Rutherford, making an eerie and compelling unity.

Quartet Sequence is a half-hour track with Stevens, Watts, Herman and the guitar and voice of Julie Tippetts. Herman's bass sounds deep-rooted and subterranean and Tippetts finds a kind of harmony with Watts's chirruping soprano. On the final duo track with Stevens and Watts, the sound-blooming *Flower* recorded at the Little Theatre Club, musical empathy and comradeship tell a story of sheer sonic oneness of reed and drum, straight out of nature.

Quintessence, a double CD, is a very precious recording indeed, with Watts and Parker both on soprano, Stevens, Bailey and a young US bassist in Kent Carter.

You might expect an amalgam of such diehard virtuosi of improvised music to exercise their individualisms and put all collectivity aside. In fact the absolute contrary is true. Their performance creates a fully committed, almost selfless ensemble sound where each musician seems to be playing for his bandmates' lives, every note a message of connection and alliance.

If you follow the sound path of each man in turn, you soon determine how it leads directly into the unity of timbre. And at the heart of it all is Stevens's ever-wakeful drum inventiveness flickering, pounding, buzzing, tapping, vibrating — a whole cosmos of percussion.

This is the art of the unexpected where every note jolts the consciousness. That it happened first and once thirty-five years ago and has scarcely been bettered since is due to two men who learned their music in marching bands and wore wings on their uniforms. *Freedom* has the most surprising sources and out of such surprises an uncanny beauty is born.

January 8th 2010

Pentonville Blues

Kenny Clarke/Francy Boland Big Band

At Her Majesty's Pleasure/The Complete Live Recordings at Ronnie Scott's

(Rearward)

When the Pittsburgh-born pioneering bebop drummer Kenny Clarke emigrated to France in 1956 he soon became a magnet for visiting black US jazz musicians, performing and recording with both sojourning US and European contenders.

By 1961 he had formed a strong musical comradeship in Paris with the Belgian pianist Francy Boland. Together they created a powerful big band made up of the cream of European and ex-pat US jazz musicians.

The multiracial Kenny Clarke Francy Boland Big Band had a huge influence in bringing jazz artists of transatlantic traditions together. US players like the Chicago tenorist Johnny Griffin — a French resident — baritonist Sahib Shihab, trumpeters Benny Bailey and Idrees Sulieman and Ellingtonian bassist Jimmy Woode merged with British reedmen Ronnie Scott, Tony Coe and Derek Humble, Swedish and Dutch trombonists Åke Persson and Erik van Lier and self-exiled Canadian trumpeter Kenny Wheeler.

In 1969 the band arrived in Britain to play at Scott's Soho club. Griffin was arrested at Heathrow for minor tax offences and taken off for a night in Pentonville prison, returning a day later in time for the London gig.

Boland named an untitled piece he had written *Pentonville*, and Griffin's experiences provoked him to compose an entire suite dedicated to the British penal system, which he called *At Her Majesty's Pleasure*. After more than four decades this suite — one of my prize pieces of vinyl — has been issued as a CD, and it sounds better than ever.

It begins with *Pentonville* — a place soon to be known well by five brave trade unionists — and a hot, riffing theme which releases a scorching Sulieman, a rare Boland solo, while Scott sounds subdued and menacing over Persson's belligerent slides.

Wormwood Scrubs: *Dawn* begins the day calmly with Shihab's birdsong flute before the reeds get going. Scott and Griffin speed up the proceedings with rapid-fire tenor exchanges and there is an ensemble interlude before Humble's fleeting alto flies in.

The track *Doing Time* is a demonstration of what Clarke and fellow drummer Kenny Clare did with aplomb for the band for years. It leads directly into *Broadmoor* where Bailey's far-reaching flugelhorn, Scott's effervescent tenor and Coe's liquid clarinet all do a brief stretch.

The empathetic tenderness in Coe's tenor throughout the tense three minutes of *Holloway* breathes out in every note of Boland's quasi-Ellingtonian arrangement, while in *Reprieve* the pace and mood change into a swinging optimism forged by Bailey's soaring and swooping flugelhorn solo, Humble's agile alto and the warm, rolling rumble of Shihab's baritone horn.

All members seem to savour the closing track *Going Straight*, and among the concise solos Wheeler's sharp chorus and Humble's deft alto tones stand out. "No more prison!" the players seem to affirm with freedom-loving sounds at every juncture.

The band's eventual run of gigs at Scott's Frith Street club from February 17 to March 1 1969 was recorded on February 28, and the fired-up session brings back a whole jazz era.

The drumsets were raging for the opener *Box 703 Washington DC*, with crackling choruses from Sulieman and his Yugoslav section-mate Duško Gojković. Griffin was well on-song for his signature *Griff's Groove*, before Clarke and Clare erupted for their three joint drum features — *Volcano*, *And Thence We Issued Out Again To See the Stars* and the tumultuous finale *Kenny and Kenny*.

Now Hear My Meaning has Persson roaring and Shihab's baritone belching through the ensemble. *Rue Chaptal* unleashes the four trumpets for successive solos. The very solitary sentiments of *I Don't Want Nothing From Nobody and I Ain't Giving Nothing Away* gives space for Shihab's lonesome baritone and Sulieman's reclusive trumpet.

Sax No End is exactly that, with Griffin, Coe and a home-based Scott in full tenor fettle.

If you wondered how a fully charged and rampantly swinging big band full of brilliant musicians squeezed onto a tiny stage sounded in Ronnie's precious cavern more than four decades ago, this album is a must.

It rocks and grooves like fury.

February 8th 2011

A Revolutionary Jazz Spark

Iskra 1903

Chapter One/Buzz Soundtrack/Sequences 72 and 73
(Emanem)

Iskra (the spark) — now wasn't that the name of the illegal revolutionary newspaper of the Russian social democrats, first published in Munich in 1903 with Nadezhda Krupskaya, Lenin's partner, as its first secretary?

Few now associate the name with an astonishing trio of jazz improvisers called Iskra 1903, who made their first recordings in September 1970 at a concert at the ICA. Iskra 1903 was a revolutionary trio, in its own way. Bassist Barry Guy, trombonist Paul Rutherford and Sheffield-based guitarist Derek Bailey were soundmakers playing in a threesome like nobody else before them.

Just listen to the ICA concert tapes on the three-CD album *Chapter One* and you'll discover what I mean. Rutherford plays piano in the opening section, Guy uses his bow and Bailey plucks sounds from his guitar that are so new that you feel like the techniques are being discovered in the very moment that you hear them.

When Rutherford switches to trombone some way into the first improvisation another dynamic comes to the fore from this extraordinary slide-man, who learned his instrument within the strict and straitened confines of the Royal Air Force. Nothing could be less military than this.

All kinds of sounds pervade. As Rutherford blows with a soft, almost tender eloquence, there are taps and creaks emanating from somewhere within Bailey's crackling guitar, and the howls and growls from Rutherford's slides in *Improvisation 3* dissolve the boundaries between the players.

For much of the recording Guy's bass does not lay down time so much as transcend it with his sawing bow, creating not a beat or a rhythmic grounding but layers of timeless sound, each one lying on the one set down before, over which Bailey twangs and scrapes and Rutherford wails out his guttural cry with excruciating artistry. As you listen, you uncannily realise that this music is now forty years old and has had very little exposure over these decades. You also come to understand, after hearing just a short section of their music, that Iskra is an entirely correct and proper name.

Iskra 1903's music was and still is entirely original and new while also being revolutionary in its ensemble form. It is also a thoroughly collective endeavour. There are few outright solos, although often one of the trio takes leadership of the moment — such as Guy in his long bowed section towards the end of the twenty-five minutes of improvisation.

Their music is a collective assertion of sound, mutually supportive, a declaration of solidarity, of oneness made by three.

The tapes of Iskra 1903's soundtrack to the long-lost and unobtainable film *Buzz* were found by Rutherford in the year 2000 and made into the album *Buzz Soundtrack* in 2001. The listener can only imagine the images that the music accompanied. Darting, quivering, pointillist, the phrases more brief and less developed than in the *Chapter One* album, the listener hears the record with a certain frustration at being a deprived watcher, but the sounds are still captivating — in particular the Rutherford/Bailey interplay on *Buzz Trio 5.*

By September 1972 the trio had become a dozen, so accordingly the name was changed to Iskra 1912. The new recruits included some powerful players, with saxophonists Evan Parker and Trevor Watts, Toronto-born trumpeter Kenny Wheeler, pianist Howard Riley, vocalists Norma Winstone and Maggie Nicols, and Sheffielder Tony Oxley providing live electronics.

The *Sequences 72 and 73* album weaves an engrossing and unprecedented texture of sounds, with Rutherford's unaccompanied slide essay on *Non-sequence* and Bailey's beguiling preface to *Sequence 73* particularly memorable.

With all the musicians present, Iskra's separate sparks fuel the fire of consistent surprise which is jazz at its most real and unified. I think that Krupskaya would have loved it with a true seditious empathy.

June 24th 2010

If Music Could Stop War...

The Revolutionary Ensemble

Vietnam 1 / Vietnam 2

(ESP)

In 1971 at the apex of the war in Vietnam, soon after president Richard Nixon had declared of the Vietnamese people: "The bastards have never been bombed like they're going to be bombed this time," three eminent jazz musicians formed an astonishing trio calling themselves The Revolutionary Ensemble.

The violinist was Leroy Jenkins, born in Chicago in 1932 and an ex-student of the luminous DuSable High School where he came under the tutelage, like dozens of other future jazz musicians, of the formidable Captain Walter Dyett. He joined the Association for the Advancement of Creative Musicians, worked briefly in Paris with other free spirits — saxophonist Anthony Braxton, trumpeter Leo Smith and drummer Steve McCall in the Creative Construction Co — returned to the US and settled in New York where he founded The Revolutionary Ensemble. On bass was the outstanding Sirone — born Norris Jones in Atlanta, Georgia, in 1940 — with his superb bow technique, who had played with altoist Marion Brown and pianist Dave Burrell. The percussionist was an oft-times minimalist Jerome Cooper, another Chicagoan, born in 1946.

Together they produced expressively free and interactive improvised music creating a threesome of sheer jazz collectivism that lasted throughout most of the decade until 1977, cutting few albums but including a gem — *The People's Republic* — in 1976.

Vietnam 1 and *Vietnam 2* were recorded in 1973. Nixon had launched the 1972 Christmas bombing campaign of Hanoi hoping to secure concessions from the Vietnamese at the Paris peace talks in January 1973. The US invasion forces had been defeated after nearly a decade of murderous aggression and by March 6 1973 all US military personnel had left South Vietnam, although lower-intensity conflict still ensued.

The Ensemble's album was made during a period of upcoming victory and here was the music of three startlingly creative African-Americans registering their sonic solidarity with the Vietnamese people and their armed forces at New York's "Peace Church", a fitting enough venue for the recording.

When the Ensemble first started playing Sirone remembered how the local jazz musicians expostulated at their powerfully unusual instrumentation. "Violin, bass and drums, you must be crazy!" many of them declared. And yet this was a narrative of war in a place of peace and their sound needed to be full of that ambivalence, that terrible and real contradiction.

Vietnam 1 begins with shimmering bows, high and low, violin and bass strings skimming off each other as if they were locked into a life and death combat. It is a unique sound new to jazz, new to all music — a sonic picture of war by two virtuosi of peace. As Sirone turns to plucking, the dualism becomes even more extreme with Cooper's background cymbals becoming gradually stronger. When Sirone continually thuds the same dark note and Jenkins scrapes an agonised sound above him, the war's terrifying edge becomes explicit for both sides, the invaded people and their drafted and compelled US aggressors.

This is truly audacious music of its time. Its meanings are not hidden by abstraction but made more awful by their sensuous truth. Perhaps it needed such an unprecedented jazz trio to conjure it, a wilful commentary on all that is wrong and excruciating, yet its torment of improvisation is so full of artistry and brilliance.

It is the *Guernica* or the *All Quiet On the Western Front* of jazz, a sound portrait of invasion since visited upon the peoples as the targets of terror in Iraq or Afghanistan.

As an unaccompanied Sirone darkly twangs out the sound of such shock and awe from his deep and pulsating strings we hear one of the peerless jazz solos inspired to create a timbre of consternation, dread and suffering from the very fingers of life and hope.

Jenkins's violin shrieks and cries as the human voice is also perceptible inside his toxic and beauteous notes that shake with the sound of a dream of bliss. And when Cooper strikes his solo his rolling drums seem to unleash a thunderous freedom that promises peace and reconstruction.

Essential music for those times and these.

September 22nd 2010

Alpha Boy

Joe Harriott
The Joe Harriott Story Box Set
(Proper Box)
Alan Robertson
Joe Harriott: Fire in His Soul
(Northway Publications)

From Jamaica, Guyana, Trinidad and all the jewelled islands in between they came after a world war. Migrants, nurses, teachers, soon to become railwaymen, bus drivers, factory workers: all Caribbean peoples whose families and forebears had so much taken from them during the four hundred years of slavery, colonialism and imperial bondages.

And with them arrived Joe Harriott, come to blow his horn.

As a ten-year-old boy he had found himself, like Louis Armstrong, in an orphanage. This was Kingston's Alpha Boys' School, where among a colonial curriculum he found the food and freedom of music. The clarinet — and the alto sax which followed — gave him the work and opportunity for a life of brilliance and a reason for taking the Windrush wake to Britain, to pursue his love of jazz, fired up but never dominated by the alto sax genius of Kansas City's Charlie "Bird" Parker.

In London, from 1951 he began his long sojourn of saxophone glory as a relentlessly jobbing jazz musician. Never more than a few luminous notes from poverty, he took any work that he could get, from gigs in quasi-New Orleans bands like that of Chris Barber to dance bands, bop outfits and audacious new jazz formations on the very sharpest edge of the music.

Hear his unique reed beauty all through the new boxed set *The Joe Harriott Story*, and compare his linear and piercing Antillean lines to the blues-drenched gyrations of the great Parker while you read of his brave, rebellious and meanly appreciated sound in the compelling and beautifully written biography by the Scotsman Alan Robertson, *Fire in His Soul*, which has just been republished.

In my 2004 *Star* review of Robertson's rightly acclaimed book I wrote of Harriott as "a proud, self-directed and lonely seer of jazz, a black musical prodigy in a white British underworld of the music where it was so much more easy and comfortable to be an imitator." Harriott was never that and, after his faraway death from cancer in Southampton in 1973, not for nothing does the inscription on his

Bitterne churchyard tombstone quote his own defiant and spiky words: "Parker? There's them over here can play a few aces too."

Such aces abound from the 50s tracks with drummer Tony Kinsey's quartet, through standards like *April in Paris*, or the wringingly moving *Everything Happens to Me*, to his performances on *Band* and *A Night in Tunisia*, with the short-lived power of the Ronnie Scott Big Band and a volcanic Phil Seamen on drums. And he blows a seething solo on *The Big Fist*, composed by another alumnus of the Alpha School, the crackling trumpeter Dizzy Reece, a Jamaican brother of jazz eminence.

But it was in November 1960 that Harriott began to forge his most potent contribution to the jazz canon.

Three members of his new pathfinding quintet were Caribbean through and through. Beside Harriott was fellow Jamaican bassist Coleridge Goode and the startling trumpeter and St Vincent poet Shake Keane, with his exquisitely pitched lyrical expressivism. The pianist was Scottish lawyer and ex-RAF pilot Pat Smythe, and the pounding drums of Burton-on-Trent's Seamen earthed the band while creating an almost levitating buoyancy.

Eight tracks composed by Harriott made up the hugely innovative album *Abstract*. His quicksilver chorus at the outset of *Formation* is a marvel, as is the ever agile Keane's puckish solo and the tiptoe ensemble over Goode's sucking bass.

Smythe's chordal surprises create an undertow of unity in *Coda*, and in *Abstract* Keane blows a burning high-rise release followed by Harriott's twisted, whirling beauty. Shake is razor sharp too in *Straight Lines*, with Harriott's geometrical sound patterns above a plunging Goode. Through *Caribbean Sketches*, Keane and Harriott transform the visual to the timbral as blazing lights and tropical seascapes are rendered in sound.

Seamen's British drums sounds are deeply rooted in Africa, provoking the growling, honking and pealing of the Caribbean horns.

Within this small box is a feast of Harriott and some of his closest and most powerful musical comrades — half a century old now, but still ripe, beautiful and full of the narrative of the migration and struggle of an entire generation.

January 17th 2012

Saturday Afternon Resistance

Joe McPhee & Survival Unit II with Clifford Thornton

Live at WBAI's Free Music Store, NY, NY

(hatART)

A key sonic text of its troubled times, Joe McPhee's October 1971 broadcast from New York's WBAI Free Music Store tells as much about its social and political context as any newscast or newspaper.

Protest against the war of aggression in Vietnam was rampant — 12,000 anti-war demonstrators had been arrested in Washington in April and, the month before the broadcast, 1,500 armed police backed up by helicopters had attacked Attica state prison to crush an inmate rebellion, killing thirty-one prisoners and nine hostages.

The anger, resistance and determination come pounding and crying out in this music, made by McPhee playing trumpet and tenor, Byron Morris on soprano and alto, pianist Mike Kull and drummer Harold E Smith. A special guest was the rarely recorded Philadelphia-born baritone horn player and trumpeter Clifford Thornton, whose first album *Freedom and Unity* was recorded one day after the funeral of John Coltrane in July 1967, with McPhee making his debut recording.

Redolent with black pride and notes of defiance, the band — called Survival Unit II — sound out the jazz message of their era through this newly remastered recording of the original broadcast of WBAI-FM, a New York radio station that gave open support to the contemporary Civil Rights and anti-war protests.

The announcer tells us this is live jazz on a Saturday afternoon and the music store's shelves must have been shaking as McPhee rasped and roared out his saxophone notes at the beginning of the opener, *Black Magic Man*, with Smith's thunderous drums behind him.

McPhee introduces the band and then it's directly into *Nation Time*, the title tune of McPhee's 1970 live album and a tribute to the poet, dramatist and critic Ameer Baraka. First McPhee's tenor, Morris's piercing soprano and Thornton's delving and plunging baritone horn take their solos while Kull scatters his chords inside their notes and takes his own solo journey. The mood changes for the love ballad *Song for Lauren*, the third of all six McPhee compositions on the album. His solo boils up to an ecstatic climax before the moments of calm which presage Kull's choruses and Thornton's poised and echoing solo.

The spirit of resistance radiates all through *Message from Denmark*, sounding from McPhee's caustic and free trumpet fanfare which soars out of its opening. The track remembers the brave defiance of the freed slave Denmark Vesey (1769–1822) who conceived, planned and organised a slave rebellion in his home city of Charleston, South Carolina in 1822, but whose efforts were betrayed by informers on the eve of the uprising in which more than 9,000 slaves and free blacks had committed to taking part. Vesey was captured, tried for the would-be insurrection and hanged.

1971 had its own Denmark Veseys, women like Angela Davis or men like George Jackson, killed in San Quentin prison in the act of resistance two months before this recording.

All three horns blow with a fiery, rebellious fury and Smith's drums call out for action in the sounds of turbulent and insurgent times. From hero man to hero woman as the music leaps from Denmark Vesey to Harriet Tubman. *Harriet* is the final track on the album and McPhee's corrosive trumpet is perhaps seeking the authority of her voice, the voice of a woman risen up from a brutal slavery in Maryland where she was almost killed by an overseer who threw a metal weight at her head, a woman whose long life from 1820 to 1913 shone as a relentless abolitionist and organiser of the Underground Railroad which carried hundreds of slaves to freedom in Canada, and a campaigner for women's suffrage.

Morris's alto hovers and sweeps over Kull's grounded comping, Smith's skins crash out their message and McPhee's saxophone tells Tubman's proud life narrative.

As the applause rings all around the Free Music Store it carries a then-times and now-times understanding of those like Vesey and Tubman, those still incarcerated yet struggling in the prisons of New York state and California, and those still campaigning in the aftermath of the Civil Rights contests in Alabama, Georgia and Mississippi.

Jazz is their storyteller, true, beautiful and immediate, and McPhee and his fellow musicians are their griots, then and now.

June 30th 2011

The Last Monk

Thelonious Monk Quartet

The Last Concerts

(RLR)

Well, I never realised before that there was a Wolverhampton boy playing bass on some of Thelonious Monk's last recordings, but you can hear Dave Holland, agile and plunging, on a new discovery session on the RLR label.

RLR is short for "rare live recordings" made from private tapes often carried by members of the audience, so don't expect world-class sound engineering.

But the glorious and enigmatic Monk sound it is, and they represent some of his final testimonies.

Through much of 1972 Monk was touring with the all-star Giants of Jazz band, including Dizzy Gillespie on trumpet, altoist Sonny Stitt and Art Blakey on drums, and he made his last studio recordings with them in Berne in November 1971. But in June 1972 he played at New York's Village Vanguard with a quartet which included Holland, tenorist Paul Jeffrey and Monk's son TS 'Toot' Monk on drums.

Jeffrey, born in Harlem in 1933, had met and studied with Monk's longtime tenorist Charlie Rouse in the 1950s, and shortly before the Vanguard date had toured with Monk in the Carolinas and Japan. It was also around this time that Monk, having left his New York flat and wife Nellie, was withdrawing further and further inside himself, finally moving into the house of his friend Nica von Koenigswarter in Weehawken, New Jersey.

So the Village Vanguard tapes register a crucial time in his own personal and mental deterioration.

Full of life and vibrant music they are too, from the slow, disguised beginning of the first notes of *Straight, No Chaser* and Jeffrey's loping solo, the music takes off with Holland and Toot creating an easy flow. Holland takes a deft solo with Monk comping behind him, and the pianist's own shining chorus sounds as if he is truly enjoying himself.

Off Minor and Jeffrey's solo make a fascinating comparison with all those of Rouse, who played with Monk regularly for over a decade. Jeffrey's sound is completely different, a long way from the breathy, almost adenoidal timbre of Rouse. His is a lot less gruff, much more riverine and lyrical, almost sweet-sounding at times, as on *Round Midnight*.

Twelve minutes of *Hackensack* offer some vintage Monk after Jeffrey swings though a buoyant and sparky solo. His notes bounce off the keys with Toot tapping his snares behind him as he explores the familiar but still unexpected angles and different levels of the tune.

Toot comes in for a powerful solo, playing all over his drums and cymbals as Holland plays unaccompanied, bringing Midlands musical genius to the famous New York club, his notes twanging eerily all through the shuttered space. *Evidence* follows, and there is plenty of that of Monk's still very nimble brain and keyboard co-ordination as he dives into his tune.

Jeffrey is confidently creative and full of fire — what a pity there were no studio recordings made of him and Monk, who flies in his solo, lifted up by the near-levitating beat of Toot and Holland. The familiar theme of *Blue Monk* sets Jeffrey on more original pathways and Monk himself is so far inside his notes that it sounds like pure autobiography.

In July 1975 Monk's sound was given its final recording by an audience member with a portable tape recorder at the Lincoln Center during a Newport Jazz Festival in New York session. It was the same quartet, except that Larry Ridley replaced Holland.

I Mean You begins the performance, and as Jeffrey takes the first solo his sound seems to have changed since the 1972 Village Vanguard sessions — it is fuller, more surly, even approaching Rouse's coarser sound in some phrases.

Monk plays with force and verve, clamping down as he comps with words seeming to pour from his fingers in his tunes like *Ba-lue Bolivar Ba-lues-are* and *We See*, where Jeffrey takes another impressive solo flight as Monk thumps out his chords.

The ponderous and blues-edged *Misterioso* is powerful indeed — Monk's penultimately recorded tune expresses a complex joy in sadness from his solo notes which is hard to forget.

As for his very last, it is his most famous — *Round Midnight* — and its first phrase heralds a brief shower of applause. A journey through the theme with Jeffrey, some crying notes from the saxophone, Monk's own stamping solo, the theme again with his son hitting the rimshots, and finish.

The rest was silence.

August 16th 2011

Never to be Erased

Derek Bailey

Fairly Early Derek Bailey with Postscripts/First Duo Concert London 1974/Domestic and Public Pieces
(Emanem)

I remember the first time that I heard Derek Bailey and his guitar live. It was at a benefit concert for the Communist Party of Great Britain in the mid-70s.

As he sat alone on the Roundhouse stage playing unaccompanied acoustic guitar I listened and could only think "what is this?" I had grown to love the sound of the guitar, from the blues-sodden notes of Muddy Waters to the melodic and lightning-fingered jazz virtuosi like Django Reinhardt and Wes Montgomery, but I had heard nothing like Bailey.

His timbre was atonal, acerbic, raw and naked, an epic scraping of sound. I took it as a challenge. I listened closely to his albums and almost unknowingly began to hear a strange beauty pouring from his fingers.

A Sheffielder born in 1932, he had spent the 50s in theatre and dance bands playing bread and butter music, from the pit of the London Palladium to a band accompanying Gracie Fields. I tried to imagine him playing *Sally, Pride of Our Alley* or *The Biggest Aspidistra in the World*. What would have been in his mind?

From this world of commercial music he moved to its opposite extreme, turning to free improvising jazz in his home city with drummer Tony Oxley and bassist Gavin Bryars in the 60s and finally moving to London to play with other brilliant but impoverished improvising pioneers like John Stevens, Evan Parker and Paul Rutherford in groups as diverse as the Spontaneous Music Ensemble and Iskra 1903.

He eventually toured with his band Company through the 70s, playing through Europe, Africa, the Americas and Japan. He established an unprecedented sound and technique, making music which was frequently emulated but never equalled.

The Emanem label documented much of his musical life — he died in 2005 — and has produced some key recordings of his work.

Fairly Early Derek Bailey with Postscripts spans 1971 to 1998 from solo, duo and trio performances.

The *Six Fairly Early Pieces* use a six-string guitar with pedal-controlled amplification and are full of tinkling string echoes and juxtapositions of curt, amputated and lingering notes making seemingly astral sounds.

There are two *Rehearsal Extracts* from 1974 with the Chicagoan reedman Anthony Braxton playing sopranino saxophone and flute. Bailey has a nineteen-string guitar which he plays with a bow, creating a low, pulsating groan with brusque interruptions while Braxton warbles and caws as if birdsong were formalised. *Tunnel Hearing* of 1980 has dislocated blues echoes, with Bailey rambling "Some people smoke, some drink and I talk to myself."

Luckily he played guitar too. Stevens plays drums and Kent Carter plays bass on *A Bit of the Crust* and *A Bit of the Dumps*, two extraordinary yet brief tracks where an improvising hornless trio sound almost orchestral.

The Last Post-Morning and *The Last Post-Afternoon* were recorded in May 1979 in the kitchen of Bailey's Hackney flat and sent to Emanem's Martin Davidson in the US on the eve of Thatcher's election victory. Interspersed with astonishing acoustic guitar runs and the most unexpected sound images, Bailey curses Thatcher, describes his neighbour's scrapyard, plays tapes of Thatcher and Heath — "the old twat and the new twat" — and ironically concludes that it is all "the price of freedom" with a brilliant and caustic coda.

Bailey's 1974 duo concert with Braxton at the Wigmore Hall is a fertile meeting. Braxton plays soprano, sopranino and alto saxophones, flute, clarinet, soprano and contrabass clarinets while Bailey plays amplified and nineteen-string guitars.

Two masters at work, here finding unity from entirely separated skills and consciousnesses, making sound the catalyst of coalescence. Braxton melodises, spits and chokes through his reeds, blowing beauteous sounds next to arresting whistles, while Bailey's strums and brusque phrases break open into surprising moments of unexpected loveliness.

So much guitar improvisation of *Domestic and Public Pieces*, including the 1976 clinical account of the burned Unity Theatre — the home of the Musicians' Cooperative where Bailey often played — with his dry voice over the graphic, fiery, irrepressible strings that chime out, almost with an invention of their own throughout the performances both in Bailey's former Islington home and the more stellar venue of the Institute of Contemporary Arts.

"Music is self-erasing," he said. Not quite — these powerful Emanem recordings and many others remain.

January 14th 2011

True Woman Pioneer

Mary Lou Williams

A Grand Night for Swinging

(High Note)

Mary Lou Williams was one of the most brilliant and versatile musicians of jazz. She was a true pioneer of the music, ever discovering.

Born Mary Scruggs in Atlanta in 1910, her family moved north and she grew up in Pittsburgh, where she learned piano from the age of six and went on to perform at parties and in vaudeville. She married saxophonist John Williams in 1927, moved to Oklahoma and, by 1928, she was arranging for Andy Kirk's band, which, largely due to her swinging arrangements, soon became renowned.

She also contributed compositions and arranged for other prime swing bands, led by Earl Hines, Benny Goodman and Tommy Dorsey.

Williams was at the centre of the emergent bop scene in the 40s, writing scores for Dizzy Gillespie's big band and becoming a close companion of Thelonious Monk and Bud Powell. In the 50s, she lived in England and France for two key years, performing in trios and quartets, before returning to New York, converting to Catholicism and founding a charity dedicated to aiding musicians struggling with depression and the abuse of drugs and alcohol.

She returned to performing in 1957 and subsequently made some of her finest recordings, many of them at live dates in intimate club settings, where, sparked by responsive audiences and superbly inventive sidemen, she played with astonishing skill and originality.

A Grand Night for Swinging is typical of such dates.

Cut during a live hotel performance in Buffalo in 1976, Williams is accompanied by Roy Haynes, one of the truly supreme jazz drummers and veteran of recording sessions with masters from Charlie Parker, Monk, Powell, Lester Young to Eric Dolphy and John Coltrane, plus bassist Ronnie Boykins. The session concludes with a brief interview with the ever-effervescent Williams, who asserts that jazz is at the centre of US music because it "beats love and is healing to the soul."

And you can believe it too as the trio open up with the title song. Boykins tethers down the springing beat while Williams's notes spin everywhere above Haynes's dancing brushes.

It is difficult to give original ring to such an overplayed standard as *I Can't Get Started*, yet this trio achieve it. Williams's choice of pauses, stresses and embellishments and her two-handed artistry make it almost seem like a new tune and, as you listen closely to *My Funny*

Valentine, you get a strange sense that there are two pianists at work, so hard is each hand working along the keys.

Bag's Blues is a tribute to the pioneering vibes man Milt Jackson. Jackson was a master of the blues himself and Mary Lou's fast lick would have set his appetite grooving.

Williams had an uncanny way of transforming blues-song into joysong and she does this again all through the *St Louis Blues*.

WC Handy's familiar theme is turned upside down, first in her unaccompanied intro and then with Haynes and Boykins skipping beside her in a zestful romp full of swinging heat and concoction. When she turns to saxophonist John Stubblefield's contemporary praise-tune for his newborn son *Baby Man*, there is beautiful gentleness and sense of wonder arising from her notes us they vault from her keys.

Williams worked as an Ellingtonian arranger in the mid-40s, and the trio's version of *Caravan* shows her empathy with the Duke.

This is very much a Haynes feature and, after the pianist lets go with some tearing choruses, the drummer moves from virtual quietude to a blast of skins that must have sent the hotel's cocktails splashing in frenzy.

A Grand Night for Swinging it's called and it certainly was. It serves as an excellent introduction to an often neglected genius of jazz piano.

December 17th 2008

Her Flying Voice

Norma Winstone

Somewhere Called Home / Well Kept Secret / Distances / Stories Yet To Tell

(ECM)

During the early 70s, when I was teaching in Poplar, East London, one of my colleagues who cleaned our old Victorian secondary school building was a woman in her late fifties called Ruth. She was an ever-busy, friendly work companion who took huge pride in her job — you could see yourself darkly in the waxy, glowing parquet floor of the school hall. She lived in the pinnacle of a tall council block looking straight into the throat of the north entrance of the Blackwall Tunnel. Ruth loved music, in particular the singing of Frank Sinatra, and one afternoon after school as I was stacking up chairs in my classroom she asked me about my choice of sounds.

"Jazz!" I replied. "Oh, me too," she replied.

"You know, my niece is a jazz singer. A very good one. Have you heard her? Norma's her name, Norma Winstone." She was right, for sure.

Norma had been born in Bow in 1941 but moved further east to Dagenham with her family after the war, sharing the same school with that prodigy of comedy and jazz piano, Dudley Moore. From a teenage beginning in East London pubs, by 1960 she had become a successful vocalist, singing with jazz groups led by Michael Garrick and Mike Westbrook.

In the mid-1970s she formed the trio Azimuth with pianist John Taylor and trumpeter Kenny Wheeler, making albums with her sometimes wordless and other times song lyrics for the Munich-based ECM label.

Hear, for example, *How It Was Then* on the Azimuth album with the same title. In this Winstone — with her buoyant, hazy passion, Taylor's rippling runs and Wheeler's piercing notes — rejects any compromise with the injustices of the past, in the cottonfields of memory and history.

"How it was then, never again," she reprises many times over.

In 1986 she recorded *Somewhere Called Home* — her first ECM album as a lead singer — with Taylor and the Canterbury-born reedman Tony Coe.

Her voice hovers airily over Taylor's notes, finding the same levitating level as Coe's caressing tenor in *Prologue* and *Celeste*, or his piercing clarinet interventions in *Café* and *Sometime Ago.*

Photo by Lisa Valder.

There are surprises too, with Coe's spiky clarinet introducing a ruminative Winstone thinking out her way through *Hi Lili Hi Lo* and floating through the American Songbook classics *Out of This World* and *Tea for Two*.

Her 1993 album, recorded in Los Angeles with the pianist from Spokane, Washington, Jimmy Rowles — who had accompanied Billie Holiday and Lester Young — was given the most apt of titles with reference to Norma Winstone, *Well Kept Secret*.

Rowles had bounce and verve in his every sound, and with bassist George Mraz beside him Winstone swings through Ellington (*Prelude To a Kiss*), Strayhorn (*A Flower Is a Lonesome Thing*), Clifford Brown (*Joy Spring*) and more songbook ballads like *Where or When* and *Dream of You*. Her weightless lyricism is a foil for both Rowles and the twanging Mraz, and the album skips, soars, reflects and glides from its first to very last note.

Winstone was 67 when she recorded *Distances* for ECM, following this with a further trio album, *Stories Yet To Tell*, in 2010. Both albums featured the bass clarinettist and saxophonist from Düsseldorf, Klaus Gesing, and the Italian pianist Glauco Venier.

Still in her prime and "climbing in heights of invisible air" as she sings in the first album's title song, her empathy with these two cross-generational musicians is complete and powerfully moving.

Her winnowing voice, whether in familiar songs like *Every Time We Say Goodbye* or through her brief calypso — spurred by Jamaican Andrew Salkey's poetry — *A Song for England*, is perfectly poised, sometimes aching, sometimes full of wonder, wit and dance.

But it is always beautiful, particularly *Giant's Gentle Stride*, inspired by Coltrane's *Giant Steps*.

As for *Stories To Tell*, the musicianship is just as fine and it is as if Winstone has found her perfect partners. She moves the pitch of her voice with a parallel skill to Gesin's changes from soprano saxophone to bass clarinet while fusing with the precise chiming of Venier's keys.

Their harmony is rare and beautiful, particularly on the exquisite *Cradle Song* where she sings with words and wordless with a marvel of meaning and sound.

A few weeks ago I walked past the old Poplar school where Ruth and I had worked. I saw a converted block of luxury flats, gated and exclusive for the banking fraternity of nearby Canary Wharf.

The old playground of many a child's joy and discovery was now a car park. Ruth's shining corridor and classroom floors, glossed in pride for local working-class children, now took the footfalls of the government-subsidised new rich. Another story to tell for Winstone.

And truth to tell, every time I hear her flying voice and storyteller's words I think of her aunt and my dear colleague Ruth, her jokes and humanity ringing across East London.

February 15th 2011

Clarity and Beauty

Bobby Bradford
Love's Dream
(Emanem)
John Carter and Bobby Bradford
Tandem 1/Tandem 2
(Emanem)
John Carter and Bobby Bradford Quartet
Seeking
(hatOLOGY)

Born in Cleveland, Mississippi, in 1934 and raised in Dallas, Texas, Bobby Bradford is one of the most innovative and yet overlooked of jazz trumpeters.

As a youth he played with other local contemporaries soon to be eminent, like the Jazz Messengers' pianist Cedar Walton and Ray Charles's future tenorist David "Fathead" Newman. But Bradford took a very different tack after he moved to Los Angeles in 1953, serving his time in the USAF and at university, and he began playing with Eric Dolphy and in the Ornette Coleman Quartet in 1961-63.

He missed out on some key recording sessions with Coleman which established the quartet's music as a revolutionary new sound in jazz. So instead of sudden musical renown, Bradford became a teacher — a profession he has pursued for most of his life. In 1973 Bradford came to London staying with the creator of the Emanem label Martin Davidson and finding kindred spirits in drummer John Stevens and altoist Trevor Watts.

I remember John's excitement at the prospect of playing with him and he brought him down to one of our Stepney poetry sessions at the Half Moon Theatre — a converted synagogue in Alie Street where John, Trevor and Bobby, accompanied some local poets, played rampant music which shook the old pews and rafters.

That trio, plus US bassist Kent Carter, is the personnel of *Love's Dream* recorded at "Le Chat qui Pêche" — a Paris Latin Quarter club — in 1973. It's a marvellously skilled and fresh live date with Stevens playing furiously on a full kit and not the smaller set he played with the Spontaneous Music Ensemble. Watts is in tremendous mettle, his notes splashing out in all directions.

Bradford rips free on the title tune laying back on Stevens's rippling drums, and on the first take of *Coming On* at breakneck speed Watts's fiery alto bursts out of Carter's delving bass and Bradford's horn sparks rebellion. The very slow and dirge-like *She* — also called *Woman* — makes an extreme contrast. Carter uses his bow, Watts wails forlornly and Bradford blows out alone.

Roswita's Dance is also Stevens's dance of drums and flickering cymbals, and Watts's gyrating chorus is wondrous. *HM Louis 1* is the quartet's salute to the mighty Armstrong who had died two years before and it is Bradford's acknowledgement to tradition as well as musical insurgence. Watts plays out of his skin with superb poise and invention in his interplay with Bradford, who catches Satchmo's fire.

When Carter returned stateside he paired up with the Fort Worth-born (in 1928) clarinettist and another LA arrivant John Carter. Together they had formed the New Art Jazz Ensemble in 1964 and had the closest musical connections. The two volumes of *Tandem* are taken from live sessions at UCLA in 1979 and Worcester, Massachusetts, in 1982 with Carter playing his completely demilitarised cornet.

Horn duets with nil rhythmic accompaniment should and feel what they are — adorned with air with no hiding place. The two men play brilliantly and the avid listener misses nothing. No wonder that Coleman said of Bradford: "He is one of the greatest trumpeters alive."

He whips in and out of breath conjuring stupendous sounds, lung-dancing with Carter's own dextrous and high-pitched quivering notes. The clarinet lyricism on *Petals* is tender and beauteous, and Carter's

birdsong sounds on *Angles* are as nature itself. Bradford takes his own solo track as if it were his own true voice. *Woodman's Hall Blues* recalls an old venue in Fort Worth and is a colloquy of horn genius, each breath sparking from the other.

Finally there is the quartet album *Seeking* which preceded Bradford's English sojourn and was recorded in Los Angeles in 1969. This was the New Art Jazz Ensemble with bassist Tom Williamson and drummer Bruz Freeman, a Chicagoan and brother of two other fine musicians — tenorist Von and guitarist George. At this point in his musical life Carter was still a multi-instrumentalist playing alto and tenor saxophone as well as flute and clarinet.

The Californian prospect of *In the Vineland* suggests the vines being hit by sweeping winds with Carter's seething alto blasts, while Bradford's horn calms the storm. Freeman's drums flutter with fury. *Sticks and Stones* feature Carter's whirlwind clarinet and Williamson's pounding bassline, while in *The Village Dancers* Bradford blows a solo of pristine clarity and radiance.

But the finale *Song for the Unsung* is Bradford's own composition that could almost be the story of his own life, except there is so much excellence, skill, originality and beauty to his sound that for him at least the overlooked was never overcome.

October 13th 2010

A Greenwich Horn

Paul Rutherford and Paul Rogers

Solo in Berlin / Rogues / Chicago 2002
(Emanem)

Growing up in south London — rather than the streets of New Orleans, Chicago or Harlem — of all the virtuoso trombonists blowing through a century of jazz, none had more uniquely creative brilliance with their tricky slides than Paul Rutherford, born in Greenwich, London in 1940, the son of a socialist ex-soldier who worked at the Woolwich Arsenal.

His elder brother, a Charlie Parker devotee, encouraged him to learn the alto saxophone, but he turned to the trombone. In 1958 he joined the RAF as an expedient to study and develop his musical skills at its Uxbridge music college, and there he met two other recruits, altoist Trevor Watts and drummer John Stevens, thus ironically making the authoritarian and class-divided ranks of the Royal Air Force the true birthing place of British free jazz.

In 1963 Rutherford was demobbed and enrolled in London's Guildhall School of Music, and by 1966 he had joined up again with Stevens and Watts to create the Spontaneous Music Ensemble, and was organising free-improvising sessions on a regular basis at the Little Theatre Club in Covent Garden.

His first entirely solo album *The Gentle Harm of the Bourgeoisie*, recorded in 1974, expressed not only Rutherford's outrageous improvising skills but also his mastery of multiphonics, whereby he blew and sung down his horn simultaneously, also employing mutes and sophisticated spittle techniques which were entirely new to the sonics of jazz.

Much more of this original musical genius pours out of *Solo In Berlin 1975*, a compilation of Rutherford's performances in the city that, for a generation before his, had held the directorate of a jazz-hating fascism.

Now there was a British musician in full mettle who believed that "improvisation and any avant-garde work is progressive," and that "artists can be the greatest gift that any new socialist society can have." In the Berlin solos, Rutherford is speaking, proclaiming, joking and professing through his horn with seventy-five minutes of extraordinary slide narrative.

Listen to the brass speech of *A Song My Granny Taught Me* and imagine her in full relish, or the battery of sardonic notes of *Not a Very*

Wonderful Ballad and its amused self-awareness. As for the foursome of pieces, *Primus*, *Secundus*, *Tertius* and *Quartus*, they take the trombone as far out as it has ever gone in jazz, and perhaps in any other musical genre — an astonishing achievement which makes you wonder at the state of Rutherford's lip at its finish.

On to 1988, when Rutherford paired with the arch-bassist Paul Rogers — born in 1956 and part of the Mujician quartet with Keith Tippett, Paul Dunmall and Tony Levin — to record the album *Rogues* in a Birmingham pub called the Cannonball, which for jazz lovers finds itself on Adderley Street.

So the only accompaniment to this duo is not the great Florida altoist but clinking beer glasses, cash tills and dry throats, hardly heard below the improvising delights. And what a pub night that must have been. Hear Rogers's sheer artistry with fingers and bow on the first track, the thirty-nine minutes of *Rogues 1* and Rutherford's declaiming and chattering brass. Such co-operative exuberance with contrasting sounds in such bizarre unity in a Midlands bar is remarkable, and the recording's sound quality is as excellent as it is authentic.

Rogue Bass is all Rogers, and *Rogue Trombone* is more solo Rutherford, but it is the pure empathy of strings and breath that you remember, as if two contrary sound elements have been reconciled as one.

April 2002 found Rutherford performing at the Empty Bottle Festival of Jazz and Improvised Music in Chicago, alongside old mates soprano saxophonist Lol Coxhill, Swedish tenorist Mats Gustafsson, local fellow slideman Jeb Bishop and other free improvisers.

Beginning with *Bottling Up*, a thirty-two-minute Rutherford solo, the CD *Chicago 2002* reveals him in customary dexterity, wailing, howling, aching, spluttering, witticising and melodising all the way through.

Loliloquy brings Coxhill away from his 70s busking spot on the Hungerford Bridge to the Michigan lakeshore.

A kindred spirit to Rutherford, the two inspire each other and their bandmates as if the fiery breath of London was blowing its jazz message all through the Windy City.

As for the superlative Rutherford, he continued to blow with enormous brain, soul and imagination until he died in 2007. Thank Emanem recordings that we still have his brilliance astride our ears.

September 22nd 2011

Inca's Message

Keith Tippett's Ark

Frames: Music for an Imaginary Film

(Ogun)

Keith Tippett

Mujician 1/Mujician 2

(FMP)

In 1971, the singular Bristolian pianist Keith Tippett assembled a studio ensemble called Centipede, which comprised fifty musicians, to cut a record called *Septober Energy*. The mere twenty-two who took part in the *Frames* session of 1978, including two bassists, two pianists and two drummers, seemed almost miniscule in comparison.

With the musicians playing in pairs, Tippett very appropriately called his band the Ark, but the assembly also framed the various ensembles that he had helped create during the previous decade, including his piano duo with Stan Tracey and his Ovary Lodge Quartet with bassist Harry Miller, percussionist Frank Perry and vocalist Julie Tippetts.

The Ark set free the invention of many other fine musicians too, from altoists Trevor Watts and Elton Dean, trumpeters Mark Charig and Henry Lowther, trombonist Nick Evans and the tumultuously artful South African drummer Louis Moholo.

"May music never just become another way of making money," proclaims Tippett from the sleeve notes and how powerfully sound those words from the very first notes of *Frames*, now reissued on the Ogun label, as the two bassists Miller and Peter Kowald share a duo of timeless sonic unity and discovery.

Julie Tippetts's lyrics to the first movement of *Frames* are about the flight of British birds — swallows, seagulls, magpies. And, as the ensemble takes flight too, it is the reeds that thematise the sounds of swirling, cooing and cawing.

The second movement presents the most filmic and pictured of the album's sounds, with the orchestra crescendoing in full joy until Moholo and Perry turn their drums and percussion towards duo creation. Tippett's naked piano plus Larry Stabbins's soprano, Dean's alto and Kowald's tuba foment the strange earthly unity of the soundscape. It is as if Blake's words and images have, as a miracle, turned to notes.

Tippetts sings the opening of the third movement with "the sigh of dawning" extended by Tippett's lonely piano notes. As Tracey's keyboard begins to sound in its more strident timbre and Lowther's pellucid horn soars out, the sunrise has grown to day and a sense of optimism prevails.

The upbeat, rapidly marching pace of the final movement prefaces a spiralling Watts over a wordless vocal chorus fast morphing to the whole orchestra playing wood flutes, recorders and bird whistles and the singers invoking "the children of the dawning." *Frames* isn't always an easy piece of music, but it's one of immense power, beauty, musicianship and sonic solidarity — all the qualities that you associate with Tippett.

It was Tippett's infant daughter Inca who mispronounced her father's profession and, in doing so, gave the name to both his thematic 1981 *Mujician* album and the later co-operative quartet in which Tippett played a key part.

The 1981 solo piano session, plus another from 1986 in Berlin, have been reissued on the German FMP (Free Music Production) label and they offer a fascinating contrast to Tippett the orchestrator. There is the same level of intensity, utter originality and musical brilliance, but his piano performance offers the listeners the opportunity to follow his artistry more nakedly, step by step as he propels his sound forward. The orchestra has become piano.

The 1986 session includes the two parts of *Dan Sing Music* and, to me, it is more evidence that what Blake did to language, Tippett does for sound — a profundity in the childlike, the wisdom in innocence. *Mujician* is an infant vision and saying that is not to demean it but to glorify it. Inca was right and wise when she named her father.

December 10th 2008

Tempos of Our Time

Max Roach and Archie Shepp

The Long March

(hatOLOGY)

The year 1979 was an ambivalent time for world politics. Reaganism was about to enter the ascendant and Margaret Thatcher was elected in London. Yet it was also a year of people's revolutions large and small, from the overturning in Iran to upsurges in much smaller states like Nicaragua and Grenada, called by the Grenadian revolutionary leader Maurice Bishop "big revolutions in small countries."

In August 1979, two of the great revolutionaries of jazz, drummer Max Roach (born in Newland, South Carolina, in 1924) and tenor saxophonist Archie Shepp (born 1937 in Fort Lauderdale, Florida) united at the Willisau Jazz Festival in Switzerland to make the album *The Long March*, composed of two CDs.

Roach was a militant of the first bebop generation. A confrère of Charlie Parker, Dizzy Gillespie, Thelonious Monk and Bud Powell, his astonishing technique transformed the conventional drumkit from a rhythm instrument to a force for breaking up and redirecting the beat, creating more complex solo patterns and shifting the pulse from bass drum to ride cymbal.

His drums also brought an emphatic political focus and solidarity to the music, combining his huge instrumental prowess with Civil Rights and internationalist protest in key albums like the *Freedom Now Suite* (1960), *Percussion Bitter Sweet* (1961) and *Members, Don't Get Weary* (1968).

Shepp became a jazz prophet of the post-bop generation. A companion of Coltrane, his tenor sound was harsh and intense, often caustic, and his albums like *Fire Music* (1965), *Poem For Malcolm* (1969) and *Attica Blues* (1972) were a sound commentary on the George Jackson era, a chorus of struggle for black justice and freedom, and an end to racist incarceration.

JC Moses is the name of the opening track, named after another pioneering bop and post-bop drummer who played with Shepp in 1963 as part of the iconoclastic New York Contemporary Five.

It is an essay in unaccompanied drum artistry by Roach, striking every spot of his drums' surface area, making them speak and echo with the narrative of a percussionist's life and skill. Next up is Shepp and Ellington's *Sophisticated Lady*, the solo horn breathing a sometimes gentle, sometimes rasping fire, aware of tradition yet breaking and extending it into a new era.

As the pioneers finally combine for the album's title piece, the middle section of *Sweet Mao* — a suite written by Roach in 1976 and commissioned by the Italian Communist Party following the death of Mao Zedong, commemorating the 6,000-mile march across China by the Red Army in 1934-5 with Chiang Kai-shek's forces in pursuit — the twenty-six minutes of relentless power from Roach's drums bespeak the burning courage of the liberating army and Shepp's heralding horn rising between the earth and crescendo pitch, calls out a battle cry of their will and dedication.

Shepp's *U-JAA-MA* follows and is taken at headlong pace remembering Julius Nyerere's cry, note after note by tenor and drums a message of solidarity to Africans building socialism and seeking to transform their continent from centuries of colonial underdevelopment.

In another solo drum track *Triptych*, Roach remembers the brilliantly innovating groundwork of two of his predecessors, Basie's great drummer Jo Jones and the giant from Evanston, Illinois, "Big Sid" Catlett, drum star of the bands of Fletcher Henderson, Coleman Hawkins and Louis Armstrong.

Roach's cymbal work in the final part of the piece celebrates Jones's trailblazing work with the hi-hat. Then Shepp bursts in to remember his friend and co-horn John Coltrane with Trane's classic composition *Giant Steps*, played as only Shepp can, with guttural cries and breathy rhapsodies.

Roach declared that "the newspapers are filled with cries for freedom in every corner of the world. The artist should reflect the tempo of his time. He should also endeavour to bring about changes where possible."

No more so in 1979 than in South Africa. The Civil Rights campaign had won huge advances in the US South, the anti-apartheid struggle was pursuing similar ends of racial justice and now "Mississippi Goddamn" had become the twenty minutes of *South Africa Goddamn*, with Roach's tapping heartbeat grounding Shepp's rumbles, wails and howls for a free and equal South Africa.

The finale is *It's Time*, which Roach had originally recorded with a choir in 1962, with Clifford Jordan on tenor. The imperative behind the title is urged on by Shepp's boiling solo, as Roach's drums throb for freedom now in the US, Africa, Germany, everywhere.

It was time then, in 1979, and the music still impresses us, it is still time now..

November 11th 2010

In Walked Don

Don Pullen

Don Pullen Plays Monk

(Whynot)

Thelonious Monk and Don Pullen were both southerners from different places and different generations, and both arrivants in New York — Monk from Rocky Mount, North Carolina as a small boy in 1922 and Pullen from Roanoke, Virginia, as a rapidly maturing pianist in 1964. Yet for Pullen, Chicago was also a prime birthing place for his unique Monk-inspired artistry.

Before coming to New York he had imbibed the avant-garde power of fellow pianist Muhal Richard Abrams and his Experimental Band, as well as the explosion of new musical ideas generated by members of the Association for the Advancement of Creative Musicians. By 1973 Pullen's percussive, rampaging keyboard sounds were recognised by Charles Mingus, who brought the pianist into his band.

In 1979 Pullen reunited with two other Mingus alumni, tenorist George Adams and drummer Dannie Richmond, and so the Pullen/Adams Quartet was an inspiring jazz fixture for almost a decade. The early 90s found him recording for Blue Note both as a soloist and with his African-Brazilian Connection band. He died in 1995 shortly after recording his *Sacred Common Ground* album with a choir of Kootenai and Salish singers, a salute to his own partial Native American Cherokee roots.

Don Pullen Plays Monk, recorded in 1984 in New York City, has never been issued on CD before now, and its eight tracks include four Monk tunes, two homages by Pullen and two alternate takes.

Pullen takes the opener *Well You Needn't* at a breakneck speed, much faster than the composer ever played it. Full of outrageous surprises and breathless verve, Pullen makes his characteristic charges up and down the keys like a man late for the most important meeting of his life while also softening his hurry as if his keyboard is morphing into a Pennine stream.

It is a strange contrast to Monk's most romantic and famous theme, the sheer melodism of *Round Midnight*. The familiarity of the tune gives added resonance to Pullen's drum-like interpretations, as if this midnight were an hour of percussive ritual mellowed by moments of lyrical beauty.

Then he reflects Monk's lifelong playfulness and musical mischief in his own very Monkish tribute, *Monkin' Around*. One hand pounds out the grounding chords while the other makes its successively thumping and stomping keyboard excursions.

You wish Monk could have heard it — and what he would have made of it as the hail of notes peal out of his own city of sounds. *Gratitude* is another dedication from one piano drummer to another, except this performance is sublimely reflective, as if each note and cluster of notes is a thought, a memory, an eternal second of admiration and loving recognition of a musical brother, creator and innovator.

Its melody is both tender and quietly rapturous, reminding me of those of *Sacred Common Ground* like *Resting on the Road* and *Reservation Blues.*

Trinkle Tinkle — certainly an onomatopoeic title — with its hurtling twists and sudden corners is a test piece for any pianist. For Pullen it is a rapid-fire improvising outing full of dips, instant rises, onrushes of notes and extraordinary moments of departure and arrival played with an exuberant brilliance.

There are two versions of *In Walked Bud*, which Monk wrote as a celebration of his friend and fellow bop piano magician Bud Powell. As Pullen plays it, his strangely pausing beginning on the first take makes you wonder if he was considering how a fast friend writes a tribute to a close musical comrade.

Pullen was to write his own praise song to George Adams after his death in 1992, the haunting *Ah George, We Hardly Knew Ya* on Pullen's *Ode to Life* album, released on Blue Note.

In fact, he plays *In Walked Bud* almost straight, but with some characteristic tumbling cadences and unexpected curves, showers and flurries of cascading notes.

How does one powerful musical originator acknowledge and honour another as a provocation to further creative flights? This record will show you, note and note again.

September 28th 2011

Sounds of Genius

Steve Lacy and Mal Waldron

At the Bimhuis 1982

(Daybreak)

The two New Yorkers, Steve Lacy and Mal Waldron, both of whom died recently, became one of the great duos of jazz history.

Both had extraordinary beginnings. Lacy, born in 1934, was a white soprano saxophonist who began in the early 1950s playing in Dixieland bands and with New Orleans men like Red Allen and Ellingtonians like Rex Stewart. But he crossed a bridge during stints with the arch-modernist Cecil Taylor in the late 50s and then with his great tutor Thelonious Monk, whose tunes he would play for the rest of his life, most powerfully in a completely solo context. Years of exile in Europe pitched him with his long-lasting quintet, including altoist Steve Potts and his violinist wife Irene Aebi.

Mal Waldron was eight years older than Lacy, had bop beginnings in the 1950s with a spate of Prestige recording sessions and became Billie Holiday's pianist, as well as a part of the experimental groups of bassist Charles Mingus and altoist Eric Dolphy.

Like Lacy, Waldron spent much of his performing life in Europe and the white horn man and black keyboard genius frequently teamed up, creating an unforgettable jazz amalgam of kindred but very distinctive spirits.

At The Bimhuis 1982 catches them both at their apex of innovation, playing three Monk tunes, plus Lacy's *Blues for Aida* and Waldron's earthy *Snake Out* at the now defunct Amsterdam venue.

Waldron always said that his piano was as a drum, so the lack of a bass and drums is never an impediment — the pair's sense of space, pause and rhythm and their empathetic understanding make their music as whole as anything in the entire canon of jazz.

Waldron's percussive chords, shadowed by Lacy's troubled, mysterious notes, open *Blues for Aida*. All through the piece, the duo strike and blow sounds which reflect each other as on a dark pool, staring into each other's sounds.

Snake Out crashes out as a contrast. Waldron's pounding opening solo is a cavalcade of angry notes which finally merge with Lacy's howling soprano fanfare. The sound cracks into a desperate whistle as his choruses race forward in a frantic sonic chase which sprints for a breathless fifteen minutes.

Lacy's horn snarls, rasps, sobs and exclaims before a solo Waldron creates a hypnosis of the ears through the repetitive drama of his inventive patterns, which provoke incessant change and surprise.

When Lacy returns to finally reprise the startling theme, as a listener, you can only wonder about the journey that you have just travelled. The elegaic beauty of Monk's *Reflections*, one of his most perfect melodies, was blown through Lacy's horn a million times, each one different.

Waldron, too, was much influenced by Monk, but his notes express less the "brilliant corners" and explosion of a multitude of directions, than the almost mesmeric piling up of only very slightly different repeated phrases, each one tipping the improvisation further and further towards a world of new pathways.

Lacy's lyricism takes the familiar *Round Midnight* and makes a host of new tunes inside it with his inventive and intelligent breath.

It is, of course, Monk's most eternally played composition and it is not easy to make it sound new and unexpected. But this duo weaned themselves on Monk and because they knew his work so intimately, his tunes are their palimpsests on which they paint their own musical worlds, as they do over *Epistrophy*, one of Monk's most provocative themes.

Where would recorded jazz be without its legion of amateur sound engineers who take their machines into unlikely clubs and dare to cut the sound of genius? So, thank you, Sjaak Willemse and your portable tape machine.

Not only is this recording pointedly clear, it fixes in jazz history one of this duo's most brilliant nights in a lively Dutch venue long since demolished and disappeared.

January 24th 2007

Jazz Internationalist

Trevor Watts and the Moire Drum Orchestra
A Wider Embrace
(ECM)
Trevor Watts
Moire Music Trio
(Intakt)
Trevor Watts and Veryan Weston
6 Dialogues
(Emanem)

Powerful innovator of the alto and soprano saxophones, musical internationalist and pioneer of British free improvising music, Trevor Watts was born in York in 1939, but spent his boyhood in Halifax.

A brilliant and rebellious self-taught musician, he developed his reed in the RAF between 1959 and 1963 while stationed in Germany. There he met fellow airmen, drummer John Stevens and trombonist Paul Rutherford, and when he was demobbed he found himself playing in all kinds of genres, from Sonny Boy Williams's blues to Rod Stewart's pop. In 1966 he found Stevens and Rutherford again and they formed the epochal free jazz combination the Spontaneous Music Ensemble and established a performing base at London's Little Theatre Club.

The records that Watts made with Stevens, Rutherford, fellow saxophonist Evan Parker, bassist Barry Guy and fellow Yorkshireman, guitarist Derek Bailey, were daring harbingers of everything that came later in the British free jazz scene, and Watts is a true musical ground-breaker with a life spent in audacious artistic exploration with few financial rewards.

In 1982 he formed Moire Music, originally a tentet, but by 1993 when *A Wider Embrace* was recorded in London, it was composed of five Ghanaian drummers — Nana Tsiboe, the veteran Nee-Daku Patato who performed as part of Kwame Nkrumah's independence campaigns and played with Bob Marley, Miriam Makeba and the Afro-rock group Osibasa; Joyo Yates, Nana Appiah and Paapa Jeh Mensah, Watts and the Scottish bass guitarist Colin McKenzie from Dunfermline.

A Yorkshireman, a Scot and five Ghanaians making astonishing music together. As the words of the album's opener *Eguga* testify, "To be in tune is to be together in spirit. Whatever happens we will live into another day in harmony"-Watts's watchwords which have guided his life's journey in music.

And *A Wider Embrace* is just that. Hear Watts's compelling liquid soprano on *Free Flow* between the pounding drums of the two parts of *Tetegramatan*, the swirling alto above the orchestra of percussive sound rhythms of *Otublohu*, the story of Accra or the beauteous melodic undertow of *The Rocky Road to Dublin* and the seething *Southern Memories*, inspired by Moire's 1992 tour to a South Africa newly free of apartheid. Altogether a prime and marvellous album is *A Wider Embrace*, a true and equal rendezvous of Africa and Britain.

In 1995 Watts recorded the album *Trevor Watts and the Moire Music Trio* in London with McKenzie and just one drummer, the virtuoso Mensah playing kit drums, Indian finger drums, African tana drums, cabassa, ankle bells, djembe and zebra skin drums.

This album has an extraordinarily original and continually surprising soundscape. Watts blows melody as he finds and creates it with a skittering beauty as in *End of the Road* or *Gentle Love*, with the natural timbre of naked birdsong, an English-sounding very Pennine birdsong which I hear around me every day, but sung here over Mensah's African earth and out of Ghana's shrubs, grass and trees. Hear nature's keening lyrics in *Yatra Groove*, for example.

Yet other lands are invoked too, as in *Latino Shuffle* where sounds imbibed in Venezuela pour out of Watts's global horn, all grounded by McKenzie's relentless heartbeat and Mensah's ever-inventive variety of percussive rhythms streaming from their African source.

The Cornish pianist Veryan Weston is also an ex-member of Moire, but the *6 Dialogues* recording with Watts on the Emanem label is a very different kind of session. Instead of the thrusting drum rhythms, dogged riffs and swooping melodic turns of quarter of a century of Moire music, Watts, with Weston as an improvising partner, returns to the form of free interactive sounds he originated with Stevens and Rutherford in the mid-60s.

Yet as soon as the opening sonic conversation *Unrest Assured* begins, this is a different Watts from those early days of the SME and Amalgam. He is full-voiced, persistently melodic, as much of the earth as of the sky and its birds, as if he has collected and become something of Africa and the entire world of music along the way.

Weston's notes seem to stream endlessly from the imagination of his fingers, falling like permanent sunlit rain all through the music.

This is a colloquy of experience, played with a profound reach of empathy, with both musicians playing and voicing out their lives. Music of the world it is, the real world where Watts has always belonged. Long live his sound.

January 19th 2011

Music of Human Flesh

Anouar Brahem

Thimar/Astrakhan Café/Le Voyage de Sahar/ The Astounding Eyes of Rita
(ECM)

A Devonian blowing soprano saxophone and bass clarinet, a bassist from Wolverhampton who is a veteran of Miles Davis bands, led by a virtuoso of the lute-like oud born in Halfaouine, Tunisia — playing as a trio in March 1997 in an Oslo studio. Their tunes are mostly Arabic except one, *Kernow*, which is the Cornish word for Cornwall.

Quite a jazz syncretism here, producing an early album by Anouar Brahem called *Thimar*, which is Arabic for "fruits." And such fruits for the ear — Brahem has been playing the oud since 1967, when at the age of ten he began his studies at the Tunis National Conservatory of Music. As a young man he became a musical master, migrated to Paris in the early 80s, returned to Tunisia in 1985 and two years later was appointed director of the City of Tunis Musical Ensemble, returning to classical Arabic music, inspired by the great oud genius and his early tutor Ali Sriti.

Thimar is an album of astonishing tenderness — the three musicians playing with a rare sonic unity, as if separate genres of music never existed and music itself were one, and only one essence.

In opener *Badra*, John Surman's breath caresses a mind-tingling soprano solo and Dave Holland's eternally plucking fingers create what Brahem called "a sound so beautiful. Powerful but rounded. Not at all aggressive or harsh." And that is how the album continues and manifests itself, with Brahem's strings as serene as you could imagine and as fleet as those of Django Reinhardt or Wes Montgomery, an amalgam of Arab melody and peculiarly British jazz improvisation.

Listen to Surman's solo soprano on the track called *Wagt*. Then directly into Brahem's unaccompanied oud on *Uns*. What is this music? Is it jazz? If you have to ask the question, you're not absorbed in the music. Just savour its extraordinary beauty.

Then on to *Astrakhan Café*, an album recorded in 2000 with the Turkish clarinettist of Gypsy roots Barbaros Erköse and fellow Tunisian percussionist of bendir and darbouka, Lassad Hosni. This trio invoke an entirety of the world in their music, melodies from the Balkans to Turkmenistan, from Tanzania to Azerbaijan.

Hosni's dark beats and Erköse's sonorous notes begin opener *Aube Rouge*, a tale of Grozny's horrendous bombardment, while Brahem's felicitous oud gives a sound picture of cosmopolitan food-sharing in the title tune.

Every track is a message of a world with a unified humanity, played with neither pretentiousness nor sermon. Erköse's clarinet is filled with human juices, as if fire could be liquid. Brahem's lower strings fill in for a bass and Hosni's drums are everywhere in the music. Hear *Blue Jewels* or Brahem's portrait of his birthplace Halfaouine and you will know that at this café the menu is truly global and the meals are cooked in sheer solidarity.

On to 2006 and the album *Le Voyage De Sahar*, made with two Frenchmen — accordionist Jean-Louis Matinier and pianist François Couturier. They collaborated on the 2002 album *Les Pas Du Chat Noir* and both albums exude Brahem's Parisian years.

The musical montage of Brahem's perfectly cut notes, Matinier's rolling lines and Couturier's sparse chords is a unique one indeed and the journey that the threesome take, across the Sahara, through *Les Jardins de Ziryab* and *Nuba*, to *Cordoba* and *El Andalous* and *Halfaouine* again is one that the listener takes too with immense surprise and reflection.

Brahem's new album *The Astounding Eyes of Rita* is dedicated to the great Palestinian poet Mahmoud Darwish (1941-2008) and recalls his poem *Rita and the Rifle*. "And I remember Rita. The way a sparrow remembers its stream."

German Klaus Gesing plays bass clarinet, Swede Björn Meyer bass and Lebanese Khaled Yassine is the percussionist with darbouka and bendir. Uri Avnery, the progressive Israeli writer and pro-Palestinian campaigner, wrote that "Darwish was the poet of anger, of longing, of hope and of peace. These were the strings of his violin."

And his strings join with those of Brahem in expressing the deepest feelings and history of his people. Rita's eyes shine through the sounds of this quartet, making, as Darwish called his most telling collection of poems, "the music of human flesh."

Whether it is Gesing's forlorn horn on *The Lover Of Beirut*, Yassina's earth-inspired drumming on *Galilee Mon Amour* or Brahem's sublime artistry throughout, this is a golden record, as precious as its inspiration.

April 7th 2010

Brass Trickster

Lester Bowie
The Great Pretender
(ECM)
Lester Bowie's Brass Fantasy
I Only Have Eyes for You
(ECM)

Jazz has thrown up a number of great tricksters of the trumpet, from Rex Stewart and his horn vocalese at the centre of the pre-war Ellington orchestra to the post-war puckish humour of Clark Terry and Dizzy Gillespie's fierce brass wit. But there has never been another horn Anansi like Lester Bowie.

His influences were born from an astonishing eclecticism. Born into a music-loving family in Little Rock, Arkansas, he began learning trumpet at ten and was soon exposed to music at school, church and through his military service. He worked with R&B groups around St Louis, his teenage home, and through the south. By 1965 he was playing in Chicago and became the second president of the Association for the Advancement of Creative Musicians (AACM), proclaiming his allegiance not strictly to jazz, but to "great black music."

With fellow AACM members Joseph Jarman, Roscoe Mitchell, Malachi Favors and Don Moye he founded the Art Ensemble of Chicago, which fused the avant-garde with a host of past and current black musical influences. He also developed "avant pop," which brought together jazz, funk, pop and soul in brass and percussion ensembles like Brass Fantasy, and other outfits such as The Leaders and the New York Organ Ensemble.

In 1981 he recorded his album *The Great Pretender* for ECM, and it has recently been reissued in their budget Touchstones series. The title track is a love song which was a huge hit for the 50s vocal group The Platters.

Seventeen minutes long, it gives ample opportunity for Bowie to blow out a succession of wails, howls, grunts, an artillery of half-valve effects, bent, abortive and smeared notes accompanied by Donald Smith's piano, Fred Williams's bass, Phillip Wilson's drums and Hamiet Bluiett's baritone. Bowie's wife Fontella Bass and David Preston add their background vocals.

A marvellously audacious performance, *The Great Pretender* synthesises the meaning of "great black music." When Bluiett's gruff horn growls out its expletives, followed by Bowie's raucous lines, it is as if jazz is all-inclusive, a true syncretism in sonic action.

Some Jelly Roll Morton-like hokum prefaces *It's Howdy Doody Time*, and Smith turns to organ on *When the Doom (Moon) Comes Over the Mountain*, with funky sounds from Williams's electric bass. *Rios Negros* gives Bowie's horn a stuttering Latin edge, in *Rose Drop* the percussive effects tinkle and chime alongside his sighs and Wilson's crashing drums.

In the final track, *Oh How the Ghost Sings*, there are echoing and eerie sounds all round, and Bowie's brass snorts and eeyores contrast with some soaring, almost stratospheric phrases. So much trumpet in so little time, the story of Bowie's life.

In 1985 Bowie's Brass Fantasy recorded the album *I Only Have Eyes For You* in Brooklyn, with Wilson on drums and eight brass horns. Bowie, Stanton Davis, Chicago ace Malachi Thompson and Bruce Purse played trumpets, Craig Harris and Steve Turre trombones with Bob Stewart on tuba.

The title song is a slow march, mostly ensemble with regular trumpet phrases leaping over the riff. Thompson's *Lament*, dedicated to the bop trumpeter Ray Copeland, begins with some breathy snorting mouthpiece effects and anguished wails before the ensemble threnody begins, out of which Davis breaks with his shimmering solo, leaping further and further upward as he progresses. It is as if this lament is a praise song for trumpeters everywhere, so universal is its reach.

Many great jazz musicians came from there — from Tricky Sam Nanton to Wynton Kelly, from Joe Harriott to Dizzy Reece, that Bowie's ska-driven tune *Coming Back, Jamaica* has much epic jazz history in its notes.

Stewart's growling beginning to his own composition *Nonet* develops into a dialogue between his cavernous tuba sound and the other brassmen playing in ensemble before, in turns, they leap out into individual breaks.

We don't have to wait long for it to come back for the final track, *When the Spirit Returns*. Bowie's melodic unorthodoxy and the sheer discovery of his sounds fires all the players.

Life-inspiring all the way.

July 14th 2010

Birdsong Along the Lea

Mike Westbrook

On Duke's Birthday / Westbrook-Rossini

(hatOLOGY)

Mike Westbrook is nothing less than a British jazz genius, an utter original and virtuoso of the big band as well as much smaller groups.

I remember in the early 70s, when Westbrook was living in East London, he brought his small marching band — very close to a Salvation Army formation — to the E1 Festival on Bigland Green in Stepney, as well as to demonstrations for causes from Troops Out to the imprisoned Shrewsbury building workers. I started to wonder then whose influence drove forward his huge musical brain and imagination. I should have known, and *On Duke's Birthday* reveals it completely.

Westbrook was born in High Wycombe in 1936 but grew up in Torquay, combining painting and an extra-curricular love of music at Plymouth Art School after National Service — partially served in Germany — and a dose of accountancy. In 1962 he moved to London and before long he was sharing house band status at Ronnie Scott's jazz club in Soho with South African Chris McGregor's Brotherhood of Breath.

A series of powerful big band albums on the Deram label — including what I believe to be his greatest, the anti-war suite *Marching Song* of 1969 — anticipated his music for Adrian Mitchell's play about Blake, *Tyger* in 1971, which itself preceded albums such as *The Westbrook Blake — Bright As Fire* and his 1999 suite to Blake, *Glad Day*.

On Duke's Birthday is a fusion of Ellington, Blake and Westbrook, and a very considerable achievement indeed. Westbrook's solo piano sketching at the outset of the opening track, *Checking in at Hotel Le Prieure*, has a nervous, valedictory air, but builds up through Tony Marsh's unleashed drums and Chris Biscoe's haunting baritone to a state of relentless activity and a sense of preparation for a large-scale orchestral performance.

The entry of Dominique Pifarély's sprightly violin and Brian Godding's twanging guitar shatters the tension and the ensemble takes off. There are two versions of the title theme, both grounded in an aura of sonic sadness and tribute — Ellington had died in 1974, a full decade before this 1984 recording.

Georgie Burns's mournful cello is at the heart of *On Duke's Birthday 1*, and the complex of trombonist Danilo Terenzi's slides suggest something of the incomprehensible networks of musical brain-power that throbbed in Ellington's head all through his long jazz life.

It's fascinating to prelude the twenty-one engrossing minutes of

Westbrook's *E Stratford Too-Doo*, recorded in Le Grand Théâtre of Amiens in May 1984 by the three-and-a-half minutes of Bubber Miley's muted mystery and contradictory jauntiness of *East St Louis Toodle-oo*, recorded in a New York studio in December 1927 by the Ellington Orchestra. East St Louis and Stratford, London E15 are oceans and continents apart yet miraculously fused in music.

There is birdsong at the beginning of Westbrook's movement, even along the mudbanks of the ferociously urban river Lea, and the ambience of a worrying peace expressed by the quickening force of Pifarély's violin and Biscoe's rampant baritone horn. You wonder what Harry Carney, Ellington's pioneering baritonist on the 1927 waxing, would have made of it all. Then Marsh's drums come in a-pounding, Biscoe's horns find their mark and suddenly, in the way of Ellington, the mood is metamorphosed and the sound is citified.

In 1986 Westbrook recorded *Westbrook-Rossini*, a suite founded on the music of another hugely popular composer, Italian opera man Gioacchino Rossini.

With a seven-piece band of unusual instrumentation including sopranino saxophone, two tubas and a piccolo, Westbrook's arrangements of extracts from *William Tell*, *The Thieving Magpie*, *The Barber of Seville* and *Otello* resonate with powerful ensemble passages and some stinging solos from altoist Peter Whyman, sopraninoist Lindsay Cooper, trombonist Paul Nieman and Westbrook himself, like Ellington an often under-rated pianist.

Tell was a people's rebel hero of Switzerland, and the five versions of the *William Tell Overture* were commissioned by the Festival du Theatre Contemporain in Lausanne.

Westbrook gives Rossini's music a true insurgent mood and, when the final explosive theme of the *Tell Overture* arrives, those notes which exploded in my boyhood head as the theme of *The Lone Ranger and Tonto* during the post-war years of the Saturday morning pictures at the Romford Odeon made me realise again how deeply music stays in the blood and how jazz stirs and transforms it into now-times.

Hear Cooper's sopranino brilliance all the way through the album, or Nieman's dextrous slides conversing with Andy Grappy's thundering tuba, or Westbrook's musing notes on *L'amorose e Sincero Lindoro* from the *Barber of Seville.*

Jazz at the opera and opera at the heartsblood of jazz — Westbrook manages it with aplomb, syncretic artistry and not a small dose of the blues.

April 7th 2011

Caribbean Heart

Courtney Pine

Transition in Tradition

(Destin-E)

Playing Courtney Pine's 1990 reggae-based album *Closer To Home* recently reminded me how much the saxophonist's jazz was plunged in the Caribbean and how his family's Jamaican background were central to his music's bloodstream. Unlike any US jazz musician — with the possible exception of Sonny Rollins — Pine's proud Caribbean heart beats in his every note.

Two decades later, Pine's new album *Transition in Tradition* celebrates the achievement in jazz of one of the music's first great soprano saxophonists — Sidney Bechet, who was born in New Orleans in 1897.

New Orleans is really a Caribbean city and its people, who invented jazz, had countless bonds with the necklace of islands to its south. So here is a contemporary Caribbean reedman blowing his tribute to a great Caribbean jazz pioneer in a unique album, invoking places and people that express one unified Caribbean nation and a musical culture of huge diversity.

Pine has been around a long time now. His first album *Journey To the Urge Within* goes back to 1986 and his last two decades have been a relentless process of imbibing absorbing and expressing diverse musical influences — Coltrane, Ornette Coleman and Charlie Parker within the jazz canon and reggae, funk, ska and hip hop elsewhere.

Pine's sumptuously deep bass clarinet begins the album's opener *Haiti*, with some stirring ensemble work from his band, a pan-Caribbean assembly including Dominican guitarist Cameron Pierre and Cuban violinist Omar Puente. But also present are Ghanaian drummer Robert Fordjour and Stefon Harris, the renowned vibist from Albany, New York, who follows Pine's lung-bursting chorus with a sparkling marimba solo while the band riffs on behind him.

Pine's vaunting theme *New Orleans* follows, his soprano marching down Bechet's streets and Pierre's fleeting guitar matching every step until Derbyshire-born pianist Alex Wilson takes the lead, joined by the irrepressible Puente. *Le Matin Est Noire*, taken from an Archie Shepp song, has more superb Pierre, this time on mandolin, and a solo from Puente that begins with echoes of Grieg's *Peer Gynt* suite.

The tailgate-sounding slides of trombonist Harry Brown begin the title tune with Darren Taylor's bass also dominant. Pine's swirling soprano comes in, meshing cultures in its wake and manifesting his sleeve dictum, "When cultures meet there is either conflict or positive union, what's for sure is that both cultures will never stay the same" — a commentary on the astonishing hybridity of New Orleans.

Toussaint L'Ouverture is a tribute to a powerful Caribbean hero with, as Wordsworth put it, an "unconquerable mind." The Haitian revolutionary is given a noble melodic theme by Pine, embellished by the vibrato of his bass clarinet and a stomping piano chorus by Wilson. A tribute to a Jamaican jazz eminence, *The Tale of Joe Harriott*, follows, a moving solo outing for Harris and more eloquent Wilson, with Pine's tender notes on alto flute.

Throughout *The Sound of Jazz?* Pine's soprano gyrates as if he were a part of the second line of a New Orleans funeral parade, with echoes of *Flee As a Bird*, Delta rhythms and Puente's resonating violin.

In *Creole Swing*, Harris dazzles a chorus and Pine's bass clarinet bubbles and gurgles, while *Afropean* remembers the generation of exiled South African free jazz musicians who arrived in Britain in the 60s, including, as Pine reminds us in his sleeve notes, bassist Johnny Dyani and drummer Louis Moholo-Moholo. Their imprint is all through this music.

The album's final track *Au Revoir* is a bold, assured performance to conclude Pine's most accomplished album, an expression of what he notes is the "boundaryless imagination" of fused cultures — African, European, Caribbean — which once became one in New Orleans and, through the century-long journey of jazz, have never stopped harmonising.

May 27th 2009

And Why Not?

Schweizer-Nicols- Lewis-Léandre-Sommer
The Storming of the Winter Palace
(Intakt)
Omri Ziegele Where's Africa Trio with Irène Schweizer and Makaya Ntshoko
Can Walk on Sand
(Intakt)

Is it possible to successfully tell the story of such a momentous historical event as the storming of the Winter Palace in Petrograd in 1917 through jazz, a form of music which emerged a century ago from the cosmopolitan heart of New Orleans, a city where the Delta of the Mississippi meets the Gulf of Mexico?

And also when the jazz narrative is told by three women — a Swiss pianist, a Scottish singer and a French bassist — and two men, a German drummer and an African-American trombonist born in Chicago?

Perhaps these questions are summarily answered by vocalist Maggie Nicols, who wrote this sonic essay with pianist Irène Schweizer, and who at one point in the ten-minute proceedings — recorded live in March 1988 at the Taktlos Festival in Zurich — declares from the midst of her mostly wordless lyrics: "And why not? And why not?" Audacity here certainly, and brilliant jazz musicianship too — mostly in a free ensemble setting, stirred up into a relentless excitation by the five revolutionary improvising spirits.

The album's first track, the twenty-six minutes of *Now and Never*, begins with an astonishing collective passage, with George Lewis' gruff slides tunnelling beneath Nicol's embroidered, lyricless vocals, Jöelle Léandre's bass buzzing like some monumental insect, Günter Sommer's flickering cymbalism and crashing drums before Schweizer's rampaging entry of keyboard runs and flourishes.

The frantic present tense of the piece continues with Nicols suddenly breaking into words, their English creating a strange absurdity as she sings of a mad rush for bargains at a jumble sale, and you wonder exactly what her aroused and hyper-engaged bandmates are making of it all in their own diverse languages and ways of living.

But the meaning is in the music as Schweizer's pace becomes lightning, with Sommer's sprinting snares and Lewis' snorts and Nicols declaring: "I wish I was a liar!"

No lies either in *The Storming of the Winter Palace* which follows. I would play it with John Reed's *Ten Days that Shook the World* beside you and a DVD of Eisenstein's *October*, then see how each fills out the other.

Lewis' trombone is fearsome and prophetic with Schweizer's pianism groundshaking. Léandre plays a pulsating bowed bass, breaking up the earth and concrete as Sommer's drums roll and pound as if they are signalling and urging the revolutionaries.

The piece moves with the sound of a crippling system and its power at last being ruptured, a sheer invitation to the imagination.

There's a very different musical ambience throughout the album *Can Walk on Sand*, which in its own way celebrates another profoundly welcomed defeat of reactionary power.

The Where's Africa Trio — made up of the redoubtable Schweizer, Swiss alto saxophonist Omri Ziegele and the septuagenarian South African drummer Makaya Ntshoko — plays a selection of diverse tunes, some of which are compositions by South African revolutionary musicians who were exiles of apartheid and living in Europe for up to four decades. These include pianists Dollar Brand — later Abdullah Ibrahim — and Chris McGregor, and bassist Johnny Dyani, all of whom were Ntshoko's contemporaries.

Ntshoko was the drummer in the Brand Trio in the early 60s and on the pianist's seminal album of 1964, *Duke Ellington Presents The Dollar Brand Trio*.

Schweizer must have known the second track *Tintinyana* like his own drumsticks, so often did the Brand trio play it. Ziegele's gyrating alto spins out his notes and there is a romping chorus from Schweizer.

Mal Waldron's tender melody *Soul Eyes* is given a moving testimony and the trio skips through the briefest versions of Ornette Coleman's *Giggin'*. The African rhythms of McGregor's great Afro-European band The Brotherhood of Breath burst out of Schweizer's jumping choruses of *Andromeda*, and Ziegele's airy timbre rises from his own compositions, *Can Walk on Sand* and *Rare Bird*.

But is is in the final two tunes — *Ithi Gqi* and *Mbizo* by the mercurial Dyani, where a second altoist Jürg Wickihalder is added — that the long years of the South African's musical defiance of apartheid is powerfully recreated by Schweizer, Ziegele and survivor Ntshoko for our own times, like a sonic beacon from past decades of brave struggle.

September 7th 2011

Salvation Blues

Harry Beckett

Maxine

(ITM)

I first heard his trumpet blowing red-hot and rhapsodic through the cigarette fog and chatter of the dingy public bar of a South London pub — the Plough in Stockwell — in the early 70s alongside two other rockets of British jazz from London, pianist Stan Tracey and drummer John Stevens.

Harry Beckett, who died in July 2010, was born in St Michael, Barbados in 1935. As a boy he learned the cornet in order to play in a Salvation Army band. He came to England as a nineteen-year-old as part of the formidable post-Windrush generation of West Indian arrivants which included some brilliant jazz horns — Jamaican saxophonists Joe Harriott and Wilton Bogey Gaynair, trumpeters like the Vincentian Shake Keane and the Jamaican Dizzy Reece. With Beckett they lit up British jazz in the post-war years, bringing a faraway Antillean strength and poignancy to a transplanted music which had its provenances along the northern mainland shores of their region.

They shared their seas and had been born within a Caribbean sound and spirit. That spirit was at the heart of all Beckett's notes, breathy, powerful and ever-inventive as they were. And as they still are too when you listen to their clarion cry on the anthologised album *Maxine*, a selection of some of Beckett's post-1987 work with his close, Europe-based musical comrades.

Coltrane's *Bessie's Blues* — the opener recorded in London in 1995 — begins with a stirring blast from John Burgess's tenor before Annie Whitehead's growling trombone adds a muscled chorus. Beckett comes in flickering, nimble, in perfect control of every note and full of fire and beauty.

Les Jardins du Casino is a duet recorded in 1991 with the British pianist Django Bates. Gentle and softened by Beckett's melodic breathiness and full of feeling, he explores the piano and trumpet duo context — one that he frequently essayed — with a surprise at every turn, guided by lyricism and tenderness.

I Don't Want To Know, recorded in Germany in 1991, finds him with the Leipzig-born pianist Joachim Kühn and the French bassist JF Jenny-Clarke.

Beckett was a prime balladeer as well as a passionate player and here his story is one of pained regret, told in a crying tone beside

Kühn's more direct, objective notes, creating an conversation of contrasting moods.

The same trio plays *Amsterdam* with its slow, almost anthemic opening and Beckett sounding almost like an ancestral bugler, moving to a faster pace with Jenny-Clarke's pummelling beat, Kühn's chiming keys and then Beckett in full brass audacity, striding across the melody.

With *Maxine*, Beckett is in another piano-trumpet duo, this time with the Umtata-born South African of the Blue Notes, Chris McGregor. It's another ballad, blown airily against McGregor's grounding chords.

Beckett's influence on succeeding generations of Anglo-Caribbean jazz musicians was profound. He raised up their hopes and determination.

The twenty-four minutes of 1987's *Cozy 'n' Rozy* put him beside McGregor, bassist Fred Thelonious Baker, US drummer and Sun Ra Arkestra veteran Clifford Jarvis and a springing twenty-three-year-old Courtney Pine on tenor, his Jamaican roots bursting through his horn and fusing with the Barbadian breath of the older player.

Baker begins with a dub-sounding bass, then the horns and McGregor unite for the lilting theme before Beckett sets out on an adventurous solo journey with sudden leaps and cadences, half-notes and frantic phrases, repeated soulful paradigms and exclamations of Caribbean sonic glory.

When Pine enters — clearly inspired by his horn partner — he sounds assured and confident enough to try out all manner of sounds and configurations. When McGregor steams in for his own compelling chorus — a white man of Africa hounded by apartheid — jazz has provided its own brand of musical unity.

Beckett's musical achievements were huge and radiantly eclectic, from the free collective improvisations of the London Improvisers Orchestra to his glorious solo outings on the succession of Graham Collier big band albums of the late 60s and early 70s such as *Songs for My Father* and *Darius*.

His last album *The Modern Sound of Harry Beckett* was a Caribbean journey much closer to reggae and dub. Beckett was a singular, distinctive and inspirational jazz genius with an untrammelled beauty of sound all of his own.

And oh, for those Stockwell nights again...

March 1st 2011

Echoes of Indignation

Joe McPhee, Lisle Ellis and Paul Plimley

Sweet Freedom: Now What?
(Hat Hut Records)

In 1994 the multiple hornman Joe McPhee, born in Miami in 1939, recorded his trio album *Sweet Freedom: Now What?* with the bassist Lisle Ellis and the Canadian pianist Paul Plimley.

It was a drummerless trio giving a tribute to the great bop drummer Max Roach's pioneering 1960 album in support of both the Civil Rights movement and the struggle against apartheid, *We Insist! The Freedom Now Suite.* Roach died in August 2007 after a lifetime of jazz brilliance and powerful political commitment, so the reissue of McPhee's epochal album is both timely and urgent, for it continues Roach's tradition of jazz for liberation and the freedom of all peoples.

In his sleeve notes McPhee writes: "Fifty years after the end of World War II, neonazi skinheads kill Gypsies in Austria, terrorists poison thousands with nerve gas in the Tokyo subway system and a black family finds a burning cross on their lawn in a community near where I live in New York State."

The first thing to say about this record is that the listener should listen very carefully first to *We Insist.* Not only because *Sweet Freedom* creates many echoes of its testimony and of the heroism of its times but because McPhee's record is a sound essay of a different era, a different reality when "civil and human rights fall prey to expediency" and where freedom itself needs new definitions — "for just when you think you have it firmly in focus it jumps, changes and becomes something else entirely."

We Insist! included a profound sense of jazz history and tradition. Not only in the lyrics of the songs Abbey Lincoln sang, which stretched back to slavery and slave rebellion but because among its musicians were the Nigerian drummer Michael Olatunji, emphasising the jazz kinship to Africa, and the veteran tenor saxophonist Coleman Hawkins, who helped establish jazz itself and carried within his sound the very beginnings of the music.

Sweet Freedom begins with McPhee's version of *Mendacity*, from the 1961 Roach album *Percussion Bitter Sweet*, a song of the corruption eating at the US political and electoral systems.

McPhee's soprano edges the tune with flickering allusions, while Plimley and Ellis play beneath with darker sounds. *Driva' Man*, a portrait of a tyrannical slave overseer has McPhee's tenor digging into the blood of oppression while Ellis' bass resonates.

Roach's *Self Portrait* is welded with the black freedom anthem *Lift Every Voice and Sing*. It begins with almost inaudible taps and whistles before McPhee's unaccompanied tenor blows out the rousing theme and Plimley's keys with Ellis's plucking fingers search out new routes to freedom. It precedes the pure alto clarinet melodism of a solo McPhee and the spiritual *Singing With a Sword In My Hand*.

Garvey's Ghost is also from *Percussion Bitter Sweet*. McPhee plays the homage to the Jamaican Africa-inspired mass leader. It is a haunting threnody, with McPhee's tenor mourning above Ellis's tingling bass.

Roach recorded *The Smoke that Thunders* on his 1984 album *Survivors* as a drum solo and evocation of the great falls of the Zambesi. Ellis transforms it to an astonishing solo bass performance, one of the finest you will ever hear, as his twanging strings evoke the progress of the great river to the very lip of the precipice, and over.

The Persistence of Rosewood is a trio tone poem in Roach's effusive spirit, remembering the 1923 massacre of a small black community in a Florida village by a white mob enraged by a false accusation of rape. Rosewood was razed, with an unknown number of dead.

There is an amalgam of lived pain and historical memory in McPhee's alto clarinet notes and Ellis' bowed bass, a pain that is sustained for almost ten minutes as the pace quickens and the anger boils. Plimley's chords echo with indignation.

Here are performances which continue the truth and beauty of Roach's great album and formulate the concluding question of McPhee's title — what now?

In his notes he remembers the walls in apartheid Israel and along the US southern border with Mexico. Obama is there now, but so are the continuing guns in Iraq and Afghanistan. McPhee still questions all who listen, as did the notes of Roach — what now?

July 28th 2010

Like a Melodic Seagull

Lol Coxhill

Coxhill on Ogun

(Ogun)

I wonder how many of us, upon approaching Hungerford Bridge from the Charing Cross side during the 70s, would have heard from a distance the sometimes piercing, other times tender notes of an unaccompanied soprano saxophone soaring into the London sky?

If so, it would have been the busking sound of a jazz master — and Lol Coxhill is his name, now seventy-seven years old and looking back over a musical career of extraordinary diversity. The early 50s found him doing national service in the RAF and a member of Denzil Bailey's Afro-Cubists. He toured US air bases in England, playing Chet Baker and Gerry Mulligan compositions with the Graham Fleming Combo and guested with giants of the time such as Joe Harriott and Tubby Hayes.

During the 60s he accompanied visiting US performers from the Motown sound of Martha and the Vandellas to bluesmen Otis Spann and Champion Jack Dupree, while also playing with the exiled South African bandsmen of Chris McGregor's Brotherhood of Breath and deepening his free improvisation experience with the Spontaneous Music Ensemble and Trevor Watts's Moire Music.

The CD *Coxhill on Ogun* is an amalgam of two albums made in the late 70s — *The Joy of Paranoia* and *Diverse* — and together they show some of the many dimensions of Coxhill's singular artistry.

The Wakefield Capers, recorded at Bretton Hall, Wakefield, is a collective improvisation of nearly nineteen minutes with three guitars — Ken Shaw on electric, Richard Wright on Spanish and Paul Mitchell-Davidson on bass.

Coxhill's opening salvo is searing and gripping and when he returns he sounds like a melodic seagull, then as an argumentative partner in a colloquy with a Derek Bailey-sounding Shaw. The guitars stew up a formidable rhythmic undertow and Coxhill's soprano flies powerfully above them, and sometimes within them.

Cornish pianist Veryan Weston is his partner on *The Cluck Variations*, described in four movements and full of continuous perturbations and improvising empathy. The "cluck" is sometimes that of a virtual chicken, but one full of rhythmic groove in its soul, while the *Joy of Paranoia Waltz* is Coxhill joyously overdubbed four times over with different saxophones.

Unexpectedly, the listener is suddenly thrust into Michael Garrick's arresting electric piano accompaniment to *Lover Man*, with Coxhill filigreeing in and out of the familiar melodic theme with a deft assurance, making you wish earnestly that he had recorded more standards. The twosome then go hurtling into *Perdido*, first Garrick in unconstrained keyboard leaps, then Coxhill, swinging as if performing a folk rhapsody, contriving to give the Ellingtonian theme a creative burst of original sound that would have surprised and startled even the Duke.

The album *Diverse* was recorded at the Seven Dials in London in 1977, and the first long track *Diver* has Coxhill as many a street passer-by might remember him with their ears, except for the echoing interior sound, playing this time — according to the sleeve notes — with only a "loose floorboard" as accompaniment. He blows an astonishing sonic essay of solo reed improvisation, touching every aspect of an endless saxophone beauty and discovery, fulfilling the instrument's true glory.

The final track *Divers* finds him with the British arch-bassist Dave Green, bowing and plucking beside the percussionist John Mitchell.

It is a trio of authentic jazz-surprisers, with Green plungingly resplendent in his entirely comradely artistry and Coxhill ripping out a relentless storm of reed creativity for nearly twenty-one full and pulsating minutes, so that the listener wonders if he can ever stop.

He hasn't so far, more's the joy. So get hold of this unique testimony, and if he comes to anywhere near you, grasp the chance to hear him live. For with Coxhill, live is the word.

April 23rd 2010

Music to Every Ear

Francine Luce

Bò Kay La Vi-a

(Ogun)

Francine Luce's Caribbean homeland is Martinique, the island of Frantz Fanon and Aimé Césaire.

She writes: "The frogs, crickets and birds from Martinique are good improvisers too. In their own rhythm together they create such a unity. The keys to the house of life are never too far away from us. We just need to use those keys to open the door and make our house of life a home worth living in."

This she does in her first album *Bò Kay La Vi-a*, Creole for "Next to the house of life" with a band of truly momentous musicians with their roots deep in the free and unbounded jazz traditions of both Africa and Europe. The recording was cut in September 1996.

The three horns include the veteran Bristolian tenor and soprano saxophonist Evan Parker, who over his sixty-six years has managed to coax almost every sound conceivable from his instruments; the South African trumpeter Claude Deppa who has played with virtually everyone from Miriam Makeba and Art Blakey to Carla Bley and Chucho Valdés and the miracle-worker of the free trombone, Londoner Paul Rutherford, who played his final slides in 2007.

The bassist is Paul Rogers, another formidable figure of British free jazz, and the pianist is his confrère in the quartet Mujician, another Bristolian Keith Tippett, a master of the avant-garde for nigh on four decades. The drummer is Cape Towner Louis Moholo-Moholo, the last survivor of the Blue Notes and a percussion supremo.

So quite some accompanists here and it is as if they mutate to Caribbean bird and insect life in the album opener, *Le La Te Ka Klere* (When The Earth Is Illuminated). "Stop/Look/Listen/what life tells you/Stop/ Understand/Search/Why are we on the earth?" Luce sings. And all in Creole, a neglected and barely recorded jazz language, with Moholo-Moholo's proud drums underscoring the words.

Parker's birdsong horn and Tippett's tinkling music box are beside Luce's almost agonised voice through *Au Fil du Temps* (As Time Goes By), all prefacing Deppa's lonely trumpet tones. The brief *A Round 7* celebrates the seven musicians, all singular in their soundscapes but unified in their ensembles. And the climactic line in *Quand La Vie Nous Sourit* (When Life Smiles On Us) is "Change-toi et tu Changeras La Monde" (Change Yourself And You Change The World). Luce declaims the song with a true sonic drama and a rousing sense of the moment.

Pokeya is a trio performance, with Parker and Deppa discovering even more new sounds for Luce (the sleevenotes assert that the three of them are playing "water"), while in *Déjà Vu* Rutherford's trombone joins with Rogers and Moholo-Moholo in a short anthemic piece of empowering breath and note finding. *Not Why!* is a stirring free jazz blow like the South Africa inspired Brotherhood of Breath of old, with Rutherford's part-growling, part-whining slides setting the sound parameters beside the astonishing reed chuntering of Parker's rampant tenor.

Tippett's lone piano opens the love-worn notes of *L'Amour Vaut Bien un Chanson* (Love deserves a song). It is ten and a half minutes of Luce and Tippett, the pianist's blue phrases unifying with the mood of the singer's pining words, this time in both English and French. *A Petits Pas D'Toi* (Little steps of you) with the intense emotive contrariness in its lines (Life, life is like this/B for bliss/C for crying), shows Luce's extraordinary vocal range, at times bringing to mind the youthful Abbey Lincoln. Even now, with Lincoln at eighty, what a duo they would be!

Rencontres is a quartet encounter — Luce, Parker, Deppa and Rutherford, the three horns mixing with Luce's sighs and exhalations as if she were the fourth. The final track is *Luna*, a duet with the audacious bowed bass of Rogers who strokes the depths of the melody as if he were striving to reach its deepest birthplace, down, down in the Caribbean earth.

What has become of Luce? Much more recently she sung on a 2009 Moholo-Moholo album, *An Open Letter to My Wife Mpumi*, also on the Ogun label but we need to hear much more of her. Her final sleeve message in the Creole of her people is simple but telling and applies to us all. "Tiebe' red, pa moli!" as we say in Martinique. "Keep going, never give up!"

November 18th 2010

Ramon the Toms

Ramon Lopez

Songs of the Spanish Civil War

(LEO)

Walking through the Peace Gardens in Sheffield I passed the memorial to the South Yorkshire members of the International Brigades in the Spanish Civil War. It made me reflect on the part played by the music I love in that momentous struggle which began seventy-five years ago, and its long aftermath.

Jazz always had a potent relationship of solidarity with the democratic forces of the Spanish Civil War. While the Republican and International Brigades were fighting for a democratic Spain during its dark years, jazz musicians in the US — among them the Duke Ellington, Count Basie and Fletcher Henderson orchestras, Sidney Bechet, Benny Carter, Teddy Wilson and Frankie Newton — were playing benefits and fundraising concerts alongside singers and campaigners such as Paul Robeson and Josh White.

After Benny Goodman organised the Stars for Spain benefit in 1937 he was confronted by pro-Franco pickets outside his Carnegie Hall concert, while Wilson — the 'Marxist Mozart' — helped form the Harlem Musical Committee To Aid Spain, and its concerts included contenders like Basie, Cab Calloway and Fats Waller. By 1940 many jazz musicians were combining to support benefits for the Spanish Children's Relief Fund.

Then in 1969 — three decades on and with Franco still in power — Charlie Haden's Liberation Music Orchestra cut their pathfinding eponymous LP.

Among the tunes included on this and succeeding albums were a number of Civil War tunes played with a rampaging urge and energy, together with Haden's tribute to the Spanish Communist leader Dolores Ibárruri, *La Pasionaria.*

Ramon Lopez, born in Alicante in 1961, began his life as a drummer in the mid-70s, and his musical consciousness was transformed in 1980 when he heard the epochal pioneer bop drummer and US Civil Rights activist Max Roach.

In July 2000 he gathered together a group of kindred spirited jazz musicians to make his own tribute to compatriots of earlier generations, *Songs of the Spanish Civil War*, and it is entirely apt that such freedom-evoking marching songs and melodies of struggling comradeship become jazz messages.

Lopez is a unique multi-textured drummer whose sound is vitally connected to his own Spanish folk tradition, with sounds very different from those of other European and US jazz percussionists. In 1997 he made an album of drum solos called *Eleven Drums Songs*, and his luminous tribute to multi-reedman Roland Rahsaan Kirk arrived in 2001.

Since 2006 he has been recording with the German free pianist Joachim Kühn and the Moroccan guembri virtuoso Majid Bekkas, and now teaches tabla and Indian music in the National Conservatory of Paris — an outcome of his intense study of Indian classical music.

Lopez assembled a small, virtual international brigade of free-improvising jazz heads to help him cut his record. Two French hornmen in bass trombonist Thierry Madiot and the alto and baritone saxophonist Daunik Lazro join him with the virtuoso British bassist and member of the Mujician quartet. Paul Rogers, playing a five-stringed bass with vocalist Beñat Achiary contributing to three songs.

Madiot's fierce slides ground Achiary's words with a growling undertow on the opener, the Catalan anthem *Els Segadors*, and Lopez's drums are everywhere while *El Quinto Regimento* is introduced by the birdsong notes of Lazro's breathy alto, with Roger's bowed bass buzzing inside them and Lopez's bell-like tapping percussion. It is an astonishing amalgam of sounds.

Lazro comes blazing in above Lopez's cymbal brushes and Rogers's throbbing strings in *El Paso Del Ebro*, with Madiot spluttering out quasi-tailgate guttural cries. Rogers's talking, proclaiming bass sounds furious and enraged, as it does at the opening of *El Tren Blindado* next to Lazro's chirruping alto.

Who knows what thoughts and dreams beset the Republican combatants as they sang *En Le Plaza De Mi Pueblo?*

Lazro blows the melody above a percussive storm and Rogers's heartbeat flickers, hums and leaps as he saws with his bow. *La Santa Espina* is a rampant hornless bass and drums duet full of Anglo-Spanish fire and conviction. Rogers' twanging bass accompaniment to Achiary's inflamed voice stirs the blood at the beginning of *Los Cuatro Generales*, and as the quartet reassembles the impassioned collective sounds grow in defiance and musical testimony.

La Sardana De Les Monges has a clear narrative as a horn duet with Madiot's gruff obbligatos sometimes veering off the story, other times taking the melodic lead.

A reprise of *Els Segadors* is the finale, with the drums of Lopez spinning out of a dream of freedom.

There is determination, resistance and huge creative flair resounding from this free and fiery ensemble as the sounds fly through the world as the plight of Spain did in history, picking up support and huge anti-fascist solidarity, as it still does in these streaming notes of jazz.

June 15th 2011

Rhythms of Freedom

Louis Moholo-Moholo's Viva-La-Black
Exile
(Ogun)
The Louis Moholo-Moholo Unit
An Open Letter to My Wife Mpumi
(Ogun)

The volcanic drummer born in Cape Town in 1940, Louis Moholo-Moholo, original member of the Blue Notes who came to live in London as an exile from apartheid in 1965 and stayed here until that cursed system's demise in the early 90s, declared during a talk at the 2010 London Jazz Festival: "I like stories! I play stories!"

He spoke about resisting the "heavy manners" of the South African police against black musicians or the multiracial bands like the Blue Notes. He told how the Cape Town police picked him up one night for carrying the "weapons" of his drumsticks. When he told them he was a jazz drummer, they ordered him to demonstrate on the police station counter.

"I didn't pass the test!" said Moholo-Moholo and he was locked up. "Under that system we were forced to repress ourselves," he explained. "So when we came here to exile we tried to set ourselves free in another land. And we still didn't know then how much the Boers had messed us up."

Perhaps his album *Exile*, cut in London in 1991, the year after the release of Mandela and the agreement for the release of political opponents of apartheid, is Moholo-Moholo's musical commentary on the swiftly moving political events in his birth nation.

"Of course, all music is political, must be political, and as long as the Boers are in power we cannot rest," Moholo-Moholo had declared five years before and there is nothing restful about the sounds of this album.

Viva-La-Black, the drummer's band, was a multiracial, internationalist outfit of powerful confrères. Fellow Cape Towner Claude Deppa was the trumpeter with two other South Africans, tenorist Sean Bergin and percussionist Thebe Lipere, plus the prime British bassist Paul Rogers, Caribbean Londoner Steve Williamson on alto and tenor, and Frank Douglas, the guitarist from Curaçao.

Moholo-Moholo remembers his departed Blue Note comrades in *Dudu Pukwana*, named after the altoist who had died in 1990 and featuring Bergin's caustic alto, and *For The Blue Notes*, which has more rampaging Bergin, a twanging chorus from Douglas and

Williamson's more ruminative tenor, with Deppa's piercing brass pointillism.

Rogers's delving notes and Moholo-Moholo's quasi-military snares introduce *Plastic Bag*, with some lively vocal hokum before Williamson takes a sprinting chase and Deppa goes stratospheric.

Visions is Douglas's tune, and besides Lipere's forest of percussion and Deppa's astonishing valve effects, Williamson's serene and measured solo is a revelation of promised freedom.

The longest track is the seventeen minutes of *Wathinta Amadoda*, with Moholo-Moholo's incessant drum heartbeat, Deppa's shrieking chorus and Douglas's effervescent strings all suggesting perhaps that an enigmatic freedom is impending for an apartheid-free South Africa.

By November 2009 Louis, back in London from his restored home in South Africa, was recording with another band also composed of South African, Caribbean and British improvisers. Black Londoner Orphy Robinson was there with his vibes alongside Martinique-born singer Francine Luce, Jamaica-rooted baritonist and altoist Jason Yarde and the prime English bassist John Edwards.

South Africa also provided pianist Pule Pheto and altoist Ntshuks Bonga. Their album *An Open Letter To My Wife Mpumi* is a free-spirited, rampantly open session in which Luce's wordless and Creole vocals swing over the fiery horns, Edwards's pulsating beat and Pheto's grounding keys.

Moholo-Moholo is the earth of it all, rocking through all the diversity of sounds. The most vivid and compelling feature of the album is the way in which rich sonic dialogues so frequently develop between unexpected protagonists.

Fine Line is a duet where a strident Moholo-Moholo and Robinson converse, their sticks and mallets finding a surprise amalgam. Moholo-Moholo's lightning pattering and skittering drums move right inside Robinson's flashing chords and gyrating cadences and the Cape and the Caribbean seem to be made as one inside a London studio.

Then in *Two Alto Hit* this South African and Caribbean oneness is consolidated, with Bonga and Yarde in a hot-pursuit alto saxophone colloquy, spurred on by drums, vibes and Edwards's ubiquitous bass, forging a cosmic unity which has always characterised Moholo-Moholo's intentions and achievements.

It's still there after seven decades — just listen.

July 27th 2011

Message to the Real World

Horace Tapscott

The Dark Tree

(hatOLOGY)

If you think that music in southern California in the 60s was all about sun, surf, The Beach Boys and The Mamas & the Papas, then listen to the incomparable sounds of pianist, composer and relentless community activist Horace Tapscott.

Tapscott was born in Houston, Texas, in 1934 and moved with his family to Los Angeles in 1945. He began his musical life as a trombonist, but while in the USAF (1953–57) he learned the piano before a serious car accident while touring with the Lionel Hampton Orchestra forced him to give up the slides and concentrate fully on the piano.

In 1961 he finished with touring and settled back in LA, forming the Pan Afrikan People's Arkestra which became an essential cultural arm of the black community. Despite his widely acknowledged musical brilliance, Tapscott only made records for small local labels and rarely performed away from his community base.

The Arkestra was grounded in a neighbourhood church in South Central LA and with its free concerts and workshops, for many years he mentored and developed the musical and social skills of local youth, including the prodigious young altoist Arthur Blythe, who made his debut recording *The Giant Is Awakened* with Tapscott in 1969.

In 1989 Tapscott recorded his most celebrated album *The Dark Tree*, cut while his quartet were playing at the Catalina Bar and Grill in Hollywood, and issued on the Swiss-based hatOLOGY label.

And what a foursome — the prime bassist from Tulsa, Oklahoma Cecil McBee, who has recorded with all the post-bop masters from Jackie McLean to Wayne Shorter, from Yusuf Lateef to Abdullah Ibrahim; New York drummer Andrew Cyrille, long-time Cecil Tayor colleague who is one of jazz's great percussionists, and on clarinet the astonishing Fort Worth-born John Carter, like Tapscott a dedicated LA community man and composer/performer of the five-album suite charting the history of black people in the US; *Roots and Folklore*.

As soon as the 21 minutes of the title track of *The Dark Tree* begin, the resolve of McBee's pulsating bass and Tapscott's thundering chords are immediately contrasted with Carter's high notes, and you know that the quartet are messaging the real world around them, that this is a sound poem about the civilised hugeness and determination of an entire people, shut into the enormous cell of a city's urban hell in the innards of the state most identified with a dream of release and the pursuit of betterness.

It is music of communal drama and resurgent hope with Tapscott's keys at its centre, promising growth, unity and unrestrained understanding. He plays with an intensity unlike any other jazz pianist, paralleling that of Bud Powell, but whereas Powell's frantic and abused self, his head beaten by racist police was splitting through his naked notes, Tapscott's sound is thicker, more congealed, as if a community are gathering and rebelling with his Africa of sounds, now transported to the Pacific coast of the Americas.

It is as if in this quartet there are three drummers and an exultant horn.

McBee's relentless plucking and shaking strings, Cyrille's heartbeat of snares which never ceases, Tapscott's complex strikes along his keyboards and Carter's wailing, hierophantic reedsong — as Tapscott announces it, the voice of a "big black clarinet" issuing a narrative of realism to those closest to him and beyond.

The record is a double CD lasting more than two hours, with the titles reflecting Tapscott's world of reflection and action — references to family in *A Dress for Renee* or *Sandy and Niles*, Africa in *Nyga's Theme* or memories of a neighbourhood vagrant recalled from Tapscott's Houston childhood in *Sketches of Drunken Mary* where an addicted, desperate woman staggers from the quartet's notes, or *Lino's Pad*, where Cyrille's marching snares and Tapscott's storm of sound make the music seem as if it is calling its listeners on to the streets.

The Dark Tree is one of the essential records in the century of jazz, revealing the intellectual and imaginative hinterland in the technical prowess of four of its finest and most visionary players, all of whom see the real world in every phrase they invent and perform.

Consider the sleeve photograph if you wish to delve deeper into its meaning — a vast, complex and many-sinewed tree trunk and its tributary branches, full of rampaging hidden life. That is in the music too, redolent of the times when it was born and expressive of its makers' artistic genius for all time.

August 26th 2011

Forty-one Notes

The Roy Campbell Pyramid Trio

Ethnic Stew and Brew
(Delmark)

Born in Los Angeles in 1952, the searing and rampaging trumpeter Roy Campbell came to live in New York when his family changed coasts while he was a child.

He began on the piano when he was six and switched to trumpet while at secondary school. He had two formidable trumpeters as his tutors and models — Kenny Dorham, who had been Charlie Parker's front-line horn partner, and the audacious Jazz Messenger Lee Morgan.

Campbell blew his way through many trumpet traditions, from bop, funk and R&B before settling within the compelling influence of the Chicago-based Association for the Advancement of Creative Musicians with such free spirits as pianist Cecil Taylor, altoist Henry Threadgill and drummer Sunny Murray. He cut his first two innovative and hard-blown albums, *New Kingdom* (1992) and *Tierra Del Fuego* (1994), with the adventurous Chicago label, Delmark.

In *Ethnic Stew and Brew*, cut in 2000, he is one part of an outstanding threesome of interacting musical genius that forms the Pyramid Trio. The bassist is William Parker, the Bronx-born giant born in the same year as Campbell and already a veteran of New York free jazz circles having played and recorded with pianists Taylor and Matthew Shipp, tenorists Charles Gayle and Frank Lowe and violinist Billy Bang, and never as a mere accompanist, always as an equal.

As did Hamid Drake, born in Louisiana in 1955, a drummer of profound power and empathy with his fellows, who moved northwards to Chicago with his family. He was tutored by the drummer son of the legendary tenorist Fred Anderson and finally became the drummer in Anderson's regular group in his Velvet Lounge club.

There is an aura of internationalism about *Ethnic Stew And Brew*. Like many great jazzmen before him from Tricky Sam Nanton and Wynton Kelly to Sonny Rollins, Campbell has Caribbean lineage and his sound carries a rich cosmopolitanism, not only through his own Trinidadian and Barbadian roots, the African longing of his sound, but also evocations of Asian soundscapes as in the tracks *Impressions of Yokohama* and *Heavenly Ascending*. As he says in his sleevenotes, "to me the Pyramid Trio is about world music with a touch of jazz."

And quite a touch too. Right throughout the opener *Tazz's Dilemma*, Parker's twanging life-pulse and Drake's grounding drums give a ceaseless earthbound movement for Campbell's belligerent horn.

When Parker's bow saws its choruses it is as if a great African tree is shaking. The transoceanic message of *Malcolm, Martin and Mandela* fuses resistance in two continents. March-like in parts, it suggests mass protest, with Campbell's high-note peals a call to permanent vigilance.

All the album's tunes were composed by Campbell and the jaunty *Imhotep* continues the forward movement with the trumpeter's breathy, pacy runs provoked by Parker's vibrant bow and Drake's pulsating rhythmic engine.

Impressions of Yokohama has Parker playing a Japanese shakukachi flute with Campbell's horn sounding as if he is ascending Mount Fuji, whereas the title tune has a definite Caribbean flavour with bass, drums and Campbell's stop-time theme providing meshed tastes of dasheen, yam, bread-fruits, plantain and pigeon peas.

"You have to take people on a journey," says Campbell of his music. This one ends back in the Bronx and with the story of the death of Amadou Diallo, a 23-year-old Guinean immigrant worker shot down by four New York Police Department officers in February 1999 with forty-one bullets, within the lobby of his own apartment building. The police were acquitted of all charges.

Campbell's tune to him begins with Drake's solo African drums and some agonised horn vocalese. As Parker's bass comes resonating in and Campbell plays a mournfully beautiful, pure-toned chorus which bursts into crescendoed leaps in an amalgam of anger, tenderness and a cry for justice, we think too of our own Diallos, of Jean Charles de Menezes, Blair Peach, Ian Tomlinson and all those who came before and we understand how Campbell's brave music enfolds them too in its defiant and indignant notes.

Forty-one times he blows the same repeated note to end his narrative. And as you listen, transfixed, you don't forget it.

August 26th 2010

Walking the Lyne

Terri Lyne Carrington

Jazz is a Spirit / Structure

(ACT)

I remember well the first time that I heard the drumming of Terri Lyne Carrington over ten years ago. She was playing alongside two jazz veterans, pianist Herbie Hancock and vibesman Bobby Hutcherson at the Barbican, and her huge sound was like a subtle tempest blowing in my ears.

She is a true storytelling drummer. Angela Davis wrote of her, in the sleeve notes of *Jazz is a Spirit*, that "her own music embodies profound lessons about our social and personal lives, about the histories that produce us and how we might free ourselves from these histories and simultaneously carry them forward."

Born in 1962, her own life narrative started in Boston where she began playing the drums as a child in local clubs with powerful musicians like Oscar Peterson, Clark Terry, Rahsaan Roland Kirk and Pharoah Sanders. Her great musicianship meant that she became a part of tenorist Wayne Shorter's band in the late 1980s, and she subsequently began to lead her own bands, breaking down and unifying jazz genres as she progressed.

The sessions of *Jazz is a Spirit* were recorded in 2001 in Burbank, California. She was joined by some prestigious players, including Hancock, trumpeters Wallace Roney and Terence Blanchard, guitarists Kevin Eubanks and Paul Bollenback and tenor saxophonist Gary Thomas.

With a reminder from bassman Malcolm-Jamal Warner that jazz is "collective storytelling," the opening track *Jazz Is* leads into *Little Jump*, with horns Roney and Thomas in powerful voice and Hancock's piano incisive and inventive. Carrington's drums are prominent, as they are in *The Corner*, where she combines with percussionist Darryl Munyungo Jackson to create a powerful rhythmic undertow.

Samara is a tribute to her old leader Wayne Shorter. Thomas traces out the theme with a melodic beauty, and Hancock's solo is full of feeling for a hornman who was his longtime bandmate too.

An unaccompanied drumburst all through *Journey Agent* leads on to *Journey East from West* and *Journey of Now*, where Roney's Miles-inspired trumpet soars and crackles over the pounding drumbeat.

Middle Way is Blanchard's only track, with Hancock filling in the spaces left by the ensemble and striking into his own choruses with bounce and verve. When Thomas's quizzical tenor and Blanchard's bent New Orleans notes interplay, it is a colloquy of enigmatic eloquence.

Mr Jo Jones is a recording of the great Basie-ite drummer speaking to Carrington in 1984, with her drums superimposed alongside his voice.

It radiates a sense of jazz history as well as setting down her percussive lineage. "As long as I'm here, if you have any problems — call me," declares Jo, and you can believe it's sincere, even now, so much is she his offspring.

In November 2003 Carrington cut the album *Structure* with a new quartet comprising guitarist Adam Rogers, bassist Jimmy Haslip and the altoist and leader of many a Blue Note session, Greg Osby, whose distinctive, jerking timbre offset by Carrington's potent thrust gives the album a truly original sound.

Mindful Intent is the title of the opening track and there is plenty of that in the album. Rogers' stringplay is pointed and discursive, and Osby's quirky lines are customarily unexpected.

In his own composition *Black Halo*, melodic lines are side by side with sudden narrative changes, putting the listener on extreme edge. *Ethiopia* begins with a beauteous, unaccompanied saxophone fanfare by Osby before Carrington sings Joni Mitchell's pungent lyrics. *The Invisible* is by Rogers and features his fleet-fingered guitar brilliance.

Throughout the album the dynamism and sparking rhythm of Carrington's drumwork provides the energising foundation, illustrating Angela Davis' considered assessment: "She has significantly transformed the way we think about jazz women, and thus also how we think about jazz. Jazz is a spirit and thanks to Terri Lyne Carrington, that spirit is extricating itself from its exclusively male history."

Get these albums and hear for yourself.

May 10th 2011

Photo: Tracy Love

The Lament of a City

Sonny Rollins

Without a Song: The 9/11 Concerts

(Milestone)

On the morning of September 11 2001, Sonny Rollins had just spent the night at his New York apartment, some six blocks away from the World Trade Center in Lower Manhattan. The world's greatest tenor saxophonist, a New Yorker born in 1930, witnessed the catastrophe at very close quarters. He was in that street outside his apartment when the second tower fell and was evacuated a day later, shocked and shattered.

Anyone who knows Rollins's music also knows how important his home city is to his work and artistry.

One of his finest albums, *The Bridge*, reflected how he used the Williamsburg Bridge as his open-air practice venue, wood-shedding there regularly for hours and hours during that period of the early 1960s when he lived on Manhattan's Lower East Side. New York was his home, providing his childhood streets and his growing places, and has always surged through his sound.

Four days after the attacks, on September 15, the septuagenarian Rollins was scheduled to play a concert at Boston's Berklee Performing Arts Center. Despite the trauma, he decided to perform and this extraordinary recording is the evidence. It is a huge memorial in music to all those who perished — firefighters and office cleaners, catering staff and clerical workers, ordinary people with local yet global roots.

The choice of tunes was significant. They are resilient popular ballads with deep, questioning themes and huge melodic centres. *Where or When, Without a Song, Why Was I Born?* plus a Rollins tune which tells of another massive man-made disaster facing the US — global warming.

And with him were his regular colleagues — the marvellous young pianist Stephen Scott and veteran bassist Bob Cranshaw, plus trombonist Clifton Anderson, drummer Perry Wilson and percussionist Kimati Dinizulu.

Rollins's all-powerful saxophone seems strangely subdued and contemplative throughout the concert, but it is beautiful nonetheless. The usual relentless improvisational attack is replaced by a resounding sense of loss and pain, the sound of a great artist thinking every note, feeling every sound.

Without a Song sounds almost like a lamentation, with Rollins restrained and low-key. Anderson, often used by Rollins as a colourist rather than a virtuoso soloist, plays several moving choruses, finely poised and sadly melodic.

Rollins invokes childhood memories of his hero Paul Robeson in his words of introduction and his own solo has a sense of the singer's depth and human solidarity.

Global Warming has Scott switching to Kalimba, with Dinizulu's thudding congas featured on a Caribbean-inspired theme, close to Rollins's own Virgin Island roots from which his own long solo takes fire. Listening to *A Nightingale Sang in Berkeley Square* now, after July's London bombings, only adds a haunting historical irony to Rollins's 2001 version.

He almost weeps out the theme in the foreground of Anderson's mournful horn until Cranshaw's chorus and Scott's reflective solo only build the sadness and visions of the square's huge swooping plane trees.

Why Was I Born? taken at pace, changes the ethos, as, after an unaccompanied intro, Rollins surges into the tune with all his customary gusto, followed by a resplendent Scott, whose every note bounces with creative energy.

By the album's final tune, *Where or When*, Rollins's notes are approaching their most massive.

The roar of those present is immense, their applause unstoppable. A New Yorker rejoicing for his own wounded city, proclaiming its people's continuity yet using his storm of music to consider causes too.

For, deep inside this music, the questions never stop arising from within the grandeur of its sound.

June 21st 2006

Batting for Jazz

Cameron Pierre
Pad Up
(Get Ready)
Robert Mitchell
The Greater Good
(Jazz Services)

Here is a marvellous West Indian jazz guitarist who names his new album in the terminology of cricket and the glory of its Caribbean pitch of life. Such is *Pad Up* by the Dominica-raised Cameron Pierre. He hasn't got Viv Richards or Brian Lara in his band, but with him are the Swedish organist Anders Olinder and US drummer Rod Young, who has played with Jazz Jamaica.

The session begins with the pacy *Right Arm Over* and it's hard not to think of Malcolm Marshall or Wes Hall as Pierre races all over his strings and delivers a fleeting opening solo. Olinder follows with some clicking, gurgling choruses as Young's drums throb and scintillate.

Spike Lee's *Mo' Better Blues* exercises Pierre's prodigious technique, close enough to that of John Leslie — which was the great Wes Montgomery's real name — swinging with a rhythmic aplomb and assurance, his solo zipping off his fingertips.

The title tune has Pierre and Olinder opening the innings, with the guitarist springing between the wickets, pulling and cutting like Gordon Greenidge with sheer Caribbean invention, while Olinder stays more orthodox, his drives more classically realised.

Yeah Mon has a calypso undercurrent, played with a restless verve, while such is the power of titles that *Backfoot Drive* brings back memories of Clyde Walcott, the powerhouse Barbadian backfoot genius, as Pierre swings zestfully through some vibrant choruses. Two versions of *Ayo Nubia*, dedicated to Pierre's daughter, are tender, reflective and purely acoustic, while *Karifuna* is in tribute to the indigenous Carib peoples of Dominica and has a full-pelt speed, stomping joy and pride.

The fast bowlers are taken off for Brubeck's *In Your Own Sweet Way*, which is played with a Latin edge. The narrative of *The Bartender and the Thief* is given a rumshop scenario with Courtney Pine's bass clarinet adding a Caribbean depth and Pierre's strings quivering with life.

Pad Up is certainly the most dexterous and original guitar album I have heard for years and Pierre is a powerful contender indeed.

Another jazzman with roots in the Windward Islands is the young Ilford-born pianist Robert Mitchell, who has a Grenadian father and a Barbadian mother. His new trio album is *The Greater Good*, with bassist Tom Mason and drummer Richard Spaven. When you hear the opening track *Cumulus* the sound is tremulous and impressionistic, with Mason's bass filling the sky with a darker menace. *A Map of the Sky* is similarly spacious, galvanised by Spaven's clicking rimshots.

It is not until Mitchell becomes embroiled in tenorist Wayne Shorter's 1964 tune *Dance Cadaverous*, from his Blue Note album *Speak No Evil*, that the intensity winds up, the pace quickens and the pianist moves into a series of fervent, intricate choruses. Mitchell's own *Quantum* is slow, suspenseful and mysterious, with Spaven's cymbals showering Mitchell's sparse notes with sound-spray.

It is as if *Ochre* is discovered as it is conceived, so shapely are its individual notes and phrases, so much beauty is wrapped in the spaces between its sounds, and *Crystal Eyes* is as pellucid as its title, a succession of diamond-like piano raindrops.

All through *Teardrops*, it is Mason's bass that is weeping behind the melody, while Mitchell's chiming notes sound like messages of solace and reassurance. The bassman also sets out the theme of *The Blessing*, his notes quivering from fingers and bow while Mitchell showers his phrases behind him. This is an exquisite track.

As Mitchell completes his album with the title tune, again in the closest of musical comradeships with the outstanding Mason, you know you have been hearing a unique keyboard voice, fragile, terse, aching and passionate in turns, but a musician of brilliant poise and sound. And all from Ilford too.

February 10th 2009

Challenging a US Jazz Mould

Vijay Iyer

Your Life Flashes/Blood Sutra/In What Language

(Pi)

During his interview with the jazz writer Kevin LeGendre at the London Jazz Festival, the Indian-American pianist Vijay Iyer traced his jazz lineage through the music's radical and liberatory tradition — directly from Max Roach and the musicians at the centre of the Civil Rights movement.

Born in 1971 and raised in Rochester, upstate New York, Iyer is the son of immigrants from South India. He began learning classical violin at three years of age and taught himself piano when exposed to classical and religious music. He completed a degree in mathematics and physics at Yale by the age of twenty, and then studied for a doctorate at Berkeley. He once said: "Jazz has been this essentially hybrid form since the beginning. Putting jazz next to Indian music sort of presumes that both forms were pure to begin with, and really they've always been open forms."

As soon as you hear the opening of the album *Your Life Flashes* of March 2002, with the bassless trio of Iyer, drummer Elliot Humberto Kavee and tenor saxophonist Aaron Stewart, you realise that a new syncretism has been created. Without the bass the rhythmic centre flutters, the thematic core turns outwards with Kavee's splashing drums and Stewart's horn exploring every space beside Iyer's teeming keys. Listen to the enveloping ensemble on *Sublimation* or *Generations*. The trio call themselves "Fieldwork," as if their musical agronomy is seeding something new from old jazz husbandry.

Blood Sutra of 2003 has a more conventional quartet form with altoist Rudresh Mahanthappa, Stephan Crump on bass and drummer Tyshawn Sorey. Iyer's sleeve notes are intensely carved: "This album is our multi-thread conversation on the densely clotted subject of blood, our fluid process of associative meaning, our flowing, pulsating, collective meditation" around ideas such as "health, kinship, identity, race, violence, liquidity, desire." Quite a thematic axis here, expressed by a powerful foursome playing in and out of each others' skins with an integral empathy. Declared as a "fiscally sponsored project of the Asia American Arts Alliance," *Blood Sutra* has the sound of a jazz annunciation, of a new tradition at work, of Asian connections challenging a US jazz mould.

In *Brute Facts* Iyer pounds and chimes, and Mahanthappa — fragile and thin-toned, spinning patterns of dispersal — sounds like no other contemporary horn. Sorey is ever-busy in *Habeus Corpus*, his drums leading and following simultaneously with Iyer chewing relentlessly on a theme, while *Stigmatism* has sting, swift movement and powerful interplay.

During the same year Iyer teamed up with the poet/lyricist Mike Ladd and a ten-piece band to record the album *In What Language?* The title stems from the dark experience of the Iranian film maker Jafar Panahi at New York's JFK airport in 2001. He was arrested, chained to a bench in a cell for several hours and sent back to his place of departure — Hong Kong.

"I'm not a thief, not a murderer," he protested. "I am just an Iranian, a film maker. But how could I tell this, in what language?" Following this, Iyer and Ladd put together this album: "a song cycle about people in airports, narratives of lives in transit."

So what is here? What world is this, stemming from these words and music, what truths and nightmares?

The fusion of African-American and Asian-American narratives in a post-Twin Towers world, of "lands dismembered," the pounding of Iyer's keys, the discomfiture of Crump's twanging bass, the struggle of futility to reconnect a world which is severed, Trevor Holder's incessant, thumping drums, the lives, deaths and travels of porn wallahs, toilet scrubbers, lotto ticket sellers, Iraqi ex-businessmen now refugees, the jerking dreams of Mahanthappa's agonised horn, Ambrose Akinmusire's striving, fleeing trumpet notes.

Yemeni refugees, illegal and migrants from Calcutta, St Thomas, Ivory Coast, Senegal — asylum-seekers from Sierra Leone, lost in the world's traffic, airports their only realm, "passers-by who are passed by," facing life with their backs to the world.

It is all here, in this album, where jazz stares the world in its face. One to get, one to ponder, where music is a call to action.

February 12th 2010

Foundry of Drums

Alan Skidmore, Tony Oxley and Ali Haurand
SOH Live in London
(jazzwerkstatt)
Cecil Taylor and Tony Oxley
Leaf Palm Hand
(jazzwerkstatt)
Tony Oxley and Derek Bailey
Tony Oxley/Derek Bailey Quartet
(jazzwerkstatt)

He was born in the Steel City of Sheffield in 1938 and, like many would-be percussion innovators, as a young conventional drummer in the 50s he found himself tied to the beat dogma of his contemporaries. But when he formed a free jazz trio with fellow Sheffielders guitarist Derek Bailey and bassist Gavin Bryars, his life as a jazzman changed, despite a period in the mid-60s when he became house drummer at Ronnie Scott's accompanying visiting stellar swing and bop-playing US musicians from Bill Evans and Ben Webster to Sonny Rollins and Johnny Griffin.

Oxley's brilliance and dedication made him one of the great free jazz drummers, and these three albums on the German jazzwerkstatt label show him in different combinations and with musical partners who have all brought out diverse aspects of his jazz genius.

The first was recorded live in 1983 at The Roundhouse in Chalk Farm when Oxley was a third of the SOH trio with tenorist Alan Skidmore and Dutch bassist Ali Haurand. Hear his cymbals sizzle like a storm of sleet as his polyrhythmic drums pound relentlessly alongside Skidmore's Coltranish tones on the openers *Low the Morn*, which sometimes has echoes of Coltrane's *Alabama*.

So lovingly has Skidmore internalised and emulated the great reedman's power, while resolutely creating his own very personal buoyant sounds. The astonishing bass solo that opens *Dutch's Dreams (Ali's Waltz)* is unprecedented in jazz sonics — tinkling, pulsating, twanging, farting, quivering rhapsodies all.

Then Oxley's drums and Skidmore's soprano enter with Oxley sounding as if he is playing with hands and sticks simultaneously, before his solo where bells are rung, skins are thrashed, cymbals rattle, sticks clatter and vibrate and a universe of percussion fills the ears.

Weaver of Dreams is a movingly eloquent balladic tenor gift by Skidmore, while *Percussion 10* expresses the Oxley drum cosmos as a multidimensional solo of astonishing hybridity, and his two colleagues join him for the wickedly fast and fleeting *Ruby Doo*.

From 1998 to 1992 Oxley regularly accompanied the Long Island City pioneer avant-garde pianist Cecil Taylor. Their duo concert in Berlin's Kongresshalle in 1988 has been released as the album *Leaf Palm Hand*.

Taylor is a drummer of the piano, creating lightning two-handed percussive effects, so there are really two drummers drumming here, with the pianist's rampaging keyboard runs creating a furious sound on the opener *Stylobate 1*, while the forty-two minutes of the title track create an unbreakable jazz unity between the black African-American and the white Yorkshiremen, forging an extraordinary musical fusion of their provenances.

Oxley makes waves of flickering sound as Taylor drums his ivory bones, and nations, cultures, races and ethnicities become one in the playing. A work of phenomenal musical and physical creative stamina is *Leaf Palm Hand*, and in the midst of all Taylor's pyrotechnics Oxley is never lost or perturbed, and his drums match and equal his partner's artistic and percussive glories.

Oxley and Bailey reunited in 1993 in Cardiff at the Chapter Arts Centre, this time in a quartet setting with Matt Wand on sampler and Pat Thomas on piano and electronics. The old Sheffield days seem more than an age away as all forms of sound emerge and Bailey plucks his atonal strings inside a tempest of striking surfaces and electronic wails throughout the opener *Two on Two*.

Oxley and Bailey lay out for the mournful and blues-aching Thomas/Wand track *Hydrolysis*, but combine as a duo for two tracks, *Monics* and *Mirage*. Oxley's fevered, clashing cymbal rhythm of the former meshes with Bailey's harping, irregular phrasing to issue a disturbing harmony, while on *Mirage* the drums sound huge and everywhere, with Bailey seeming to look for the spaces between them to fill in his sounds.

There is no other drummer like Oxley. I sometimes think that his percussive language — born from steel and the massiveness of the foundries, forges and rolling mills of his birth city — could only have arisen from such an industrial context, and with them gone. His sound too is uniquely finite.

As the final track on the album *Cymbal Pointer* tells us, vibrating metals alloyed with wood and skin make the subtlety and power of blow and clang which make his music.

October 26th 2011

Questions for George W

The Carla Bley Big Band

Looking for America

(Watt)

A true agitator, Carla Bley has been at the centre of musical irony, subversion and co-operative commitment since her first records in the late 60s.

Californian by birth — born in Oakland in 1938 — she formed the Jazz Composers Guild Orchestra with her second husband Michael Mantler and contributed her arrangements for Charlie Haden's Liberation Music Orchestra on their first *Impulse!* album in 1969. In the decades since then, she has been leading large bands, composing, arranging and producing many albums, including tributes to musical geniuses as far apart as Thelonious Monk and Kurt Weill.

Looking for America emerges at a time when huge and destructive jingoistic and imperialist energies are seething across the US. As Bley admits in her notes to the album, much of it was conceived before "the recent rush of aggressive actions by the present administration," but the US invasions of Afghanistan and Iraq give her musical satire an even sharper historical piquancy.

She writes, too, that she found that, almost subconsciously, sudden infections from a "patriotic virus" were finding their way into her musical compositions — snatches from *The Star Spangled Banner*, for example.

Can you imagine trying to write an original piece of music and repeatedly finding that you were unknowingly setting down bars from *God Save the Queen* or *Rule Britannia*? Quite a shock. But Bley decided to positively employ these quirky musical trespasses and *Looking for America* is the compelling result.

During the second track, *The National Anthem*, with martial overtones and an even more peppery irony, it is the burnished tenor saxophone tones of Wiltshire-born Andy Sheppard that give a brilliant riposte to Blair's sickeningly toadying Congress speech of a few weeks ago, as Bley's reworkings of chauvinistic themes give them new — and now post-Iraq — meanings.

Within this assembled eighteen-piece orchestra, there are some marvellous musicians making some extraordinary sounds. *Los Cocineros*, for example, which is dedicated to the Latin American kitchen workers of New York, has powerful solo contributions from baritonist Gary Smulyan — an ex-kitchen man himself — and Gary

Valente's harsh trombone, blowing over Don Alias's subtle percussion variations.

Running between the more explicitly "American" tracks of the album are thematic fragments, such as *Grand Mother*, *Step Mother*, *Your Mother* and *God Mother*, with a strong womanist theme, giving the album a further dimension of structural unity and stressing the woman's contribution within an ironically conceived masculinist conception of America.

Lew Soloff takes the gripping solo trumpet lead in *Tijuana Traffic*, which began compositional life as part of a musical score for a film about the life of Cesar Chavez, the campaigning leader of the United Farm Workers of America.

But the most surprising and iconoclastic track on *Looking for America* is Bley's arrangement of the children's song *Old MacDonald had a Farm*, sounding like a rendition played by a group of musicians all high on junk food from the multinational burger-poison plantation. They play like masters though, in particular Steve Swallow on electric bass, Billy Drummond on drums and the frantic brass choruses of Soloff and Valente.

Sound satire has frequently been integral to jazz, from Jelly Roll Morton's hokum to Mingus's *Fables of Faubus*, Max Roach's *Driva Man* (from his *Freedom Now* suite), or Sonny Rollins's *Way Out West*.

Bley brilliantly continues that tradition in *Looking for America*, asking questions in her music that cut to the heart of US arrogance and power.

December 3rd 2003

Trio of Equals

Trio 3
Time Being
(Intakt)
Trio 3 and Geri Allen
At This Time
(Intakt)

Trio 3's only horn player is alto and tenor saxophonist Oliver Lake, born in Marianna, Arkansas, in 1942. During his boyhood, he played drums and picked up the alto at eighteen before going to Lincoln University and becoming a high school teacher.

Then he played in R'n'B bands and became an active member of the radical Black Arts Movement. He moved to New York and became a founder member of the World Saxophone Quartet with fellow horn virtuosi David Murray, Julius Hemphill and Hamiet Bluiett.

Seventy-year-old New Yorker Andrew Cyrille, who began his musical life in a drum and bugle corps, is the trio's drummer. He played across the jazz spectrum with hornmen and pianists from the first great jazz saxophonist Coleman Hawkins to Cecil Taylor, the first pianist of the avant-garde.

On bass is virtuoso Reggie Workman, born in Philadelphia in 1937. In his long career he accompanied the likes of John Coltrane, Eric Dolphy, Yusuf Lateef and Thelonius Monk, but he was also the rhythmic heart of Art Blakey's Jazz Messengers during their early 60s heyday.

These three masters have led a host of key sessions over the decades, so Trio 3 is truly a summation of jazz power and genius. Their 2005 Brooklyn session which produced the album *Time Being* sees Lake playing both alto and soprano saxophones on the ten self-penned tracks. Their collective eclecticism, ranging from mainstream and bop to free improvisation, bursts out in their playing.

The opener *A Chase* lucidly illustrates that here is a company of equals. No one assumes the role of lead, less still the role of an accompanist. Each musician takes his own road, but in doing so is cognisant of the band's intertwining routes. So there is true unity in free musical utterance and Workman's *Medea* has Lake blowing with huge force and improvisational will beside Cyrille's pounding percussive might, while Workman weaves deep pathways for both his soundmates to explore.

Tight Rope shows the trio's audacity. Every note is daring, requiring empathy and trust from all three both in the skill to create individual sound and open and share new sonic ground. That support and understanding is evident on Lake's astonishing opening burst at the commencement of *Equilateral*. That's followed by a retort of similar expressiveness from Workman's emulative bass, with Cyrille's cymbals extending the statement.

Every sound meshes — this is a life conversation of three jazz elders still at their apex and is as much a transparent explication of how the music works as sheer artistry in action.

The slow, droll mood of *Lope* changes to the high-pitched sopranino passages of the title tune which Lake patrols peerlessly. He sings like a nest-making bird while Workman plucks and Cyrille strikes, as if the sounds of nature were harnessed in a Brooklyn studio. A brilliant set-to.

In 2009 the trio was augmented by Detroit-born pianist Geri Allen. Younger, but with no less understanding or dexterity in the groove, she gives the new quartet an entirely different sound on the album *At This Time*. Allen brings to mind another eccentric pianist, Mal Waldron. Often sparse, intensive, percussive and immensely skilful in her use of singular repetitive phrases, she is a striking contrast to the more garrulous Lake.

For Patrick L, devoted to Intakt record producer Patrick Landolt, begins with a sawing bowed bass by Workman as Cyrille clips his rims. Lake's exclamatory phrases introduce a reticent Allen with a keyboard that sounds like another drum before Workman's humming bass completes the portrait.

All Net has Lake in full inventive passion, in colloquy with Allen's subliminal runs, while the former's *Run* is more bop oriented until the rhythmic pace slackens and then speeds up again for a relaxed and swinging outing. Time is the focus of both albums. Jazz can only emerge from the here-and-now, chronicling actuality as it is constructed and withers away.

These two albums hold on to such moments for us with an infectious spirit and skill.

December 3rd 2003

Impassioned and Prophetic Notes

Charles Gayle Trio

Consider the Lilies

(clean feed)

Nobody else but Charles Gayle sounds like Charles Gayle. Considering the Bible-inspired titles of his succession of albums through the 1990s — *Repent*, *Consecration*, *Testaments* and *Daily Bread* — you might think that they were recordings of an ancient priest. You might even be right, for the spiritual uplift in these sessions is mighty.

Gayle's tenor saxophone whacks into you like the rod of correction of old, but a lot more is happening, too. Born in Buffalo in 1939, the Niagara thunder still roars through his horn, even on his 2006 trio album *Consider the Lilies*, with bassist Hilliard Greene and drummer Jay Rosen.

The innovations from previous recorded forays is that Gayle puts aside his tenor for an alto saxophone and he also plays piano on some of his tracks.

Many of Gayle's listeners have likened his sound to that of the Cleveland-born tenorist Albert Ayler (1936-1970), whose free, hyper-abrasive and harshly lyrical horn blasted open the jazz world when he made his series of trio albums for the ESP label in 1964. But Gayle's huge saxophone voice, hierophantic and prophetic, is absolutely his own, as a hearing of *Consider the Lilies* will soon testify.

The opening track *Truley, Truley* — the spelling is his — begins with Rosen's rolling drums before Gayle enters, straining and stretching his notes as soon as his breath begins to sound. It is a rasp, a grating of sound made into beauty before Greene comes in with a series of the deepest bass cadences and plunging phrases.

There is a keening light of melodism at the centre of *Edge of Time*. Gayle pumps his notes upwards then chews on them as they fall, only to rise again.

Greene's bass shakes and vibrates until the bow smoothes the sound just as Gayle turns towards piano. The impassioned keys run away with their notes as if each one were jumping successively over the cliff of the keyboard, while Rosen's brushes pound into the cymbals and snares.

Listen to Gayle as he plays *Of Ages*, his alto vibrating with rampant breath and dedication. The final three tracks slide into each other. It is a mystery where one ends and the next begins, so intense is the improvisation over the tidal effect of Rosen's mounting and falling drums.

By Gayle's standards, this is a relatively short album, forty-one minutes of live musical performance that is but a blink in his canon.

But, as with all his recordings, it is extraordinary and engrossing, taking your consciousness to places unforeseen, a testimony of one of the most surprising of improvisers, exploring sonic worlds at the very moment that they are conceived, created and experienced.

October 8th 2008

Sounding Rod of Past Truths

David Murray
Sacred Ground
(Justin Time)
Black Saint Quartet
David Murray Live in Berlin
(jazzwerkstatt)

Born in Berkeley in 1955, David Murray is the tenor saxophone master of his generation. He has a host of epochal recordings behind him that embrace a free, eclectic range of jazz styles and genres, from post bop to the avant-garde, from sumptuous ballad performances to the pyrotechnics of his work with the World Saxophone Quartet.

His album *Sacred Ground* is steeped in the expression of jazz as cultural resistance. Four musicians of immense authority express their history, playing their instruments as their people's griots. With Murray are pianist Lafayette Gilchrist, thirteen years younger than Murray and dedicated student of the saxophonist's long-time piano partner John Hicks who died in 2006, the great New York avant-garde drummer Andrew Cyrille and Murray's old bass buddy from Brookline, Massachusetts, Ray Drummond.

"You can't talk about America without talking about all-overshading racism," asserts Murray in the album's sleeve notes. Within his tune *Banished* the quartet tell the story in sound of how thousands of black families were driven out of their homes in Missouri and Arkansas in the years between the civil war and the Great Depression.

The tune became a part of the soundtrack of Marco Williams's film of the same name — a rousing musical experience, with Murray's bass clarinet sounding a deep clarion for struggle, tossing notes everywhere.

The African-American novelist Ishmael Reed wrote that the lament "tells the whole story of the banished whether they be the United States' homeless or the refugees in Darfur."

The album's title song is sung by Cassandra Wilson with Reed's lyrics. "We've come back to claim our dearest legacy," she asserts, after ancestors were "banished from your towns of hate." Now, she sings, "we've come back to claim our very own" and Gilchrist's rolling piano chorus gives irresistible movement to her words. But it is also Murray's own true redemption song and his horn rumbles, roars, gurgles, boils, spits and demands, sounding out a fearless pitch as Wilson summatively exclaims: "We survived!"

Hearing Murray live is a sublime jazz encounter and the powerfully recorded *Live in Berlin* session with the Black Saint Quartet gets as close as possible to the real experience. Gilchrist is with him again, alongside bassist Jaribu Shahid and drummer Hamid Drake, both of whom are rocks of the avant-garde.

Murray's quartet reprise some of the key tracks of *Sacred Ground* in Berlin's Radial System V in November 2007. For Murray, *Banished* is "as relevant as it never was before," with "black people currently being driven out of downtown New York, Chicago or Los Angeles, because they can no longer afford to live there. After Katrina, Louisiana is no longer a real state, it's largely wasteland. That's the way it goes, America is a very ungrateful country."

Such was the context of his Berlin performance, a wondrous demonstration of the tenor saxophone as a sounding rod of historical truth and contemporary defiance, a horn of the deepest and most earnest collective struggle for freedom.

"I am a protester in everything I do, resistance is the tradition of black music," Murray declares in the sleeve notes. "While drums were the means of communication in Africa, we took music to another level as a means of resistance. Everything we invented was copied so many times that some people have forgotten what the origin was. We, my people, are the inventors."

And how these words strike out in the music. Hear Drake's pounding drum fury in *Dirty Laundry* and Shahid's cavernous bass introduction to *Banished.*

In *Murray's Steps*, the leader's horn traverses many a saxophone odyssey and Gilchrist's choruses journey with him in rocking and blues-laden gait.

And Waltz Again moves on a ballroom of struggle, with Murray's extreme notes, high and low, expressing the far extremes and beautiful melodism of his instrument, still sounding at the heart of jazz rebellion.

October 7th 2009

Ploughman of the Horn

Evan Parker and the Transatlantic Art Ensemble

Boustrophedon

(ECM)

There was a time when the ardent revelations of free improvising jazz found a close comradeship with progressive politics and culture. Looking through my poster collection the other day, I found the orange blaze of the Moving Left Show of April 1975, organised by the Communist Party at The Roundhouse in Chalk Farm.

A powerful jazz line-up there was, with avant-garde improvisers of huge stature. Drummer John Stevens was there, trombonist Paul Rutherford, guitarist Derek Bailey and the free soprano saxophonist and busking genius of Waterloo Bridge, Lol Coxhill.

Mike Westbrook's band turned out too, with the doyen of British free tenorists ever up for a musical challenge, Bristol-born Evan Parker.

Born in 1944, Parker settled in London in 1965, working with Stevens and Bailey in the pioneering Spontaneous Music Ensemble, with drummer Tony Oxley and frequently within the South African/ British life's blood amalgam, Chris McGregor's Brotherhood of Breath. Parker's recorded canon is enormous and his most recent album *Boustrophedon* attests to the huge admiration and respect he has within the international jazz commonwealth.

Parker is once heard, never forgotten. His horn bursts with sonic fire — life itself resounds in his every note. And in *Boustrophedon* he is in cosmic company with the Transatlantic Art Ensemble.

Three members of the Art Ensemble of Chicago are present — alto genius Roscoe Mitchell, trumpeter Corey Wilkes and bassist Jaribu Shahid, together with two other British free jazz veterans, bassist Barry Guy and drummer Paul Lytton.

Also among the ensemble of fourteen are violinist Philipp Wachsmann, born in Uganda, Brazilian cello virtuoso Marcio Mattos and other musicians stretching across Europe and the US. They made their record in Munich.

Between his overture and finale, Parker calls each section of his music a "furrow." The title *Boustrophedon* is a Greek word meaning "turning like an ox while ploughing" and referred to a means of writing where the first line would run from left to right, the second from right to left and so on. It is a reference to Parker's method of improvising, of returning to the direction of what has been accomplished but creating fresh lines with each new venture, never duplicating, always innovating.

Big Bill Broonzy created and played the *Plowhand Blues*, but it was never like this. Parker's massive collective rasp and earthbound rhythms cut through the jazz swards, turning over buried loams and sods of sound. The throbbing drums and echoing strings that pound and stroke out the opening of the overture and the first *Furrow*, followed by the flute birdsong, have a musical timelessness. Craig Taborn's piano chimes are like the discovery of dawn in the farmlands.

History moves through these sounds, the history of rural life somewhere, somehow, sometime. In *Furrow 4* you can hear the whinnying shires, their clopping across sudden hard surfaces. And when Parker's swirling reed enters there is a mighty perturbation, an abrupt disruptive frenzy as if a bucolic life is finished forever and something much more threatening is about to ensue, marked by *Furrow 5* and its clarinet annunciation and Wilkes's talking, moaning, agonised trumpet.

In *Furrow 6* Taborn's piano marches beside the two whining and vibrating basses and Mattos's chronicling cello. There is a sudden menacing stroke and either Parker or Mitchell, both masters of circular breathing, blow seemingly endless hierophantic phrases, the saxophone teeming notes before a background of sublime and worrisome chords and the gradual clashing of cymbals.

The tenor saxophone storms in like a tsunami, Parker's sheer breathless power rumbling across the fields, smothering the earth, inundating its every scooped-out groove, pursued by a morose bass coda.

The plunging basses dominate the *Finale* broken up by Wilkes's skittering brass and the last incontestable chords, as if the time of the earth is over, it can take and tolerate no more.

As with all music, the listeners invest their own interpretations, their own truths of illumination. What is *Boustrophedon* telling us in its wild and brilliant notes? No comfort, but warning a-plenty in Parker's rapturous sounds.

December 16th 2009

Reaching for the Flame

David Haney and Julian Priester

Ota Benga of the Batwa

(CIMP)

Jazz is story, story is jazz. Nowhere in the music's century-long history has this dictum been more compellingly realised than in this album by two apparently contrary jazzmen.

Born in Fresno, California, in 1955, the pianist David Haney grew up in the cold tremors of the city of Calgary, Alberta, leaning onto the foothills of the Canadian Rockies. His partner is trombonist Julian Priester, born in Chicago in 1935, who grew to musical brilliance in a period of post-bop ascendancy and who honed his slide-craft with masters like Max Roach, Jimmy Heath and Tommy Flanagan before moving into freer jazz orbits.

Their story's protagonist is Ota Benga, a captured African of a massacred Pygmy people of present-day Rwanda and south-western Uganda, brought to the US in a cage and exhibited at the 1906 World's Fair in St Louis. He was subsequently employed in the Bronx Zoo cleaning animal cages where he gradually became an exhibit himself in the eyes of spectators.

After complaints from some visitors he was dispatched first to the Howard Colored Orphans Asylum in Brooklyn and later to Lynchburg, Virginia, where he was given a room by concerned philanthropists, although he frequently slept in the local woods still longing for Africa. Eventually one night he made a fire, and in a deep yearning for his homeland he took a shotgun and killed himself beside it. All only a century ago in the land of the free, Benga's life and death is another long episode in the unending story of US racism, and the Haney/Priester duo tell it like griots with an astonishing soundscape.

Their record made me think of other inspired duos grounded in similar, sometimes more implicit narratives — Jelly Roll Morton and cornetist Joe "King" Oliver's 1924 *Tomcat Blues*, or more explicitly, drummer Max Roach and tenorist Archie Shepp's sound essay on apartheid, *South Africa Goddamn*, or bassist William Parker and drummer Hamid Drake's *Awake, Arise* of 2005.

These two musicians of two separate generations playing with such brotherly empathy and blessed with superb musicianship are true jazz storytellers.

On the opening track *Theme for Ota*, Haney's ruminative notes are gradually bloodied by Priester's distant-sounding, moaning slides and cadences of sorrow which challenge the oppressive silence until they rise and almost strike the sky with reaches and grasps for freedom and return.

A sense of sonic nakedness around these musicians radiates from Priester's solo beginning to *Variation on a Theme for Ota*, and when Haney enters with his pounding phrases, Priester's horn becomes almost hierophantic in its urgent messaging.

In *Batwa's Spirit*, Priester's repeated belching notes seem to be the breath of a determined life, and Haney's responses create a colloquy of resolution, their pace quickening, their veins swelling, almost bursting with agony and revelation.

For both musicians persuade their instruments to talk and tell, to narrate as imagined events come pouring out of their sounds. What kind of incarceration was Ota's time in *Howard Asylum*, the title of the sixth track, where the blues loneliness of Priester's winding, astringent phrases describe its ethos above Haney's acerbic grounding notes.

It is US austerity and a forbidding solitariness that they create in sound, a prison of binding notes.

The track called *Sense Her* begins with a restless flapping produced by Haney playing inside on the piano strings with mallets and Priester's straining breath-slides behind him. In *Sea of Glass* both musicians create spontaneous melodies which feed off each other, and the final *End Of Ota* is a blues for a ravaged, exiled African comrade of history, always remembered, always learned from.

Finally, a note on the sleeve picture, painted by the CIMP label's habitual illustrator Kara Rusch.

It shows hand-like flames stretching from a barred prison window, reaching for a bird-shaped flame that has separated and freed itself.

Beautiful and evocative, it recreates Ota's dream and the telling of Haney and Priester with shared dramatic insight, making a uniquely luminous artefact in both colour and sound, a unified marker of a restlessly tragic story still being made and still being told in the US and many other places. Truly, the black and white of jazz.

March 17th 2011

Hybridity and Artistry

Egberto Gismonti
Dança Dos Escravos/Zigzag/Saudações
(ECM)
Charlie Haden and Egberto Gismonti
In Montreal
(ECM)

For proof that jazz can be a music of astonishing hybridity, go to the life and recordings of Egberto Gismonti, born in Carmo, Brazil in 1947. Trained as a classical pianist in France, he returned to Rio de Janeiro in 1968 and learned the six-string guitar, found its sound palette insufficient and moved on to the seven, then eight-string models. A period of filming in Amazonia in 1977 led to a fascination with and study of the music of its Xingu peoples, which affected all his subsequent sounds.

Gismonti's bracing of a classical European tradition, a jazz instinct for improvisation and indigenous folk forms has made a unique syncretism.

In his 1988 solo guitar album *Dança Dos Escravos* (Slaves' Dance) he revisits Brazil's brutal and turbulent history of slavery and resistance, with sleevenotes quoting early Brazilian commentators and historians as a grim accompaniment.

The sheer artistry of speed in tracks like *Alegrinho* sweeps into your ears like a tornado of sound and throughout the fifteen-minute-long title track it sounds as if there is a quartet of guitars let loose in the Oslo studio, so far from the music's provenances, pains and joys.

A year later Gismonti travelled to Canada to perform at the Montreal Jazz Festival in a duo setting with the great bassist Charlie Haden, pioneer member of the Ornette Coleman Quartet from 1958 and leader of the Liberation Music Orchestra. The session powerfully expressed Gismonti's jazz sensibility with such a partner, and as well as his own compositions the pair played Haden's *First Song* and *Silence.*

Haden's huge hollow-tree bass uplifts Gismonti's multi-sounding strings higher and higher, with an added buoyancy which scrambles them into ecstatic flight. Gismonti plays piano on *Maracatu* with tides of sound and Haden plucking underwater before he surfaces with a full, throbbing heartbeat.

The Brazilian edge to the melodic serenity of *First Song* gives the tune another beauty and *Palhaço* (Clown) becomes an inseparable alloy of sadness, joy and a wayward defiance with Haden's granite bass echoes. There is the unrestrained string happiness of *En Familia* with both men celebrating those closest to them and the finale *Don Quixote* has Cervantes grooving like never before inside Gismonti's searching piano and Haden's deep twanging tones.

In 1995, again in Oslo, Gismonti recorded the album *Zigzag* with bassist Zeca Assumpção and Nando Carneiro on guitar and synthesiser. This is a marvellous record played by a boiling Brazilian trio of astounding musicianship. The notes ripple and flow like equatorial waterways small and large and the melodic invention bursts out of the choruses of tracks like the ponderous and bass-emphatic *Orixas* or the percussive *Carta De Amor*.

In 2006 Gismonti was in Havana's Teatro Amadeo Roldán where his *Sertões Veredas* (Tribute To Miscegenation), a suite in seven movements, was performed by Zenaida Romeu.

"A journey through time and space," he wrote, "in a permanent exchange between music, literature and cinema, where nothing is left untouched and everything goes through a deep transformation thanks to an intense mix."

The stuff of jazz — its mongrelism, amalgam and unity here, in plenty, played by nine violins, four violas, two cellos and a bass, as Gismonti fuses Brazilian modernism with European classicism, jazz, circus and cinema with the musical ritual of the Xingu people.

In the second movement, remembering classicism, echoes of Mozart are set beside the sound of the European whip on African-Brazilian and indigenous backs, and in the third the rhythm of the Xingu dance rituals eventually mesh with the "melodies of hope of Brazilian folk tunes." It is a dream of the miscegenation of a host of different peoples and their musics. What will emerge, what will issue forth?

Such is the first CD of the double album, *Saudações* (Greetings) — the second is a father and son Gismonti, Egbert and Alexandre, a duo of guitars playing the tunes of the father, except *Chora Antônio*, written by the son.

It is a long sonic poem of the musical continuity of generations and praise song of human affirmation and beauty made in Rio de Janeiro, the great city of mix.

The unity of sound which is the essence of the music binds every track together in glory of Brazil, its people and their living artistry.

June 6th 2011

Telling the Truth with Blues

James Blood Ulmer

Bad Blood in the City

(Hyena)

Jazz has its provenance in New Orleans and traces its global story back to the Crescent City, so jazz musicians have been eager to cast their notes and their anger about both the cruel consequences of Hurricane Katrina which blasted the city in 2005, and the feeble and inhuman responses of the US government, in particular the woeful Bush presidency.

Bad Blood in the City was recorded in the Piety Street studios of New Orleans in 2007 and its every note spells rage and indignation. The musician who led the session is the guitarist born in St Matthews, South Carolina, in 1942, James Blood Ulmer. He sang gospel with the Southern Sons as a child, moved to Detroit and New York, en route playing with giants like Art Blakey, Larry Young, Paul Bley and Joe Henderson, before teaming up with and being mightily influenced by Ornette Coleman through the early 70s, during Coleman's funky Prime Time period.

Coleman played on Ulmer's first album *Tales of Captain Black*. In 1980 Ulmer cut his most celebrated record *Are You Glad To Be In America?* on the British label Rough Trade. In *Bad Blood in the City*, Ulmer creates a Delta amalgam of jazz, Mississippi blues and black rock, stretching right back to his gospel roots and the classic blues of Bessie Smith.

His gravelly voice comes to the fore from the opening track, addressed to the survivors of the hurricane, and in the powerfully moving *Katrina*, his argument is not to curse nature — "Katrina ain't to blame," he declares.

Ulmer picks an acoustic guitar, David Barnes's harmonica wails accusingly and Leon Gruenbaum strides out on his piano as Ulmer points to the real criminals of Katrina. "Katrina ran a whole lot of people out of town/When they heard that she was comin'," he observes.

Who were these? "All the richest people could not be found." And who is to blame? "Talk to the president," repeats Ulmer.

The album moves forward with covers of songs by Willie Dixon (*Dead Presidents*) and Howlin' Wolf (*Commit a Crime*), some gospel blues (*Let's Talk About Jesus*), but it is a version of John Lee Hooker's *This Land is Nobody's Land* that peals and growls from Ulmer's throatbox as if it were really his own. A mournful, truly grounded blues.

"I wonder why we fighting over this land," sings Ulmer, when it is in fact but "a burial ground," even though "God made this land, everybody equal, for everyone." A refutation, consciously or unconsciously, to the narrative of burning optimism that runs through Woody Guthrie's *This Land is Your Land*.

And then there is Bessie Smith's commentary on the universal deluge that speaks of floods everywhere, from Pakistan to Cumbria to New Orleans, the tragic beauty of her *Backwater Blues*, sung with a grating power by Ulmer in the times of Katrina. "Thousands of poor people didn't have a place to go."

A heart-throbbing guitar solo, a harmonica that weeps teeming rain and Charles Burnham's lamentation on his electric violin for the flood-oppressed everywhere, as Ulmer cries out the words that Bessie sang eight decades ago: "Then they rowed a little boat about five miles 'cross the farm/I packed all my clothes, throwed 'em in and they rowed me along./Then I climbed upon some high old lonesome hill/Then looked down on the house where I used to live."

As I stare at the pictures of Sindh and Punjab in 2010, it is the same old story.

"Blues ain't no joke," growls Ulmer in *The Power of the Blues*. "It brings me to my knees," he says, it makes him "cry like a baby." But it does more, he asserts, for those who sing and hearken to the blues can also "use the concept of the blues to find our way around" through life like an earthy guide.

No more so in the album's final song *Old Slave Master*, cut when Bush Jr. was still in maximum power. With a romping rhythmic upsurge and Ulmer coaxing his guitar to emit a huge farting sound, it is not only the President who all but ignored New Orleans during its weeks of terror and agony ("Old Slave Master, what took you so long?") but also the President leading his nation into unwinnable, ultra-murderous wars, provoking the white heat of the blues and lines of monstrous irony.

"You take us to war in a land that can't be won/Old Slave Master, what have you done?/Slavery is a whole lot of fun."

Oh, the sheer truth of the blues!

September 1st 2010

Spirit of Unity

Rudresh Mahanthappa

Mother Tongue/Codebook/Kinsmen featuring Kadri Golpanath

(Pi)

How many times have we heard them — on buses, trains, in queues or in crowded streets or shops — racist insults or hostile comments about language when passengers, shoppers or passers-by are speaking a mother tongue other than English? I remember one incident on the top floor of a Sheffield bus when I was travelling with a group of Arabic-speaking Yemeni students. "Don't speak your Paki language here!" someone arrogantly shouted.

If Britain's arrivant peoples have had to often endure such ignorance for generations, it has been the same in the US. *Mother Tongue*, an album by the Indian-American alto saxophonist Rudresh Mahanthappa expresses this situation with potent sonic effect.

Mahanthappa, with his background in a huge nation of many diverse languages, cultures, religions and traditions, was tired of such questions as "Do you speak Indian?" or "Do you speak Hindu?" So his album creates "melodic transcriptions of Indian-Americans responding to such questions," and in doing so he blows an audacious and fascinating jazz essay with a very potent quartet indeed, including pianist Vijay Iyer, bassist François Moutin and drummer Elliot Humberto Kavee.

Mahanthappa, now based in New York, was born in Trieste, Italy, in 1971 and grew up in Boulder, Colorado. He is a graduate of Berklee College of Music in Boston and studied jazz composition at De Paul University in Chicago — an impressive jazz tutelage, certainly. As soon as the first notes of the album's opener *The Preserver* begin, with a wildly fluent chorus from Mahanthappa and Iyer in exploratory gear, the languages are peeled away — English, Konkani, Gujarati, Telugu and Tamil among others, each with their own track.

Mahanthappa's sound is powerfully distinctive and his partnership with Iyer, central to some of the pianist's albums, carries a warm and close empathy. There is sadness and sense of vulnerability on some tracks, like *Kannada* where Moutin enters for a pulsating chorus, whereas *Gujarati* sounds more confident and unhesitating.

But Mahanthappa's reed phraseology — complex, intriguing, full of surprise and bursting emotion, stays with you long after the album's end — is a common jazz language, his own sonic dialect.

Mother Tongue was his first album, recorded in 2004, and he followed that with *Codebook* cut in 2006 with a different drummer,

Dan Weiss. "The science of codemaking goes back thousands of years, following a rich tradition of applying the beauty of symbols and mathematics to communication," he writes in his sleeve notes, adding that his objective in the album is to adapt the "conventional methods of cryptography to melody and rhythm."

So how does it work out when a quartet of jazz musicians seek to bring "ciphered mysteries" and coded messages to their music? Perhaps such has always been so, for there seems little that is unusually cryptic about Mahanthappa's playing.

Listen to the full-on opening blast of *The Decider* or his bluesy sound on *Refresh*, where Iyer's fingers tread up and down his keys as if his mind is beset with uncomfortable thoughts. Or Moutin's flickering bass on *Further and in Between*, where Mahanthappa's edginess reminds me a little of Oliver Lake's scissoring alto sound.

In the album *Kinsmen* Mahanthappa meets up with the reedman who was in his original inspiration, the south Indian Carnatic saxophonist Kadri Gopalnath. Mahanthappa first heard Gopalnath's records at Berklee, and was so enthused that he managed to get a grant to travel to India to work with him. In *Kinsmen* we hear a unique amalgam of jazz and Carnatic improvisations, played by two alto saxophonists plus the musicians of the Dakshina Ensemble who, in Mahanthappa's words, "highlight the multifaceted intricacies and intersections" of two musics of two related continents.

It is truly an astonishing and beautiful album, and impossible to tell where one music ends and another begins, so fused are the two saxophones and so much does jazz prove itself again to be the music of unity.

Avasarala Kanyakumari brings her violin into this improvisational mix, and the record in one hearing abolishes separate categories and genres, sounding across vast lands and huge oceans, making the listener love the jazz spirit even more than before.

Mahanthappa's unique sound expresses that spirit. Watch out for what he does in the future.

December 16th 2010

From the Mississippi to the Tigris and Back

Amir ElSaffar
Two Rivers
(Pi)
Amir Elsaffar and Hafez Modirzadeh
Radif Suite
(Pi)

"It is based on the gasping sigh of the survivors as they dug through bodies, searching for their loved ones. The streets are said to have run red with the blood of those killed and black with the ink of the books of the Grand Library that were drenched in water."

These words of human and cultural devastation were written as a part of the sleeve notes to an album called *Two Rivers* by the Iraqi-US trumpeter Amir ElSaffar, born in Chicago but whose father was from Baghdad, the city the musician describes. Except that he was not writing explicitly about the invasion of his father's country in 2003 by US and British forces, but about the events that followed a previous invasion and massacre of Baghdad in 1258 by the armies of Genghis Khan's grandson Hulagu.

The listener is left to reflect upon the relevance of these words to now in Iraq when US combat forces have 'withdrawn' from the country leaving an occupying force of 50,000 troops operating from 94 bases, their soldiers, tanks and aircraft still marauding over Iraq's earth.

ElSaffar is a dedicated student of the Iraqi musical tradition of Maqãm, as well as an accomplished jazz trumpeter who has played with significant figures ranging from Cecil Taylor to Vijay Iyer. Maqãm is rich in polytonal and polyrhythmic elements, with sounds close to the blues, and ElSaffar has sought to fuse the musical forms of his two countries into one. In *Two Rivers* he has assembled a powerful union of jazz talents to achieve this amalgam.

Rudresh Mahanthappa plays a companion horn on alto saxophone, Zafer Tawil plays violin and lute-like oud, Palestinian Tareq Abboushi plays buzuq and frame-drum with Carlo de Rosa on bass and Nasheet Waits on drums.

Elsaffar sings in Arabic above the US-Maqãm ensemble on the opener *Menba* and as his horn sounds late in the piece, its improvising patterns have a unique timbre, as if jazz is being reborn continents away from the Mississippi Delta, between the Tigris and the Euphrates along with the plucked Baghdad blues of Tawil's clicking oud. Mahanthappa's surging alto breaks out of *Hemayoun* before

ElSaffar's soft-blown, lyrical phrase gathers pace, spurred on by de Rosa's pulsing bass.

Flood — with Waits's spirited drumming, ElSaffar's menacing choruses and Mahanthappa's empathetic solo — remembers the annual deluges of both rivers through the city while *Diaspora* is inspired by a poem full of meaning for the musicians in another country: "Why has time seperated us and made us fly away?"

Blood and Ink remembers an invader's carnage of Baghdad, the city's name meaning abode of peace. The lyrics recall "plenty of peace upon the abode of peace." But not now, and the tormented horns express it.

The sleeve notes tell us that the final track *The Blues in E Half-Flat* is "the sound of resurrection and a reminder of the resilience of the human spirit," and the mood of all members seems transformed.

Tawil's dancing oud and Waits's pounding drums underpin ElSaffar and Mahanthappa singing though their horns, as if somewhere close in the future a new, free Iraq will be born.

In the 2010 album *Radif Suite*, ElSaffar joins with the North Carolina-born US-Iranian altoist Hafez Modirzadeh to create another union of the diverse with Mark Dresser on bass and Alex Cline behind the drums. As Elsaffar said to Modizadeh: "You play Persian music and I play Iraqi music. It was about each of our dispositions as human beings, each of our desires to stretch beyond the norms and conventions of tradition and find something new."

And jazz is the conductor of the syncretism, the music of cultural reconciliation and friendship. The formation is the same as in the original Ornette Coleman Quartet, and the music has a similiar audacity.

Modirzadeh explains that "a radif is an ordering of melodies that is learned in Iranian traditional music in order to improvise from," and is thus ripe for jazz development, integrated with Iraqi Maqãm forms. As the foursome play with such a profound sense of unified sonic beauty you marvel as a listener at just how far jazz has travelled through its century of history.

Cline's gongs, ElSaffar's subtle futurist fanfares, Modirzadeh's serpentine lines of sound and Dresser's unifying bass heartbeat make one music.

ElSaffar is reticent about any political implications of his partnership with Modirzadeh. "If people read into it, they read into it," he declares.

I read out of it more than into it, and out comes peace and joint artistic brilliance by men whose people a decade or more ago were engaged in terrifying war.

Jazz can make a difference, that's for sure.

February 4th 2011

A Youthful 70

The Charles Lloyd Quartet

Rabo de Nube

(ECM)

March 2008 was Charles Lloyd's seventieth birthday and his entry into his eighth decade is celebrated by an album with a new quartet full of the brilliance of youth.

With the veteran jazz tenorist are three of the music's young prodigies — New York pianist Jason Moran, his drummer classmate at Houston's music college Eric Harland and, on bass, the Virgin Islander Reuben Rogers, who was bred amid the Caribbean notes of calypso and reggae. This live session was recorded in Basel in 2007 and is named after one of Lloyd's best-loved tunes, *Rabo de Nube* (Tail of a Cloud), which was composed by the Cuban Silvio Rodriguez. The other tunes are all Lloyd compositions, some of them going back as far as his 1960s heyday, now transformed by four extraordinary musicians.

The first is *Prometheus*, which begins with unaccompanied tenor until Moran enters with a huge chime, Rogers's bass pulsates and Harland rattles besides him. Lloyd surges forward at withering speed playing in a high register before Moran scatters his notes widely. Rogers plays an urgent bowed solo and, just as suddenly, the music slows reflectively until Moran signals Harland and Rogers to speed again. It is a track of surprising and sometimes stark variation, telling you that nothing in this quartet resides in the realm of the predictable.

Migration of a Spirit is a theme central to Caribbean life and experience and Rogers begins with a thematic burst of springing notes, perhaps reflecting his own human journey. Moran, with ancestors from Africa and Ireland, adds an enigmatic chorus and Lloyd, with his own complex mixed heritage, blows swirling passages which sweep through his home continent and far, far beyond.

Lloyd picks up his alto flute to blow a tribute to his Memphis childhood friend, the soaring trumpeter Booker Little, who flared brightly but died at the age of twenty-three in 1961. *Booker's Garden* has been well kept by Lloyd and perhaps his young confrères understand that life implicitly, for they play with the closest of empathies, particularly Moran, whose solo is compelling in its drama.

Another of Moran's spiritual New York ancestors is remembered by *La Colline de Monk* and some of the familiar phrases of the great Thelonious burst out in Lloyd's joyous choruses as he veers directly into *Sweet Georgia Bright*, a tune that he first recorded in 1964.

Moran again delivers a scorching solo with sections of pounding pace before opening the way for Rogers, whose bass twangs felicitously as he makes his way through a citation from *When Johnny Comes Marching Home Again.*

After that, it is the turn of Harland, his free, yet disciplined drums cracking through Georgia's cruel history, for there was very little that was sweet about life for black people in Georgia when Lloyd wrote his tune.

The title tune signals the end of the performance. Moran's contribution has been a sizeable one — just listen to the bell-like clarity of his notes as he plays his final solo.

Each one is separately conceived, yet their union is as beautiful, and full of meaning, as if they were only born to be an integrated force. And Lloyd's final phrases, their sudden ending as surprising as their creation, exemplify the unexpected blood in the heart of jazz.

Charles Simić's poem to Lloyd, which is printed on the sleeve, describes his sound as "close to breath, close to wind in the trees." Yes, but, as *Rabo de Nube* tells us, close to youth too.

For perhaps the standard of jazz is that, the older a musician gets, the younger is his sound. And Lloyd is certainly, with all his grey hairs and seven decades of sound behind him, a sure comrade of jazz youth.

July 16th 2008

Bandoneon Symbiosis

Dino Saluzzi

Kultrum / Once Upon a Time — Far Away in the South / Mojotoro / Cité de la Musique / Juan Condori (ECM)

Dino Saluzzi, the Argentinian master of the accordion-like bandoneon, was born in the small village of Campo Santa in 1935, the son of a sugar refinery worker. "My father was barely able to support us," he wrote. "We had no radio, no records, no electricity. We just lived close to nature, to folklore, to the primitive music of the Indians, untouched by any white influence."

In the sleeve message of his 1991 album *Mojotoro*, Saluzzi set out his version of musical syncretism. His music, he explained, is "an expression of a universal hope shared by all people, of a coincidence between different cultures, without losing their essence.

"It draws upon South American music — tango, folk, Bolivian andina, Uruguayan candombe, developing the textures of young people. It is in the end of a cultural symbiosis," — a symbiosis that certainly enfolds jazz improvisation and invention, all powerfully evident in many of his recordings.

Saluzzi turned professional while studying in Buenos Aires, and became a member of the symphonic Orquestra Estable at Argentina's pioneering radio station Radio El Mundo. In 1956 he returned to his boyhood district of Salta to work at composing, drawing in local folk music. By 1973 he was playing alongside the Argentinian jazz tenorist Gato Barbieri on his revolutionary album *Chapter One: Latin America*, and touring his continent with concerts in Bolivia, Peru, Colombia and Venezuela.

In 1982 he made the solo work *Kultrum*, his first record for the Munich-based ECM label, a series of often crepuscular sonic narratives using bandoneon, flute, voice and percussion which seem to emblematise his words: "As a musician, I'm the servant of my memories, but my memories also help me."

The lucidity of his notes and the way they shine in your ears — as in the beautiful *Gabriel Kondor*, where Saluzzi's bandoneon seems at least three separate instruments in one, enable his stories to be recreated by his listeners' freed imaginations. "Everything flows together, like clear water," Saluzzi once said of his musical aspirations, and in his 1986 album *Once Upon a Time – Far Away in the South*, he is joined by three explicit jazzmen — the bassist from

Shenandoah, Illinois, Charlie Haden, Swiss drummer Pierre Favre and the Danish trumpeter Palle Mikkelborg to further his strategy of making one music from the many.

What results is an album of sad beauty, as if Saluzzi has imbibed an Argentinian blues spirit on an instrument that somehow seems umbilically attached to jazz, so direct, multilayered and close to horn sound is its timbre. Listen to his empathy with Haden and Favre on *José, Valeria and Matias*, his harrowing solitary solo bandoneon on *Haden's Silence* or Mikkelborg's lonesome trumpet on *...And He Loved His Brother Till the End.*

A fiercely engaging record is this, ending with Mikkelborg's *We are the Children*, finishing with a playground chorus of primary schoolchildren answering the trumpeter's call of challenge and hope.

Mojotoro, an album recorded in 1992, is almost a family affair. Dino's brothers Celso and Felix join him on second bandoneon and both tenor and soprano saxophones respectively. His son José Maria is the drummer while Armando Alonso plays guitar and the bassist is Guillermo Vadalá.

It's a full sound, with Felix's tenor always sinewy and Alonso's guitar ever inventive and eager to improvise. There are stories and intense memories at the heart of this music, in particular the burning *Tango a Mi Padre* and the galloping rhythm and distant children's voices in *Lustrin.*

1997's *Cité de la Musique* has another eminent jazz presence, Omaha bassist Marc Johnson, with José Maria switching to guitar. The trio setting gives much more prominence to the senior Saluzzi, and the Oslo studio setting belies the warmth of the music which has a sense of air and buoyancy

The title tune almost skips through its paces, and Johnson's fleet and dancing bass provides a huge contrast to Haden's booming stringsound on the *Once Upon a Time* album. He is brilliantly lithe on *El Rio y el Abueo*, and he lifts the entire album skywards.

Juan Condori came ten years later and is another family project full of "memories of our ancestors who sing through us." Dino, Felix and José Maria are all present, as well as Felix's bass-playing son Matias.

"We'd gather around the dinner table with instruments," recalls Dino. "We've been doing it for so long we don't have to talk about it much. It really is a shared language. Sometimes my brother will play something, a phrase, and I remember it from long ago and realise it's something I once heard sung by the Indians — ghost narratives of living, struggling people like Chiriguano or La Vuelta de Pedro Orillas, lamenting the 'turning away from the people of the periphery'."

And all is music of serenity, nakedness and overwhelming beauty.

December 29th 2011

Worldly Neighbours

Manu Katché

Neighbourhood

(ECM)

When people ask: "Now, where is jazz going?" the best answer is "everywhere — and in places and internationalist combinations that we would never conceive."

How about this one, to start? A recording made in Munich, led by a drummer born near Paris in 1958 from a family rooted in the Ivory Coast with a Norwegian saxophonist and a trumpeter, bass player and pianist from Poland?

The life-energy of jazz that was born in the Gulf of Mexico's heat has spread to the coldest and perhaps most unlikely of settings and been waxed in a city where, for many cruel years, its sound was forbidden by fascist decree. This is Manu Katché's first date as leader. His north European amalgam comprises tenorist Jan Garbarek, trumpeter Tomasz Stańko, pianist Marcin Wasilewski and Slawomir Kurkiewicz on bass.

A cosmic neighbourhood indeed, led by a drummer forged in both the Paris Conservatory and pop contexts from Sting to Joni Mitchell and whose records include several albums with Garbarek. As for the three Poles, they have been playing together since 1994 and know every facet of each other's technique.

Katché dedicates the album to the astonishing pianist and his ex-band mate Michel Petrucciani (1962-99) who inspired and fired him.

The opener, *November 99*, featuring the ruminative piano of Wasilewski, has a sense of the ominous. His notes and phrases sprinkle while descending into thoughtful, translucent sounds. *Number One* introduces Garbarek with his lucid, shivering edge, while Katché's command of percussion has the ring and spring of Roy Haynes, with buzzing cymbals and sprightly snares.

The unique sound of Stańko, like Miles Davis playing on a cold heathland, comes to the fore in *Lullaby*, although you wonder if this sound would ever send a baby to sleep, so arresting, angular and worrisome it seems, yet so beautifully played.

Good Influence at last brings brassman and reedman together in the opening exposition of the melody before Garbarek veers off with a seething chorus, coming down again to low register before Wasilewski's solo, seeming so restrained, almost as if he is waiting gracefully for the theme to return.

You will rarely hear such an unhurried jazz musician as this Polish pianist. In *February Sun*, he waits for Stańko even as the trumpeter is playing and the following tune, *No Rush*, must have been written especially for him by Katché — the composer of all the album tracks. His drums pick up fire behind Stańko's solo, but they never change ahead of the musicians or lead by percussive fury and ingenuity as on albums with other drummer-leaders such as Art Blakey, Max Roach or Art Taylor. His drums are not urgent, neither do they raise tempests. But they hold pace and reflection superbly, at one with the restraint of his colleagues.

On *Lovely Walk*, Garbarek picks up strength and speed and Katché follows him until Wasilewski's companionship seems to slow it all down, as the walk becomes a colloquy, with the sauntering Stańko catching them up and adding a more eager contribution. In *Take Off and Land*, Wasilewski suddenly seems more prompted, as if he must travel quicker and keep abreast of Katché's relentless snare beat, while, in *Miles Away*, it is Kurkiewicz who leads the way, pursued by Stańko with some high-note exclamations and vocalised brass screeches.

What would those New Orleans patriarchs make of this quintet of far northern neighbours?

No marches, certainly, mostly easy walking. The blues of Europe suffused with thought overcoming emotion in every note? Perhaps, but with a power and beauty specially wrought.

January 3rd 2007

Newman's Blessing

David 'Fathead' Newman

The Blessing

(High Note)

He was Ray Charles' favourite hornman, whose tenor and alto sax solos roared and soared out of the gut of the ensemble. Labelled 'Fathead' by his teacher at his Dallas school, he kept the nickname all through his career as a a tenorist, altoist and flautist until until his death in January last year. *The Blessing* was his last album, made a month before he died.

Newman's musical background was the blues and before he joined Ray Charles his early leaders were bluesmen like Lowell Fulson and T-Bone Walker. He stayed with Charles for a decade and gave his band the bellowing and honking tenor sound that previous Texan saxophonists like Buddy Tate, Arnett Cobb and James Clay had created so distinctively. But Newman also brought his versatility to bear on the flute, casting his winding and unexpected filigrees out of a context characterised by hard-edged rhythm and blues.

From 1998 onwards, recording for the New York-based High Note label, Newman cut a series of fine albums in which he created a very different sound. He softened his timbre while still retaining his Texan soundscape and into the mix came a more reflective and lyrical note.

Albums like *Keep the Spirits Singing*, *Davey Blue* and *The Gift* are fine examples while the evocative *I Remember Brother Ray* is a moving tribute to his old maestro. *The Blessing* was made with a group of musicians entirely sympathetic with Newman's vision, playing a batch of tunes which span many eras of jazz expression. Pittsburgh vibesman Steve Nelson is an old Newman companion and with him too are pianist David Leonhardt, hot New York guitarist Peter Bernstein, drummer Yoron Israel and bassist John Menegon.

Opener *SKJ* is a composition by one of Newman's heroes Milt Jackson. It begins with some twanging bass work by Menegon before Newman plays a deep, velvety chorus and Bernstein's precise and cutting phrases cut through the studio.

There's a resonance to the recording. When you look at the sleeve notes and learn that the sound engineer is the veteran Rudy van Gelder, who produced all the great Blue Note sessions of the 60s and 70s, you begin to understand why.

Newman plays the Gershwin songbook classic *Someone to Watch Over Me* like a lullaby, his breathy notes soothing over the melody. In *As Time Goes By*, he takes turns narrating the theme before moving into an almost hushed chorus of his own. In *Manhã de Carnival* from the soundtrack of the Brazilian film *Black Orpheus* Israel's clipping drums base the theme before a series of brief solos by tenor, vibes, piano and guitar. Newman takes the final coda, suspirating into his horn.

Smile was composed by that comic genius from the Elephant & Castle, Charlie Chaplin, who was also a violinist and conductor of considerable skill. Newman digs deep into the message of its saddening, unheard words which pour out as testifying notes through his tenor.

During his early rampaging years as a hornman you wouldn't have associated the fiery, rumbustious Newman sound with Billy Strayhorn's Ellingtonian rhapsodies like *Chelsea Bridge* — but in old age he plays it with a touching beauty and lyricism. Leonhardt's own compositions *Romantic Night* and *Whispers of Contentment* give Newman opportunities to stretch out for longer solos, floating on the rhythm buoyantly and weightlessly.

It's as if he is reflecting in sound, reviewing his own jazz narrative of over half a century. The title track concluding the album sees Newman taking up his flute, bird-like phrases powerfully flying, just as they were when I heard him last in a Toronto pub in 2007. The vibrancy of his notes rocked the room to its rafters.

The Blessing is his final story, ailing slightly but always inventive and lucid.

Newman offers a lifetime's sound in an hour of jazz glory.

April 1st 2010

Blake Hits the Key of Life

Ran Blake and Enrico Rava
Duo En Noir
(Between the Lines)
Ran Blake
Driftwoods
(Tompkins Square)

Born in Springfield, Massachusetts, seventy-five years ago, Ran Blake has combined his singular way of playing piano with a teaching career at the New England Conservatory of Music since 1965.

You can hear the legacy of Monk in his angular lines and his sudden and surprising changes of direction, but you also hear the gospel singers he loved and emulated as a child and the drama of vocalists like Sarah Vaughan, Billie Holiday or Abbey Lincoln. His pianism carries their voices and intensity.

A deeply politicised artist, his first solo album *The Blue Potato and Other Outrages* (Milestone, 1969) used standards to refer to the oppression and struggles of the day. *Chicago* pointed to the 1968 Democratic Convention and the contestation over the war in Vietnam, *Stars Fell on Alabama* referred to the Civil Rights campaign in the South and *Never on Sunday* was a commentary on the 1967 fascist coup in Greece — all signalling the power of an allusive title.

Through the 80s and 90s he made a series of brilliant albums for the Italian Soul Note label including *Suffield Gothic* (1984), *The Short Life of Barbara Monk* (1986), *Epistrophy* (1996) — his solo tribute to Monk, and his salute to Vaughan, *Unmarked Van* (1997). In 1999 Blake recorded the live album *Duo En Noir* at the Südbahnhof in Frankfurt. A film noir journey inspired by Alfred Hitchcock's centennial, his horn partner on vinyl was the Italian trumpeter Enrico Rava, born in Trieste in 1943.

This is a duo of essential contrasts. Sometimes Rava's wispy tone merges with Blake's dreamlike notes as in the opener *Nature Boy* or the balladic *Laura*. But when Rava plays with more pointed power, as in his solo *Certi Angoli* or *The Spiral Staircase*, and Blake strikes his keys with more force and stress a different kind of amalgam is created.

In the sleeve notes Blake writes how Rava's "soulful, exquisite passion" for ballads gave him such pleasure when he played with him on numbers such as *There's No You* and *I Should Care*. He describes his own solo version of *Let's Stay Together* as "travelling through a hallucination of jetlag with an uncertainty for tomorrow's future." This demonstrates again how a jazz reading of a sentimental and predictable ballad can turn its professed meaning upside down.

The session ends with two US songbook standbys. From soft beginnings Rava's trumpet in *Tea for Two* soars like a take-off from Cape Canaveral and the hostelry of *There's a Small Hotel* is one where two veteran and exploratory musicians find unity and a precious jazz comradeship. An album of the sheer unexpected, all the way through.

Driftwoods of 2009 is Blake's most recent recording in which he remembers some of those who have forged his piano artistry. It sounds like a veteran's record, with septuagenarian reflections and acknowledgements. A measure of Blake's "story boarding" at the keyboard, it is the partial narrative of a pianist's life. And it resounds and echoes with 20th century moments, the first full century of jazz.

Listen to what Blake does in the two versions of *Dancing in the Dark*. There is no Astaire and Rogers here, but a portrait of the last century's darkness which somehow meshes in with the tune that follows, Hank Williams's *Lost Highway*, as if both tell the story of a hundred years of opportunities unfulfilled.

Songs associated with Nat "King" Cole (*Unforgettable*, with lines taken from *Tenderly*), Holiday (*Strange Fruit* and *No More*) or Nina Simone (*I Loves You Porgy*) — all tell of lives struggling with the effects of injustice and the foulest racist prejudice. Our last century, still our shame, his notes seem to be telling us. How, he implies, to make this one better?

You Are My Sunshine is a song forever breathing the subterranean lives and dreams of the miners of Pennsylvania. Blake uses it as his finale on *Driftwoods*.

Full of Monkish wit and imbued with Blake's salutary hope for the world and its ceaseless music, its power and brevity says enough.

April 1st 2010

Another Distant Land, Another Delta

Zoë and Idris Rahman
Where Rivers Meet
(Manushi)

Where rivers meet, where the waters from many sources flow and glide, where cultures merge and unify, where the Mississippi surges into the sea close to the Crescent City of New Orleans where pianos, drums and clarinets abound, to the moistening earth of Bengal, where the water seeping from the land of the Ganges Delta hears the jazz of Zoë and Idris Rahman, reflecting the sounds and people of a country so far away, another Delta land on a distant continent.

Where Rivers Meet is a record so beautiful, so tender and joyous, its music filled with the elation that its makers feel when they have created sounds that are as original as they are jubilant. If jazz is the most syncretic of musics, *Where Rivers Meet* is its proof, as diverse traditions mesh and fructify in the most rapturous of contexts.

Made primarily by a sister and brother, a pianist and clarinettist. Zoë Rahman established a powerful reputation in the hard bop quintet of Clark Tracey. She is present on two of his finest albums, *The Calling* (2003) and *The Mighty SAS* (2005). She has also recorded two strong trio albums, *The Cynic* (2000) and *Melting Pot* (2006), full of percussive drive and swinging verve, in which she combined Monkish surprise with a close rhythmic and pounding bond with her drummers.

Both drummer Gene Calderazzo and bassist Oli Hayhurst of *Melting Pot* are with her again on *Where Rivers Meet* and Hayhurst in particular is a musician wrapped in jazz diversity, having been a part of the dissident Israeli Gilad Atzmon's Levantine power and beauty in his Orient House Ensemble for several crucial years.

Throughout the album's opener, *O River*, piano and clarinet suggest the movement of waters in their every note, with Kuljit Bhamra's Bengali percussion strongly supportive. Zoë's notes lap like riverine waves all through *Invitation Missed* and Idris's clarinet, poised and liquid with a narrative all of its own, is like none other that I have heard in jazz, although, in some of his phrases, you hear Creole echoes of Johnny Dodds or Albert Nicholas and the great New Orleans reeds, but with a different geography of another huge Delta and its own musical excitation.

Sanctuary creates some sparkling interplay between Idris and Samy Bishai's sawing violin, with Calderazzo's drums and Zoë's keyboard runs close behind them. *Betrayed* has the mood of a Bengali blues, with Idris turning to flute and vocalist SC Arnob likening the twisting, meandering river to a lover's infidelities, as he sings in his own tongue.

Now You're Gone is another lament, a sister-brother duet of pining beauty and sadness, which is all too brief. *Pilgrims' Song* becomes a Bengali jazz chant, the pounding drum suggesting a journey of weariness and exhaustion. In such moments, the siblings' music reminds me of the last project of Don Pullen — his album with the Kootenai native Americans, *Sacred Common Ground* — in which he employed traditional Kootenai songs and chants as part of a musical strategy to explore and affirm his own Cherokee roots and tell the story of a proud indigenous people.

The heterogeneity of human lives and cultures can all be imbibed and expressed in jazz and *Where Rivers Meet* is further evidence of this. Listen to Zoë's swirling piano at the beginning of *Suddenly It's Dusk Again* and then Idris's teeming notes with phrases that are of his own Bengali sonic patterns, but which also suddenly remind you of a Caribbean theme that you once heard. Such moments are a part of the wonder of this album.

People will ask is it jazz or is it world music? Or folk or some other category? It doesn't matter. For me, it's a part of the endless breadth of the jazz canon, its creative surge, its collective joy, its improvising essence. And, what's more, its notes are those of sheer discovery and beauty — new rivers and winding deltas of common sound.

24th December 2008

Searching for a Home

London Improvisers Orchestra

Improvisations for George Riste

(PSI)

The story of the defiance and humanity of the Canadian hotelier George Riste has spread around the world from its provenances in Vancouver, British Columbia, and forty-five of its most prominent storytellers are the free-improvising jazz musicians of the London Improvisers Orchestra (LIO), recounting his story in sound from their regular venue at the Red Rose along the Seven Sisters Road in north London.

Riste was the owner of a small, thirty-room residential hotel called the Del Mar Inn in downtown Vancouver. He charged low rents for his predominantly poor and working-class tenants — many of them loggers and fishermen — offering carefully cleaned and maintained rooms. He would spend his days tidying the building, dealing with repairs and grounding with his tenants, while also checking on the art gallery he kept on the ground floor.

From 1981, the dominant provincial power company BC Hydro started buying up properties all around the Del Mar in order to build their new office tower headquarters. Riste refused to sell — despite over a hundred gradually ascending offers — saying that the Del Mar was a necessity for local poor people. In 1990 BC Hydro gave up and built their huge tower right behind the tiny Del Mar, with Riste declaring: "This is my life. This is what I love doing."

In his deeply insightful sleeve notes to the *Riste* album, the veteran Bristolian tenor saxophonist Evan Parker writes of how "the Red Rose protected and sheltered us from the real world of the capitalist madhouse." He tells us that "the absolutely affordable rent has made it possible to play every month of these ten years. A change of landlord and it's all over." No wonder that Riste, who died a week short of his ninetieth birthday in November 2010, remains the LIO's inspiration.

Their album radiates his humanism, with some of the music's great improvisers in full fettle.

There is Parker himself and fellow tenorist John Butcher, soprano saxophonist Lol Coxhill, drummers Tony Marsh and Mark Sanders, cellist Marcio Mattos and violinist Philipp Wachsmann, vibraphonist and percussionist Orphy Robinson and the late, stellar Barbadian trumpeter Harry Beckett, all playing within a mass ensemble dedicated to collectivism — an amalgam of improvising power.

There are four extended improvisations ranging from twelve to twenty-two minutes long, all recorded directly from the Red Rose monthly sessions.

The sound quality is remarkably good and potently atmospheric as the first free ensemble rises in waves then depletes into pungent low sonic valleys, with Marsh's crashing percussion and the mass of reeds including three soprano saxophones, a clarinet and bass clarinet, flying out of the instrumentations like wayward birds seeking different freedoms with one soprano making long, solitary moans.

It is as if each sound within the mass is searching for a home, a home perhaps like the Del Mar or the Red Rose.

Robert Jarvis's trombone and Beckett's harrowing trumpet pitch out of the opening of the more brass-emphatic second improvisation, supported by Roland Ramanan, the trumpet-playing son of another luminous Caribbean-born trumpeter, the Vincentian Shake Keane. A host of percussive and electronic effects create a shuddering groundswell.

The third section includes Annie Lewandowski playing accordion and a searing musical saw, and when the trumpets of Beckett and Ian Smith with Guillermo Torres's flugelhorn suddenly emerge from the percussive undertow, blowing breathily in diverse directions, the music suddenly bursts out of its walls and crackles across London.

The final improvisation is the longest and, as is usual with the LIO, no single musician is unduly featured — the substance is in the collective, yet strangely, and with an uncanny beauty, as you listen you can pick out and trace each single instrumental voice contributing to the massive whole.

And with an astonishing strength of communal empathy too, somehow playing with the same sonic meaning, in the same music world of humans together crossing an ocean and a continent to Vancouver, on the edge of another great ocean where the remarkable Riste's final will, with the agreement of his children, specifies that the Del Mar will not be sold.

Over its entrance his warning to global capital and property tycoons is still displayed: "Unlimited growth increases the divide."

March 23rd 2011

Songs for Humanity

Abdullah Ibrahim

Senzo

(Intuition)

The tru griot of South African piano, Abdullah Ibrahim, is an old man now and the epochs of his earlier life ring out through his notes. Perhaps that is why his new recording is called *Senzo*, which means "ancestor" in Chinese and Japanese and which was also his Basuto father's name.

Born in Cape Town in 1934, all through the apartheid and anti-apartheid era, the man first named Adolphe Johannes Brand and nicknamed "Dollar" for his imperative to have US currency to buy US recordings of Monk, Ellington and his other inspirations, played his heartsong through his homeland, Europe and the US. All his influences fused into a unique piano sound — the church, the music of the townships, Islam, to which he converted in 1968, a forty-year practice of Japanese martial arts, the struggle against white supremacy and the sounds of the world and its people.

Senzo is a record which only such an elder could make, a shamamic album full of Ibrahim's own tunes — except one from Ellington, who marvelled at him in a Swiss nightclub in 1965, took him to the US and exposed him to its jazz culture — which radiate a sense of wisdom and a narrative of a life's journey of surprise, discovery and endless absorption.

The bell-like beauty of *Ocean and the River* opens the album, a tune of meeting and confluence, a wordless message of unity and oneness, each note as large as it is possible to sound. *In The Evening* follows, not the famous Naptown blues of Leroy Carr but a strident vessel of huge cadences, falling like giant raindrops.

Next is a jaunty *Blues for Bea*, dedicated to the pianist's wife, the singer Sathima Bea Benjamin, with whom Ibrahim went into a self-imposed exile in 1962.

Aspen is an evocation of his time in Colorado among the mountains "where rivers and ancients meet," expressing a sense of permanent rendezvous that winds through all these tracks. Ibrahim travels to the birthplace of jazz, New Orleans, for his *Third Line Samba*, remembering the street parades where "the band is the first line and the dancing people the second line." And how his notes dance, gyrating through the streets of the mind's Delta.

Ibrahim jumps from one tune on a fragment, leads it to find another and sweeps onwards. From *Tookah*, a portrait of the "old times," to the long-sought African showers in *Pula*, to a tribute to his US brother in *For Coltrane*, the sound is full of boundless clarity.

Who could count the host of musicians and listeners of the world who have been stirred by Duke Ellington's enormous influence? So Ibrahim celebrates his genius by playing just a suggestion of *In a Sentimental Mood*, remembering a true and brilliant master, a creator who inspired and begat other creators all over the world. But little and on the edge as it is, it is enough.

Senzo has the sound of a summation, a digest of a defiant musical life that continues to struggle for his country, his continent and his world. Its notes permeate your heart and brain, piercing all boundaries, one by one uniting and making a song of all humanity.

February 4th 2009

Horn of Plenty

Dave Douglas

Constellations
(hatHUT)
Convergence
(Soul Note)
Witness
(RCA)

Dave Douglas, born in 1963, is a uniquely powerful and subtle New York trumpeter, skilled composer and bandleader whose albums more than often have an incisive political edge. He is also a very prolific minstrel of committed jazz, having led more than twenty album sessions since 1993 within a diversity of different bands and formations. He has also blown as a sideman with musicians as contrary as the "Hardbop Grandpa" Horace Silver and the founder of the Masada Quartet John Zorn, with his fusion of Jewish folk music and free improvisation.

In 1995, while on European tour, he recorded the album *Constellations* with his Tiny Bell Trio, with its innovative instrumentation of trumpet, guitar and drums playing what Douglas calls Balkan improvisations.

Such stark syncretisms are part of the essence of Douglas's musicianship — "I like bringing in all kinds of music," he declares in his sleeve notes. "Not to smooth over the differences but to let them sit glaringly side by side." With guitarist Brad Shepik and drummer Jim Black, Douglas creates mesmerising trio music with the Balkan element to the forefront, in particular on the track *Taking Sides*, "dedicated to all victims of brutality in former Yugoslavia." Douglas's leaping, folksy brasswork dances through the title tune and the vocalistic half-valve notes of *Unhooking the Safety Net*, while *Hope Ring True* — with Douglas's high register effects earthed by Black's startling drums — builds the strongest connection between the real world and the sonic messages of betterment.

Taking Sides has some cascading guitar work by Shepik, with Douglas's mock fanfare declaring its antimilitarism. But the climax of the album is the trio's performance of *Maquiladoras*. Here the Balkan format moves to the US-Mexico frontier, and the band extend their musical comradeship to the workers in the US-owned factories along the border and their grim working conditions.

A sense of anger blows through Douglas's storytelling horn — sometimes through repeated notes and phrases — and when Shepik's guitar bursts in beside Black's rumbling drums, real lives and struggles are transformed into expressive sounds.

Something very similar happens in the album *Convergence*, recorded in New York in 1998 by a Douglas-led quintet including violinist Mark Feldman and cellist Erik Friedlander.

In *Collateral Damages* there are more reflections on war, this time the first Gulf War, with Douglas declaring in the liner notes that: "We can't just sit back and read Downbeat. Music also has an immediate connection to world events and consciousness." The strings give a new, bustling urgency to the quintet's sound, from the very first notes of the Burmese opener and into *Tzotil Maya*, written by Douglas for the indigenous people of Chiapas, Mexico — forty-five of whom were massacred at Acteal in December 1997.

Douglas weeps out his notes of lamentation above Michael Sarin's fluttering drums. "I'm a blender by natures," declares Douglas, so it isn't surprising to hear Kurt Weill's *Bilbao Song* as a part of the mix, with Friedlander's shimmering strings well to the fore, Douglas's snorting horn and Feldman's ironic lyricism in the familiar chorus.

Collateral Damages is portrayed in the pressing indignation of Douglas's notes and Drew Gress's pulsing bass, while *Goodbye Tony* is a tribute to the great drummer Tony Williams, with all members giving virtuoso homage.

A larger band recorded the album *Witness* in 2000, celebrating the artistry and courage of an international group of writer-activists.

Douglas was on an Italian train near the Yugoslav border reading about "the rising stock of US weapons makers during the Nato assault on Yugoslavia. Not far away, half a million people were camped in a muddy field." The incident inspired *Witness*.

There are tracks dedicated to Palestinian Edward Said, the Egyptian doctor and feminist Nawal el Saadawi, Indonesian novelist Pramoedya Ananta Toer and Bangladeshi feminist Taslima Nasrin. In the twenty-four-minute-long *Mahfouz*, vocalist Tom Waits reads from the great Egyptian novelist Saadawi: "Consciousness struck at me like a policeman's fist," closely following a blistering Douglas solo in *Kidnapping Kissinger*, a tribute to the Pakistani rebel intellectual Eqbal Ahmad.

This singular album ends with *Sozaboy*, named after Nigerian Ken Saro-Wiwa's great novel.

It seethes with the author's own resistance to the multinational oil companies despoiling his nation, and shows just how effectively jazz can be a music of insurgency and world solidarity.

November 14th 2011

Life-rooted Artistry

Aki Takase Piano Quintet

Tarantella/A Week Went By

(psi)

The Japanese pianist Aki Takase, born in Osaka three years after the human catastrophes of Hiroshima and Nagasaki, was raised in Tokyo and began learning the piano at the age of three as if it were another attached natural organ. Her early influences were the sounds of Mingus, Coltrane and Ornette Coleman. By 1978, when she made her first sojourn to the US, she was an accomplished and sharply original improviser.

In 1981 she was in Europe, performing at the Berlin Jazz Festival, and by 1993 she made her first piano duet recordings with her husband, the brilliant German avant-gardist Alexander von Schlippenbach. In the early years of the new millennium she made a succession of extraordinary records for the Munich-based Enja label, digging herself deeply into the broadest of jazz traditions by reworking and reinventing the works of past genius.

St Louis Blues and *Plays for Fats Waller* followed her 1997 album with bass clarinet maestro Rudi Mahall, *Duet for Eric Dolphy*. Listen to their astonishing 21st century romping jive of *Handful of Keys* on the Waller album.

In Berlin in 1997 she cut her first album *Tarantella* for the London-based psi label with her "piano quintet," including violinist Aleks Kolkowski, Maurice Horsthuis on viola, cellist Tristan Honsinger and bassist Nobuyoshi Ino. It includes two of her own compositions, but also works by US jazz radicals Charlie Haden and Carla Bley — joint founders of the Liberation Music Orchestra — and one by her hero Dolphy.

The title tune has Takase traversing her keys with incendiary flourishes and wild, sweeping runs with intervals of redeeming lyricism, the bowed and plucked strings fizzing and mewing around her in a provocative amalgam. Bley's *Walking Batterie Woman* has Ino's sprinting bass inspiring Takase to hurtle through her notes, pummelling her keys like drums while the same composer's *Drinking Music* is a carousel of entirely unpredictable artistry with Honsinger's cello at its centre.

Takase's own *Let Those Who Appear* is lodged between Dolphy's *Hat and Beard* and Haden's requiem, composed shortly after the Argentinian revolutionary's death, *Song for Che*. Dolphy, a Californian of Panamanian roots, died in a diabetic coma in Berlin in 1964 at the age of thirty-six. The quintet plays his tune as a creatively wrought tribute to the hornman, opened by the breathless strings before Takase's tiptoed notes step out amid the plucking all around her.

As the journey moves on, the Asian-European quintet radiates a compelling unity of sound and homage, there in Dolphy's last city.

Kolkowski's tingling violin overplays an impending string storm at the commencement of *Let Those Who Appear*, a startling mesh of almost classically-aligned strings with a free piano spirit playing at the edge of dreams and reality. Who knows what humans and ghosts are evoked? As for *Song for Che*, the two continents of the quintet unify with the Americas in an upsurge of transformative sound, with Takase's hugely powerful yet emotive notes and Ino's at first splurging, then thematic bass leading the way.

Takase's artistic internationalism became even more profound on her 2008 album *A Week Went By*, recorded for psi at the unexpected venue, the Gateshead Town Hall. She is joined by two British free jazz stalwarts, drummer Tony Levin and bassist John Edwards. They come together on one track with the Danish Congolese saxophonist John Tchicai, a veteran of the 1963 New York Contemporary Five with Archie Shepp and Don Cherry, who had played on John Coltrane's epochal *Ascension* album of 1965.

She calls the opener *Surface Tension*, and perhaps she is being ironic for there is nothing superficial in her pianism. It is invented in sheer depth, delved out of the tradition of the great jazz piano inventors through a century of life-rooted artistry.

You can hear them all in her notes — Waller, yes, Monk certainly, Cecil Taylor, Abdullah Ibrahim — as her keyboard winds the world.

And when Tchicai makes the trio a duo for *Just Drop In*, his gust of notes that begins the track suddenly takes the music that began a new life in the Mississippi deltalands back to its African roots, and then out again to Europe and back to the US's eastern seaboard as he quotes Monk's *Epistrophy*.

It is a long moment of cultural and musical recognition and unity, and one — thanks to Takase's genius — neither to underestimate or miss.

December 14th 2011

Nordic Moments of Sonic Joy

Mathias Eick
The Door
(ECM)
Arild Andersen
Live at Belleville
(ECM)
Ketil Bjørnstad and Terje Rypdal
Life in Leipzig
(ECM)

You wouldn't necessarily expect the land of fjords and Peer Gynt to be a hot land of jazz, but just listen to some of the current music coming out of Norway on the ECM label and you might be a little surprised. First up is *The Door* by the twenty-eight-year-old trumpeter Mathias Eick, who is a lead horn of Manu Katché's Paris-based band.

On this, his first album, he is amply aided by arranger and pianist Jon Balke with bassist Audun Erlien, drummer Audun Kleive and, on three tracks, pedal steel guitarist Stian Carstensen. Eick is also a prodigious multi-instrumentalist and his guitar plucks out an introduction before his mellow, breathy horn introduces the theme of the title track. Balke's piano carries the sense of space and land, and as Eick blows long, heart-sung notes, the pianist breaks up his flow with fragmented, dissident phrases.

In *Stavanger*, it is Kleive's alert drums that respond almost conversationally to Eick's tender notes. *Cologne Blues* is almost dirge-like, with Balke's slow-marching keyboard beside the perfect pitch of Eick's respiring horn. As Kleive enters, spraying his drums, the sound disperses, Balke delivers a threnody and Eick returns, his notes touching beautiful places.

Eick is a most unhurried hornman, born of his musical assurance and sheer artistry. His sound eschews the affectatious or shallowly spectacular, but when he reaches upward — as he does with precision and potency in *Williamsburg* or *Fly* on this album — he creates moments of sonic joy. A powerful debut indeed.

On *Live at Belleville*, recorded in Oslo, the Norwegian bassist Arild Andersen leads a trio with Italian drummer Paolo Vinaccia and Scottish saxophonist Tommy Smith, with forty-five minutes of the seventy-minute album devoted to the four parts of Andersen's composition *Independency*.

Andersen, born in Oslo in 1945, has been recording for ECM since 1970, when as a member of compatriot Jan Garbarek's band, he cut the album *Afric Pepperbird*. He has subsequently made eighteen albums as leader. But this horn trio is a new venture and Andersen's long-developed brilliance and empathy with Vinaccia finds a sure partnership with Smith's tenor artistry.

Hear them on Andersen's tune *Outhouse*, where in turns they surge into space before Smith leads the ensemble, leaping forward beside the speeding bass and Venaccia's thrashing drums. Or on *Dream Horse*, where the echoing depths of Andersen's notes preface Smith's own forlorn and lonely message. For Ellington's *Prelude to a Kiss*, it is Smith's solo introduction, full of lyrical balm that anticipates Andersen's deeply throbbing desolate chorus.

As for *Independency*, Andersen's quivering strings give part one a haunting, glowering quality, but it is in part two that Smith takes Celtic fire in some cheetah-paced horn glory. Marvellous music!

Two Norwegians, a classically trained pianist and a rock-apprenticed guitarist, meet in a jazz concert in Leipzig, a city of huge musical history including Bach and Grieg. Here are Norway's "melodic warriors," as guitarist Terje Rypdal refers to himself and his compatriot Ketil Bjørnstad, who have performed as a duo "from Taiwan to Canada, from Italy to the Shetlands, from Lanzarote to the north of Norway."

Such is the scope of Norwegian jazz that the amalgam of these two of its sons makes a unique sonic gift to the music. Bjørnstad, as in his own *Flotation* and *Surroundings*, retains his strident classical sound, each of his notes creating a huge power, while Rypdal's choruses spin out soliloquies of his homelands, as his partner describes them, "on the very edge of Norway, with big mountains, fjords, deer and much wildlife and nature all around."

Hear his own *Easy Now* or *The Return Of Per Ulv* or Bjørnstad's *By the Fjord* to absorb a true sense of that patrimony. Then hear the pianist suddenly veer into a fragment of Grieg's *Notturno*.

Again, it is jazz beyond category, making nonsense of category — all the way from New Orleans to Oslo to Leipzig, as if boundaries and frontiers were ever foolish things.

July 16th 2009

Song for Peace

Lionel Loueke

Mwaliko

(Blue Note)

Lionel Loueke was born in 1973 in the west African state of Benin. He describes his parents as poor intellectuals, and when he first emulated an elder brother and began playing the guitar in his teens, it took him a year to earn the money to buy his first instrument. When its strings broke — and he was broke too — he would replace them with bicycle brake cables, which very soon toughened his fingers.

He found his way to the Ivory Coast Institute of Art to study classical music and gained scholarships, first from the American School of Modern Music in Paris and then from the Berklee College of Music in Boston. He earned his degree in jazz performance in 2000 and followed this by auditioning in 2001 before jazz eminences Herbie Hancock, Wayne Shorter and Terence Blanchard, then subsequently being selected for the Thelonious Monk Institute of Jazz in California. Loueke's startling jazz journey continued in 2008 with his debut Blue Note album, *Karibu*, after featuring on two Blanchard albums and two by Hancock.

When he told his story at a solo recital and talk at the 2010 London Jazz Festival he explained how his music — as complex and hybrid as it is, radiating sounds from all the episodes and places of his life — expressed its true message in his *Song for Peace*, which he said sounded out his wish for "no more war in this world."

Loueke's artistry combines a guitar virtuosity earthed in African rhythms with polyphonic percussive sounds on the strings and guitar body, plus his vocals in Fon, his mother tongue, and clicking effects inspired by Miriam Makeba, the singing genius of South Africa who made her home in the west African Republic of Guinea during the years of apartheid.

His second Blue Note album is *Mwaliko*, an amalgam of African and African-American sounds, from the traditional Beninese songs like *Vi Ma Yon* to Shorter's classic tune which gave its title to the Miles Davis album of 1967, *Nefertiti*. There are different personnel listings for virtually every track. The singers include Richard Bona, Esperanza Spalding and Angelique Kidjo, bassists Spalding, Bona and Massimo Biolcati and two drummers, Ferenc Nemeth and Marcus Gilmore.

In the opener, the felicitous *Ami O*, Kidjo's voice soars over Loueke's strumming and clicking, full of power and happiness and finishing with Loueke's satisfied coda of plucked strings. He venerates history and its long-memoried storytellers in *Griot*, which has in its centre a guitar solo of blazing jazz fire. Biolati and Nemeth — two thirds of the trio on the *Karibu* album — join him and recreate an association of deep and inventive empathy.

Loueke's unique guitar timbre frequently sounds with a beautifully muffled sound, as if he were playing beneath a blanket of kente cloth. In *Wishes* he plays alongside Bona's pulsating bass which echoes like a great hollowed Guinean tree trunk, and the duet of their combined African strings pulsates with the world's aspirations for peace and plenty.

Flying is another bass/guitar duet with voices, this time with the mercurial Spalding, whose tongue dances through her song as Loueke gives her plucked notes to leap through. Biolati and Nemeth return for Nemeth's portrait of the guitarist, *LL*, and the trio's sound is so airy and footloose that at times it seems to levitate in its own rhythm.

Drummer Marcus Gilmore is Loueke's only accompanist on Shorter's *Nefertiti*, the 60s portrait of an African woman, written during a time when black women like Angela Davis were taking leadership in the struggle for racial justice. That same power is manifest in Kidjo's surging Fon vocal of *Vi Ma Yon*, and joined by the shuddering vibrato of Loueke's strings.

Loueke's lightning fingers zip through the half-minute of *Dangbe*, which follows another trio piece, Biolati's *Shazoo*, in which his bass introduction sets off Nemeth's shimmering cymbals and Loueke's flickering strings for a brief and rapid voyage of sheer virtuosity and invention.

There was a time when the original provenances of jazz were inextricably linked with the blues guitar of the Mississippi Delta.

The advent of Loueke's profoundly original guitar dexterity adds to a formative element more deeply driving into the music's history — its origins in the percussion, strings and voices of West Africa, where the seeds of jazz were once deeply and undyingly planted by the cultural and musical genius of its people — those who stayed there and those who were chained and forced to travel to the Americas.

January 10th 2012

Trans-Pennine Message

Paolo Fresu, Richard Galliano and Jan Lundgren

Mare Nostrum

(ACT)

The Trans-Pennine express, careering between Manchester and Sheffield en route for Cleethorpes had just come through the sheer darkness of the Totley tunnel. A fellow passenger sitting opposite me across the aisle noticed that I was reading the *Morning Star*, which I had opened on the arts page, showing this column.

"Hey, I get the *Star* every day," he exclaimed to me. "And I love jazz too! I read that column every week." It was a fulfilling moment for me. What, out of the blue, somebody actually reads it!

We had a short but earnest conversation about jazz before I got off at Sheffield. "Have you heard the Italian trumpeter Paolo Fresu?" he asked me. "You should review his new album, *Mare Nostrum*," he insisted. "It's brilliant!"

"Okay," I said as I made for the door. "I'll try and get hold of it." So I did and here it is, thanks to my well-met travelling comrade.

And he was right too, for it is a most unusual and beautiful record. Consider the musicians and their instruments. Fresu is a Sardinian who learned his trumpet, like many a New Orleans horn man generations before, by playing in his local marching band. Richard Galliano is from the south of France, a master of the accordion and the smaller bandoneon — both very rare instruments in the story of jazz. Finally, the Swedish pianist Jan Lundgren, who is much influenced not only by the jazz canon but also by the classical tradition and his own country's palette of folk sounds.

René Hess, who wrote the sleeve notes, perspicaciously observes that "Fresu is convinced that the future of jazz can only be guaranteed by opening it to other musical cultures." Nothing could be truer about this heterogeneous trio who play Ravel, Brazilian songs by Jobim and a French evergreen by Charles Trenet, Swedish folk airs, a musical adaptation of a poem by the Turkish Communist Nâzim Hikmet and several originals. What a syncretism is here, a long jazz journey of circumnavigation.

As soon as the opening title tune begins, with Lundgren's piano chimes, Galliano's reassuring notes and the soft, almost cushioning brass of Fresu, you recognise that this is a trio like no other.

There's no percussion and no bass, just a mollifying and continuously inventive flow of sound. *Principessa* is a jaunty, skipping melody played with a weightlessness and buoyancy, with Galliano's joyous accordion notes gliding above Lundgren's dancing keys.

Jobim's *Eu Não Existo Sem Você* begins with Fresu's airy explorations growing in sound and power as Galliano joins him in a defiant duet. Lundgren's *The Seagull* perches on its proud and bold melody and ends with some howling blues notes from Fresu, almost as a prelude to its successor, Trenet's *I Wish You Love*. The dialogue between trumpet and accordion radiates a special and surprising beauty, a lovers' conversation bearing notes of endearment.

There is such heat of empathy between these musicians, such intuitive understanding that it seems like they have been playing together all their lives. None more so as in Lundgren's *Years Ahead*, where the interaction of their instrumental voices seems born from a common inventive impulse.

Hikmet was among the most militant, beautifully conscious and wise of 20th century poets and Fresu's free-blown adaptation of his poem *Mio Mehmet, Forse il Destino M'impedirà di Rivederti* makes a fixating musical experience. Lundgren's ominous solo introduction, Fresu's naked and vulnerable choruses and the loneliness of Galliano's notes fuse to make language in a world of sounds. Galliano's tribute to the Brazilian genius *Para Jobim* sails with a warm serenity and, through the traditional *Varvindar Friska*, Fresu blows with a genial, yet poised delicacy.

So, thank you, dear fellow Pennine-crosser. You introduced me to an outstanding musical feast, which I can now pass on with love and pleasure.

June 11th 2008

Storm Cloud of Sound

Charles Tolliver

Big Band with Love

(Blue Note)

The hot trumpeter Charles Tolliver, a Florida-born, Harlem-bred hornman who came to sudden prominence in 1964 when he partnered altoist Jackie McLean on the latter's album *It's Time*, returns to the Blue Note studio more than forty years later as session leader of *Big Band with Love*, recorded in New Jersey last year.

Tolliver established his own independent label, Strata East, in 1969 with the pianist Stanley Cowell, who also plays on the album alongside veteran baritonist Howard Johnson, searing tenorist Billy Harper and the long-established bassist and drummer duo, Cecil McBee and Victor Lewis. These hugely experienced musicians are joined by a cavalcade of brilliant younger players, creating a record of jazz passion and exuberance with an enormous storm of sound.

Tolliver is no stranger to big band composition and playing. In 1966, Gerald Wilson recorded one of his arrangements, *Paper Man*, on his *Live and Swinging at Marty's on the Hill* album, while Tolliver had been a part of his big band in Los Angeles. Its sheer expense to maintain has made the jazz big band a relative rarity, despite the huge excitement radiated by its huge sound, its ensemble beauty and the magic when a skilled soloist emerges from its forest of horns.

There are the occasionally formed big bands dedicated to keeping alive the legacy of prodigious and irreplaceable gone musical geniuses such as the Mingus Big Band or the Dizzy Gillespie All-Star Big Band, but the days when Ellington and Basie permanently toured the world and their orchestras were a galaxy of superb and instantly identifiable musicians is long gone.

Only the Lincoln Center Jazz Orchestra, led by Wynton Marsalis, plays anything like that role now.

So the first notes of *Big Band with Love*, a collective orchestral roar of reed and brass and the setting free of the theme of *Rejoicin'*, following Tolliver's sharp-edged and shouting trumpet above Lewis's crashing drums and a soaring ensemble, crystallises the very spirit of the great big bands.

When Todd Bashore surges from the saxophone section with his leaping alto solo and pianist Robert Glasper takes over as a breathless pacemaker, the listener internalises the intense joy of the music.

With Love follows, a Latin dance groove with Tolliver's trumpet sounding sometimes fanfarish, sometimes vulnerable, sometimes like a frenzied hunting horn. Then it is Cowell, twisting his notes and cutting his path until he melts into the ensemble and tenorist Bill Saxton leads the band home.

The only one of the album's seven tunes that is not a Tolliver creation is Thelonious Monk's *Round Midnight*, centred on a duet by the two old musical comrades Tolliver and Cowell, after which the onset of ensemble is explosive and complete, with Tolliver riding its rushing and menacing waves of sound.

Mournin' Variations begins like a Tudor serenade, with Craig Handy's flute dominant, until Lewis begins to pound, firstly behind the full ensemble, then accompanying Cowell and Harper's rasping chorus, then counterpointing Stafford Hunter's cavernous trombone. Tolliver enters, fiercely chirping with the full, impassioned orchestral voice mounting, before Cowell launches himself again and the flute song returns, like a rhapsodic dream. Johnson's heavy-rolling baritone sax breaks out of the ensemble after Tolliver's clipping solo on *Right Now*, which was originally written in 1964 for that Jackie McLean quintet album of the same title, on which Tolliver played.

In *Suspicion*, we hear the echoing guitar of Tolliver's son Ched, after McBee's throbbing bass and an incisive chorus from the leader.

The climax comes on *Hit the Spot* and is provided by Lewis's furious drums. He is the true revelation of the session. I had always heard him before as a subtle, empathetic and wholly creative small-group drummer, but, with Tolliver's big band, he is volcanic and beats incessantly and passionately as its true heart. It is a performance of astonishing rhythmic and multisonic musicianship.

Hear his flickering cymbals and crashing snares next to Handy's chasing alto solo and his final tempestuous signature with full orchestral unison. Big band jazz glory at its full fruition.

March 21st 2007

London to Gaza

Gilad Atzmon and the Orient House Ensemble
The Tide Has Changed
(World Village)
Robert Wyatt, Gilad Atzmon, Ros Stephen and the Sigamos String Quartet
...For the Ghosts Within
(Domino)

The Tide Has Changed is the sixth album of the Orient House Ensemble, led by the Israeli altoist Gilad Atzmon, formed a decade ago and named in honour of the headquarters of the Palestinian people in Jerusalem.

"Ten years ago I realised that beauty is the way forward," Atzmon writes in his sleeve notes. And listening to his solo work on the title song after the hokum of the introductory track, you recognise too how the sheer beauty of his sounds — a unique amalgam of Hebraic, Arabic and jazz traditions — has gained authority, sonic unity and huge emotional depth during those years.

The quartet has a new drummer — Eddie Hick — with the ever-inventive Frank Harrison on piano and the pulse of Yaron Stavi on bass. Hick's rattling snares open *And So Have We* with Atzmon's clarinet, an expression of the Atzmon dictum that "the melody is the truth".

The Ensemble's version of Ravel's *Bolero at Sunrise* sits at the very altar of melody, an astonishing piece in a surprising context where Atzmon sweeps through a complex hybrid of sound patterns. In the album's linchpin track — *London to Gaza* — the journey begins in Harrison's introductory phrases and winds through Atzmon's melody. Narratives are implied through the listener's own cultural experience, giving the impression of reading trench poems by Owen, Sassoon or Rosenberg, so much does Israel's murderous war and blockade strike at your ears, brain and heart.

Harrison takes fire too on his keys, and *We Lament* is a tailpiece of the union of agony and beauty in that besieged strip of the world. The squeeze of Atzmon's accordion sounds alongside his own alto, slowly traversing through *In the Back Seat of a Yellow Cab*, while in *All the Way to Montenegro* the journey is a dance with infectious musical joy gathering rapidity as it progresses.

The grounding qualities of ... *For the ghosts within* lie in the unity of a surprising harmony shared between Atzmon's horns, the Sigamos String Quartet led by Ros Stephen and the voice of Robert Wyatt.

Atzmon and Sigamos came together in 2008 to cut the album of song-book ballads *In Loving Memory of America* once performed by Charlie Parker. But *...For the Ghosts Within* is a very different creation indeed, made so by the addition of Wyatt's fragile, lifeworn and vulnerable voice, whose overwhelming power stems from its position as the mouthpiece of the everyman. Before Atzmon blows a chorus of huge power and tenderness, Wyatt reaches the pained heart of exclusion as he warbles *Laura* and *What's New?* and "those whose lives are lonely too" in Billy Strayhorn's *Lush Life*.

The rich string framework offered to Ellington's *In a Sentimental Mood* suddenly cracks and Atzmon blows alone, hovering over the melody like some giant-winged eagle. The strings shimmer with amazement as Wyatt — his voice shaking with astonishment — sings time and again "At last I am free, I can hardly see in front of me" over Julian Rowlands' bandoneon.

Lullaby for Irene — an elegy by Ros Stephen and Alfie Benge — is especially moving, beginning with a shuddering horn and mournful strings. Atzmon's beautifully deep, liquid clarinet chorus coupled with Wyatt's vocal completes a rare fusion of incongruous sounds. The final track is his version of *What a Wonderful World*, a song made famous and iconic by the first great superstar of jazz, Louis Armstrong. Wyatt sings it filled with the optimism of life and an bizarre balance of intimacy and detachment.

And when he tells you through the lyrics that "I hear babies crying and watch them grow/They'll see much more than I'll ever know," you believe him. As Atzmon supplements the ordinary words with the extraordinary eloquence of his chorus the album ends at the zenith of melody.

A strangely compelling album is *...For the Ghosts Within*, and one not easily forgotten.

November 24th 2010

Stan the Man that Can

The Stan Tracey Octet

The Later Works: the Hong Kong Suite/ The Amandla Suite
(Resteamed Records)

In 1997, after centuries of British colonial rule, the sovereignty of Hong Kong was handed back to China. And who was commissioned to compose and perform a valedictory suite to commemorate this significant moment of 20th-century history? It was the veteran and storymaster of British jazz piano, Stan Tracey.

It was not the first time that jazz had signalled the end of imperial control. In 1957 the great trumpeter Louis Armstrong had been in Accra to blow a stomping fanfare for Ghanaian independence. As for the Tracey band, not only did they play the final concert at Government House, they travelled to Gwangzhou and Beijing to perform the suite to elated Chinese.

In this 2009 recording five horns are added to Tracey's usual trio of himself, drummer son Clark and Andy Cleyndert's bass — tenorists Simon Allen and Mornington Lockett, altoist Sammy Mayne, trumpeter Guy Barker and trombonist Mark Nightingale. As soon as the octet strike up for the opener *Sweet Lips*, with Clark's pulsating drums and Cleyndert's thudding bass dynamo, it sounds like a much larger band. Nightingale takes his growling solo, the reeds blow behind him in unison, with Tracey comping freely.

There is no bogus or affected orientalism here, just straight-up eloquent and powerful blowing all round.

The much slower and sonorous *Lunar Lanterns* begins with some unaccompanied Tracey painting an evocative and twinkling night-time picture. Mayne's alto comes swooping in, Lockett plays beautifully all over his tenor and the sonic cityscape is almost Ellingtonian in its intensity, as if the composer had the Duke's *Far East Suite* in mind.

Tracey's opening keys of *Moon Cake* which follows are sheer Ellingtonia with the horns powerhousing forward in rousing solos, and Barker's attack particularly memorable along with Cleyndert's dark, eternal twang. *Dragon Boats* is a harbour portrait with more fine Barker and the two tenors in surging voice, and the very swift *Crackers and Bangers* suggests a people's celebration and longtime shackles rolling away.

Nightingale's slides shift like lightning and each of the horns, one by one, set off their own fireworks throughout a track of rampant excitation.

Back to 1993 when *The Amandla Suite* was commissioned by NALGO, when it merged with NUPE and COHSE to form the giant trade union UNISON, Tracey was asked to write the commemorative music.

The apartheid government had been finally defeated and toppled, so the rallying cry of the South African people of "Amandla!" — the Zulu word for power — was the suite's potent title.

Ellington is, of course, one of Tracey's great inspirations, and he too had been an active supporter of trade unions, in particular in 1941 when he helped to back the Fair Employment Practices Commission in New York — an early harbinger of the Civil Rights movement — or when in the same year he made his NBC "salute to labor" broadcast. According to Clark's sleevenotes the titles of *The Amandla Suite* are intended to "allude to events and relationships forged around the world by Nalgo."

The opener is *Cottons and Bobbins* with a characteristically wayward Tracey solo to begin the proceedings, before the horns dig in with Allen — I think — leading the upsurge followed by Nightingale blowing with a powerfully articulate precision. Cleyndert's bass trampolines in for a bouncing chorus before the ensemble leads the band out.

Perhaps only the composer knows who provoked *Humbert's Dream*, and the listener can only imagine its protagonist's thoughts and hopes.

Barker is a mainstay here, with a solo brimming with voice and colour. *The Cuban Connection* remembers NALGO's long solidarity with the Cuban revolution marked by Mayne's spirited alto and the Caribbean spice in Tracey's vibrant theme.

The trade union principle of *Building Bridges* finds its story in the next track. A slow-burner this one, with Barker and Mayne gyrating into the first choruses. Barker continues with a long soaring solo with a rockabye rhythm to uplift him. And wouldn't you like to hear Cleyndert's pinging bass and his bandmates' golden horns pounding out of the windows of town halls and local government offices all over the country as they whirl through the final track *Unison*.

The octet rocks with musical solidarity and oneness, and Clark's marvellous drums symbolise the huge strength and creativity of its members. Long live UNISON and long live the octogenarian Tracey too — what a combination.

August 18th 2010

Revolutionary Earth Music

Fred Ho and the Big Green Monster Band

Celestial Green Monster

(Mutable/Big Red Media)

The rumbling baritone saxophonist with the gargantuan tone Fred Ho was born within the Chinese-American community in 1957. An amalgam of unusually fused musical influences, Ho, both as player and composer, has unified his own traditional Chinese instruments within an Ellingtonian big band format, with strands of Charles Mingus, bop-based commitment and his own explicit socialist view of the US and its role in the world.

He wrote that he came of age during the late 1960s and early 1970s as a teenager caught up in the whirlwind of revolutionary consciousness. From 1985 he began to record on the Soul Note label with his Afro-Asian Musical Ensemble, with albums like *Tomorrow Is Now* (1985), *We Refuse to be Used and Abused* (1987) and the hugely resonant *Underground Railway to my Heart* (1993-95). He followed with musical essays on the Innova label, like his anti-rape suite *Yes Means Yes, No Means No, Whatever She Wears, Wherever She Goes* (1996) and *Once Upon a Time in Chinese America* (1999).

In August 2008 he was diagnosed with advanced bowel cancer, which was followed by radical surgery and six months of intense chemotherapy. The experience caused him to conclude: "My mission for the remainder of my time on this planet is to make Revolutionary Earth Music." Hence the extraordinary album of 2009 — *Celestial Green Monster* — a musical narrative of his view of the world, whereby the "evil behind human tenure on this planet has been a social cancer of acquisitiveness and its attendant stratified social systems, and ecological and social de-gradation."

Early on in the album comes Ho's adaptation of the Iron Butterfly rock classic *In-A-Gadda-Da-Vida*, with its epic and Miltonic connotations of Genesis and The Fall. "I thematically wanted to explore the journey of humanity's ascendancy on this planet and the dark rise of class and gender stratification," Ho writes in the sleeve notes. It is a rampaging, strident recreation with Royal Hartigan's thumping drum sound resplendent and Mary Halvorson's guitar unifying genres.

In 1975 Ho had written *Liberation Genesis* as a tribute to a decade of victories for Third World peoples. His own plunging Harry Carney-influenced baritone and Iranian-American Hafez Modirzadeh's chromodal tenor duet at its outset as if they are discussing and strategising a freedom process before the swinging ensemble wraps itself around them. The African-American trumpet reach of Stanton Davis leaps from the collective sound before Ho returns to deliver a gurgling solo.

Blues for the Freedom Fighters, another teenage composition, was created by Ho in 1974 to celebrate the victory of the Vietnamese people over years of US aggression and invasion, and its succession of eloquent solos including Bobby Zankel's alto, the trombones of David Harris, Robert Pilkington, Marty Wehner, Richard Harper and Earl McIntyre, plus Salim Washington's tenor and a summative baritone blast from the composer, shows this Monster Big Band in all its hybrid glory.

The thirty-eight minutes of *The Struggle for a New World Suite* was Ho's return to composing for the big band form to extol and exhort all efforts, activities and attempts to oppose the "monstrous evils that thwart humane social relations and threaten the very biosphere itself."

This is a work with a potent holistic endeavour and some fervent individual passages. There are the trombones of McIntyre and Wehner in colloquy during *Original, Organic and African* and the crying alto of Jim Hobbs in *Battleground Earth Blues*, followed by Art Hirahara's splattering electronic keyboard solo.

Ho's ever-present baritone has its brief exposed and salutary moment during *Patience, Passion and Praxis*, and Hobbs's serpentine runs peal through *Paper Tigers are Real Scaredy Cats*, with the piercing brass choruses of Davis's trumpet and cornetist Taylor Ho Bynum.

The suite ends with the cosmopolitan comrades stomping through *Guerrillas Gone Wild*, Hirahara's frantic piano trails beside the free, unleashed travelling song of Salim Washington's tenor and David Harris' hugely assertive trombone slides.

For Ho, "the quintessential American orchestra is not the symphony, but the big band," a musical creation not hidebound in a reactionary past but "enduring, vital and constantly relevant and revolutionary."

The *Celestial Green Monster* album is its true manifestation racked with creative originality in its surge of sound, astonishing sonic artistry, a subliminal ironic humour and an unflagging message of hope and struggle for humankind everywhere. Not bad for jazz so often overlooked, sidelined or caricatured, and not bad for the eternal message of music of every genre, everywhere.

June 3rd 2010

Old Masters Cut to the Chase

Fred Anderson
21st Century Chase
(Delmark)

In 1947 two young tenor saxophone contenders, Dexter Gordon of Los Angeles and Wardell Gray of Oklahoma City, teamed up in a Hollywood studio to record the iconic horn battle *The Chase*. The record created jubilation, wonder and controversy, establishing Gordon and Gray as tenor giants and promoting the tenor as a bop instrument.

Six decades on, *The Chase* is still ripe in the jazz memory of Chicago, and runs particularly deep in the consciousness of tenor veteran Fred Anderson. Anderson, born in Louisiana in 1929, was a teenager at the time of the classic recording. As a dedicated Chicago musician and pioneer member of the Shytown-based Association for the Advancement of Creative Musicians, Anderson has rarely left the city either to tour or record. He opened his own club, the Velvet Lounge, as a teetotal centre of jazz excellence and has kept the jazz light burning in the city for decades.

In 2009 Anderson celebrated his eightieth birthday at the Lounge. As a finale to a week of special performances he decided to unite with his co-tenorist and friend Kidd Jordan of Crowley, Louisiana, who was seventy-four years old himself, for a centennial saxophone joust — the *21st Century Chase*.

Here were two powerful Southern hornmen, who with millions of their compatriots from cities, small towns and sharecropping farms had made the great migration northwards with their families. For Jordan it had been a post-Katrina journey. Every note of this astonishing and fevered performance breathes out their provenances.

Their *Chase* doesn't have the same bounce and relentless bop energy as the Gordon and Gray performance. It has an entirely different excitation — two saxophone masters of a different era burning with a lifetime's worth of jazz fire. Accompanied by local musicians who know them as elders — bassmen Harrison Bankhead, guitarist Jeff Parker, and Chad Taylor on drums — and roused by the Chicago camaraderie of a devoted and admiring audience, they set off on their saxophone contest.

It is in fact an act of jazz union, a comradeship of horns. Yet it is Jordan whose horn bellows out the challenge to the older player, full of joy and daring, a harsh, rasping, guttural flourish before piano, bass and guitar set him down the road. Anderson comes belching in, adding his fervent counterpoint for several choruses, with Taylor's drums rocking and Jordan spluttering his high notes while Anderson stays down below.

It is a potent unity of sound, a septuagenerian and octogenarian's saxophone feast. As Anderson is fast on his solo journey, his horn cries out with staccato phrases, climbing up the scales as if to flee from the frantic rhythmic undergrowth.

Then the chase slows down but does not slacken, as if the travellers must stop and share the stories and reflections which still pour from their cogent horns. This first leg of the pursuit is just thirty-six minutes long.

The second opens with Bankhead's whining and supplicating bowed bass. The tenors enter in knowing colloquy and the quartet takes gradual ensemble fire — more passionate rendezvous than a chase.

The final track *Ode to Alvin Fielder* is a tribute to the free jazz drummer of Chicago featuring Parker's narrative guitar then honed solos from all the players.

This is a memorable album. Here are two old men considering the history of their music before, bursting with ardour and change, they relive it according to the sounds of their times and the truth of their lives.

June 9th 2010

Man of Cuba, Child of Africa

Omar Puente

From There to Here

(Destin-E World)

Hearing the astonishing sound of Omar Puente's electric violin takes me back five decades in listening to jazz. I remember the moment when, as a jazz-crazed teenager, I first heard the soprano saxophone of Sidney Bechet on a crackling 78 rpm record of what I think was *September Song*. I was used to the lyricism and juiciness of the New Orleans clarinet and was hugely impressed by the recordings I had heard of the roaring engine of Coleman Hawkins's tenor saxophone. But nothing can prepare you for the searing attack of Bechet's soprano and I heard it with a sense of startled excitation, which I felt when I first heard Puente.

Puente is a Cuban of West African lineage who lives in Bradford. Born in Santiago de Cuba, he was trained in classical violin studies at the Escuela Nacional de Arte in Havana, with extra inspiration from jazz master Chucho Valdés and traditional artists like Ruben Gonzales and Guillermo Rubalcaba, all sparked by what Puente calls the "motherland pulse" of Africa.

His more recent experiences of playing in the Courtney Pine band took him to Nigeria, a "humbling and euphoric" journey and a continuation of the travels he made as a violinist of the Nacional Symphony Orquestra de Cuba, to Asia, north America and Europe.

Puente thanks Cuba for the development of his talents. "I grew up in a new world, one that knew education and heath care were the most important things a child could have, but that valued cultural development." Such words you won't usually find in the sleeve notes of a jazz CD, but they're there on Puente's album *From There to Here*, clear and proud.

And it's a uniquely fine record, full of drama, artistry, hope and beauteous sounds. Puente has with him some marvellous British-based musicians of Caribbean roots like pianist Robert Mitchell, guitarist Cameron Pierre, trombonist Dennis Rollins and also Pine, playing saxophones and flute. As Puente steams into *My Mrs*, dedicated to his first electric violin given to him as a birthday present in 1996 by his partner Debbie, it is the Bechet effect, storming and tumultuous. Mitchell rocks out a short solo, then it is all a rampant Omar again, surging home above the pounding drums.

Somebody Backstage is dedicated to all those who make concerts happen. Musicians, sound engineers, lighting and stage managers, audience — all are acknowledged and thanked by Puente's quivering strings. In *Rumbiando* he uses his violin to emulate the sound of a Chinese trumpet to recognise the contribution of Asian immigration to Cuba.

Rollins's slides growl a chorus then soar through another. Coconut woodblocks and congas played by Oscar Martinez ground *Just Like U.* Puente saws out a chorus before Pierre brings his Dominica guitar sounds into the exchange as island speaks to island. Mitchell's chiming piano introduces the ballad *You are Too Beautiful*, arranged as a Cuban bolero, with its title saying much about Puente's own rhapsodic rendition.

Then come two tunes about travel. *Swings and Roundabouts* is about Puente's sense of culture shock arriving and living in Britain. Two contrary worlds are signalled by both acoustic and electric violins with Mitchell's keening piano. *Talking Bata* is a remembrance of the Nigeria he visited in 2008 and "the movements of festival-goers and market shoppers." A host of drums throb through the sound portrait and Puente's single amplified violin sounds like a whole orchestral string section, so powerful is its timbre.

After a Cuban excursion through the rumba and cuaguanco in *Think Carefully*, Puente ends his album with *Motherland Pulse.*

"African rhythm is the heartbeat of Cuban culture," he asserts. "My history began in Africa, it was written in Cuba and developed in the UK. Wherever I go, this is with me."

Pine and Mitchell are with him, with vocalist Eska Mtungwazi and the Harrow Youth Choir, all "searching on the journey" of music and meaning — all there in sublime abundance all through *From There to Here.* One for 2010 certainly and for all our years.

December 30th 2009

Now I'm a Believer

William Parker

I Plan To Stay a Believer: The Inside Songs of Curtis Mayfield

(AUM)

William Parker is a bass genius of jazz and one of the instrument's true innovators, a Mingus of his generation. Born in the Bronx in 1952, he came to prominence as a pioneering free virtuoso of the plunging notes in New York's loft scene of the 70s in such formative venues as the Firehouse, Studio Rivbea (organised by the reedman Sam Rivers) and Studio We. He went on to play with Don Cherry and the prime discoverer of the free jazz movement, pianist Cecil Taylor.

In the evocative double CD, *I Plan To Stay a Believer*, Parker joins with other rampaging talents to celebrate the music of Curtis Mayfield, the Chicago-born singer and composer whose "message songs" played such a vital part in the final years of the Civil Rights movement, when his songs became virtual anthems of black pride and protest.

Parker is also an accomplished poet and his powerful way with words strides out of his liner notes. "Every song written or improvised has an inside song which lives in the shadows, in between the sounds and silences and behind the words, pulsating, waiting to be re-born as a new song. Long live the revolutionary poets and musicians of the past and present, who continue to protest through their art, not resting until all things are like they should be." And of Mayfield's creations "We find our centre within his music so that we may become ourselves."

With Parker are some doyens of free jazz in a sublime amalgam — seventy-year-old Dave Burrell, the master pianist from Middletown, Ohio, and one of the young bloods of the piano, Lafayette Gilchrist. The Louisiana-born drummer Hamid Drake is in full fury with trumpeter Lewis Barnes and altoist Sabir Mateen. The poet whose voice declaims above the music like an ancient prophet is the 60s black-dramatist and seer Amiri Baraka, alongside singer Leena Conquest, who declares in the title song: "I believe in our struggle, that we shall win, I believe we need allies, the whole working class."

The shape of the recording, with the blistering choral passages from Brooklyn's New Life Tabernacle of Praise Choir, is full of echoes of Max Roach's albums with choirs reminiscent of *It's Time* and *Lift Every Voice and Sing*.

With the huge Parker twangs of its opening notes — deep, deep as they are — *If There's a Hell Below* has some soulful Gilchrist piano beside an explosive Drake, and the stygian horns of Barnes, Mateen and Darryl Foster's soprano wrestle while Conquest sings — "Stop dropping these bombs on me/This democracy is killing me/In America, you're not free."Mateen's rasping, adenoidal tenor sound bursts from the centre of *We The People Who Are Darker Than Blue*, with its overwhelming concluding riff, while the incessantly powerful vibrating beat of Parker's plucked bass underlines Bakara's dramatic vocal on *I'm So Proud / Ya He Ya He*.

And This is My Country, recorded in Paris live at the Banlieues Bleues Festival in March 2000, features a ninety-member children's choir of young Parisians singing in unity and joy — "Come together/Spray love/Reap the glory!"

Bob Marley had combined Mayfield's Civil Rights anthem, *People Get Ready*, with his own tune, *One Love*, on his 1977 album *Exodus*. Parker adds motifs from his own tune, *The Inside Song*, to his version of the song on his album. The New Life Choir steams in with the horns to create an exultant noise, a praise-song to the struggle of the people.

The seventeen-and-a-half minutes of *Move On Up* includes burning solos from the reedmen, some rumbustious trumpet by Barnes with Drake flaying his drums and pianist Burrell's constant elated comping, urging them on.

It's Alright is jivey and full of optimism, with the potent combination of the sustaining rhythm and beat of Drake and Parker's sync. "What everything is, just get the notes out free!" exclaims the arch-bassist. The horns blow with a wild, elegaic beauty through *Freddie's Dead*, which unifies joy in a life with sadness and questions on its passing.

Mayfield recorded his final album *New World Order* while lying on his back after being paralysed from the neck downwards after stage-lighting equipment collapsed on him at a Brooklyn concert in 1990.

The album's title song concludes Parker's album, with the children's choir in full cry singing of "a brand new day, a change of mind for the human race" and Parker switching to balafon, its African notes chomping through the chorus.

Mayfield's endless sense of justice courses through the ensemble's every note, completing a memorable way of celebrating the life's work of a man who always saw music as the essence of hope.

November 3rd 2010

The Healing Force of the Universe

Nicole Mitchell's Black Earth Ensemble
Black Unstoppable
(Delmark)
Nicole Mitchell's Black Earth Strings
Renegades
(Delmark)
Nicole Mitchell
Awakening
(Delmark)

Born in 1967 in Syracuse, New York State, and raised in California, Nicole Mitchell was trained as a classical flautist and played in youth orchestras. She found her first paid work busking with her jazz flute on the streets of San Diego, where she studied maths at the University of California. Perhaps this is where her musical humanism took root.

"I had the idea of creating a melody for each person who walked by," she said. "Reflecting on how people seemed to me I was trying to find a way to communicate with people through the improvisation. I was just trying to connect."

When she moved to Chicago in 1991 to work for a radical black publisher, she fell in with and was much influenced by the avant-garde stalwarts of the Association of the Advancement of Creative Musicians (AACM) and also began playing with Samana, an all-woman band. By 1997 she had formed her own band the Black Earth Ensemble and her own label Dreamtime Records, which issued her first albums *Vision Quest* in 2001 and *Afrika Rising* in 2002.

She became co-president of the AACM in 2006 and cut her first album, on the Chicago-based Delmark label, *Black Unstoppable* in 2007 with an early Windy City associate, tenorist David Boykin, the veteran free guitarist Jeff Parker, trumpeter David Young, cellist Tomeka Reid, with Josh Abrams on bass and drummer Marcus Evans.

The opener *Cause and Effect* has a huge percussive verve, with Mitchell's singing flute floating out of the rhythmic density. Abrams's vibrant bass and the urgent twang of Parker's guitar dominate the outset of the title tune before the rises and cadences of Mitchell's flute create new soundscapes.

February has the three very contrasting horns sparking delicate harmonies, while the beautiful cello opening of *Sun Cycles* meshes with Mitchell's discovering lyricism and Boykin's free and shuddering coda takes the track out.

In 2008 Mitchell recorded the album *Renegades* with the Black Earth Strings, which apart from Abrams was an all-woman band. Reid was there again with violinist Renee Baker and Shirazette Tinnin on drums and as with *Black Unstoppable*, Mitchell wrote all the album's compositions and arrangements.

The shimmering strings of Baker, a classical violinist and conductor of the Chicago Sinfonietta Chamber Orchestra, give a nimble timbre to the band on the opener *Crossroads* and Reid's cello dances agilely on *Ice* before Mitchell's flute joins her. The powerful undertow of Tinnin's drums help to fuse breath and strings in the title tune and the melodic beauty of *By My Own Grace* has a beautiful plucked-string interlude by Reid. But *Wade*, adapted from the spiritual *Wade in the Water*, celebrates the courage and relentless urge for freedom of those renegade slaves who took the Underground Railroad to Canada.

At its outset, you can hear echoes of Robeson's *Old Man River* before the anthemic traditional theme and Baker's defiant solo interwoven with Reid's cello, before Mitchell's own free-flying birdlike song.

The album's penultimate track is dedicated to the Somali activist Waris Dirie, once a refugee, then a model, now a campaigner against female circumcision. After Mitchell's long and lingering opening notes and Baker's flickering violin, the flute seems to traverse pain and solitariness, fading into the relief of silence.

In March 2011 Mitchell made a quartet album with the intention of "putting the flute more out front." Called *Awakening*, it brought her together again with Parker and long-time Chicago confrères, bassist Harrison Bankhead and drummer Avreeayl Ra. "We're just playing some tunes, having a good time, making music," claims Mitchell and from the first sounds of the opener dedicated to her daughter, *Curly Top*, there is a relaxed and beauteous virtuosity about the session.

Even the tones of the fleeting tune *Snowflakes* are hot, and the *Journey on a Thread* summarises the audacity and unity of this immensely skilled and empathetic foursome.

At the beginning of the sleeve notes to *Black Unstoppable* Albert Ayler's famous dictum that "music is the healing force of the universe" is quoted.

Mitchell and her Shytown bandmates manifest his words with every note.

November 7th 2011

The Schlippenbach Smithy

Alexander von Schlippenbach
Twelve Tone Tales vols 1 & 2
(Intakt)
The Alexander von Schlippenbach Trio
Bauhaus Dessau
(Intakt)
Alexander von Schlippenbach and the Globe Unity Orchestra
Globe Unity — 40 Years
(Intakt)

Jazz is the true music of unity and hope, and there is something both exemplary and powerfully optimistic in a German pianist born in Nazi Berlin in 1938 — his childhood passing within the long and bloody years of the defeat of Hitlerism — becoming both the instigator and source of creative combustion of a jazz orchestra of internationalist dimensions.

The Globe Union Orchestra boasts a membership of brilliant musicians from many erstwhile enemy nations and a continuing lifetime of forty-five years. Such is one of the achievements of Alexander von Schlippenbach, astonishing pianist and revolutionary improviser.

It was 1966 when this orchestra first assembled, and Schlippenbach described it as "a true pandemonium of new sounds. Forms and rhythms had opened up and offered those who reached for them — and were lucky enough to find like-minded musicians — a wide range of creative alternatives." It was the total adverse of a Nazi culture — the pursuit of the beautiful through collective sonic freedom, led by a true musical Berliner.

But let's begin with his solo piano of the *Twelve Tone Tales* of 2005, which stretches across two long albums. When he recorded these albums it was Schlippenbach's first solo recording for almost thirty years. Ever the storyteller, Schlippenbach employs his giant unaccompanied sound to create narratives where his clues fire up the listener's imaginations — in the way of all great jazz — to finish the stories themselves.

On Volume 1, his bemusing atonal artistry pounds darkly through *Devices and Desires* and the tricky corners of *K2* to reach *Allegra*

Agitato. Allegro was composed by his teacher at the Staatliche Hochschule for Music in Cologne, Bernd Alois Zimmermann, with whom he studied while simultaneously imbibing the sounds and techniques of Horace Silver and Thelonious Monk.

In Volume 2 the stories become more explicit. There are open anecdotes of self, like *Born Potty* or the key text *All Jazz is Free*. Or the three pieces by the LA alto saxophonist of Panamanian roots Eric Dolphy, who died while in a diabetic coma in Schlippenbach's home city in 1964 — one born in Berlin, one dying in Berlin. Yet hear the German piano griot tell Dolphy's lonesome story in *Out There* or *Something Sweet, Something Tender*. Inside the pyrotechnic piano breathes a tribute which is immensely moving.

The record ends with a rendition of the great Monk's *Trinkle Tinkle*, and German hands reconstitute the master's notes, spaces, turns and leaps. It sounds like an act of love.

The longstanding Schlippenbach Trio, with the English tenor saxophonist Evan Parker and German drummer Paul Lovens, came together again to record live at the Bauhaus, Dessau, in November 2009. The veteran threesome know each others' musical brains, impulses and inventiveness intimately and the bewildering brilliance of their sound is staggering. The forty-one minutes of the free triangular symphony *Bauhaus 1* is a work of compelling, fierce and tender beauty, expertly recorded as if you were inside Parker's lifegiving horn.

To move on to *Globe Unity — 40 Years* is as if you have circumnavigated the world of sounds. In his sleeve notes, the Chicago-born free trombonist George Lewis asserts that it was in the mid-60s, with the advent of revolutionary jazz initiatives like the Globe Unity Orchestra, that European free versions of the music marked a moment when the music itself had ceased to become a local subsidiary of jazz from the US.

Here, in this 2007 version of the orchestra, African-American Lewis plays beside Torontonian trumpeter Kenny Wheeler, Germans like Schlippenbach and trumpeter Manfred Schoof, the English drummer Paul Lytton beside Lovens, the ubiquitous Parker, South London slide genius Paul Rutherford and Polish reedman Gerd Dudek.

A resplendent Parker is to the fore in the title track, backgrounded by surging horn chords, until Lewis makes one of the longest and most potent trombone breaks in jazz. Schlippenbach's *Bavarian Calypso* reveals its syncretic centre with a rampant ensemble opening, a resonant chorus by Rutherford's Chicagoan slide disciple Jeb Bishop and a scorching alto solo by EL Petrowski.

The mighty Rutherford's long moment comes in a duo with Lovens in Wheeler's composition *Nodago*, prefaced by the composer's own breathy flugelhorn ascents and cadences.

The finale, *The Forge*, where music is heated, hammered and created, is Schlippenbach's piece with some ferocious Lewis and a pounding, elemental interval by the Berliner, reminding his listeners that he is still ever-present at the jazz smithy, ensconced at the heart and the brain of the music.

November 22nd 2011

From the Life-driven Tradition

Soweto Kinch

The New Emancipation

(Soweto Kinch Recordings)

The London-born, Birmingham-bred and Oxford-scholared saxophonist Soweto Kinch says about his new album *The New Emancipation* that it "challenges the comfort and complacency of our modern world, when the same conditions that enslaved and immiserated people 150 years ago are still powerfully in effect today. Yet above all it's about celebrating the endurance and resilience of the human spirit."

Quite a commission for a 2010 jazz album born in the first months of a profoundly backward Con-Dem coalition government, and quite a sonic commentary too.

Yet the best of jazz from Armstrong to Ellington to Parker to Roach, to Ornette Coleman and Archie Shepp, from Monk to Abdullah Ibrahim and Rahsaan Roland Kirk has always done these things — and Kinch is blowing his notes from the same common sound, the same life-driven tradition.

Despite his far-reaching talent, Kinch has been anything but a prolific studio man. Following his recorded outing for Tomorrow's Warriors and Jazz Jamaica from 2001 onwards, he has only recorded two previous albums under his own name, his first *Conversations with the Unseen* (2003) and *A Life in the Day of B19 — Tales of the Tower Block* (2001), a recording racked with fine expressive music and torrid social realisation.

An Ancient Worksong begins the album in the line of Caribbean ancestry before the lyrics of *Trying to be a Star* pitches the concept roundly in now times, following the vapid dreams of a new slavery of celebrity-obsessed lives of those who are "chasing fame in exchange for a chain." Then straight into the compelling, combustive notes of Kinch's burning alto in *A People with No Past*, his terse sound bringing back echoes of the pioneering South African altoist Kippie Moeketsi.

Femi Temowo has a springing guitar solo, while Justin Brown's crashing snares and Karl Rasheed-Abel's pinging bass pulsate behind them both.

Paris Heights houses the offices of a devious firm promising a "debt-free tomorrow," the "crème de la crème of debt-collection," and shows how Kinch alternates hot horn-playing and acrid and witty social satire with conjoined artistry. The profits are soaring with the rapid increase of house and flat evictions, as Kinch dramatises the orientation of a new employee advised to "hit the quotas and move up."

Suspended Adolescence features the lyrical, translucent trumpet of Byron Wallen flickering through his choruses and more earthy guitar from Tomowo before Kinch storms in with some visceral phrases.

Titles like *Trade* and *Love of Money* remind me of a Kinch performance which I heard at the Canary Wharf Jazz Festival last year and of his musings of the "accountants" made in the very shadows of the high pillars of capital. In *Trade*, Kinch's alto sets itself side by side with Shabaka Hutchings's bass clarinet with Brown's fiery drums, stirring them both forwards.

Through *Axis of Evil* the emphasis returns to words in an extraordinary versified essay bursting with quasi-Byronic rhymes — how about "is the Obama nation/an abomination/when they bomb a nation?" The narrator is "the face behind the face," the power which takes everything from the people, which "steals and resells their treasures/and tells them it's austerity measures," now times, Con-Dem times, Cameron and Clegg times and faces, or what? And reinforced by the mordant tone of *On the Treadmill*, with Harry Brown's caustic trombone slides.

The optimism of Kinch's horn and Temowo's guitar stretched through the long choruses of *Never Ending*, and *Raise Your Spirit* is a direct call for "breaking the cages apart," a chant of hope and the prospect for change. "You don't have to see the wind/to know its force," raps Kinch. But you only have to hear it when it sounds from his still young horn.

The lines remind me of other words. "Emancipate yourselves from mental slavery/None but ourselves can free our minds," said Jamaica's reggae seer Bob.

Now Birmingham's jazz crier Soweto blows out that same universal dictum into another century with the dark but resistant narratives of *The New Emancipation*. They prompt very careful listening and a call to action.

October 28th 2010

An African Spirit Lives On

John Donaldson's Unity

Nearer Awakening

(Laughing Lettuce)

He started learning the piano as a boy after an aunt who ran a South London pub bequeathed him the pub piano. Born in Brentford in 1952, John Donaldson left school at sixteen with the wanderlust and finally returned to education at a Cambridge technical college in his mid-twenties. He played in rock bands and moved to the United States in 1982, developing an intense interest for jazz in the San Francisco Bay area, where he eventually played in a trio with bassist Larry Grenadier and drummer Jeff Ballard, and with some esteemed horns like Red Holloway, Eddie Henderson and John Handy.

In 1993, Donaldson returned to London and toured with British jazz stalwarts like Art Themen, Clark Tracey and Norma Winstone. Then during the mid-90s, while living in Hastings, he met the astonishing South African pianist and tenorist Bheki Mseleku.

Born in poor circumstances in Durham in 1955, Mseleku grew up in a musical family, playing with local bands before touring Europe and the US in the 70s. He settled in Sweden, gigging with other exiles from apartheid like bassman Johnny Dyani and fellow pianists Abdullah Ibrahim and Chris McGregor. After performing at Ronnie Scott's in 1987 and taking time out in a Buddhist community, Mseleku led a band and made a series of powerful albums on the Verve label, including *Timelessness* (1994), *Meditations* (1994), *Star Seeding* (1995) and *Beauty of Sunrise* (1997).

Mseleku had a huge effect on Donaldson. "He was a great pianist and composer — to me his music was sheer inspiration," Donaldson said. "He never stopped searching, musically and spiritually. Yet he was a man of great humility. We used to talk and play piano to each other at my house hour after hour. I loved his tunes. They are full of life and brilliance and need to be much better known. That's really why I made the record, to keep his tunes alive for the future."

Mseleku, a diabetic like the great alto saxophonist Eric Dolphy, died in 2008. So, a year later in November 2009, Donaldson cut *Nearer Awakening*, his tribute album to his friend, with his Unity Quartet — tenorist Ian Price, Simon Thorpe on bass and drummer Tristan Banks.

During the 60s and 70s the presence of the precious jazz spirit of the South African expatriate genius in London of Dudu Pukwana, Louis Moholo-Moholo, Chris McGregor, Harry Miller and Mongezi Feza had a dramatic impact upon British jazz musicians. Something similar is happening on this record, with the four white Englishmen playing at the end of the first decade of the 21st century with the sonic muse of Mseleku deep inside their blood and consciousness. It is an album which pulsates with verve, fire and the rhythms of ordinary life in two continents.

The opener *Joy* is a strong, vibrant tune which Price's potent tenor makes its own and Banks's bouncing drums gives springing uplift. As Donaldson measures out the notes of his solo, each strike on the keys makes light and sparkle and tells us that joy has keen ears too.

Ntuli Street was a track on the *Timelessness* album. It is an enigmatic tune with an unknown narrative, but story there is — in volumes. Who lived in this street during the dark apartheid days? What determined their lives, their hopes? The listener adds the events as Price and Donaldson wander past the shops and dwellings, and Banks and Thorpe add the subliminal street-speech.

Nearer Awakening and *Suluman Saud* both come from *Beauty Of Sunrise*. The former is slow, balladic and serene. Price's solo is full of melodic beauty, his patterns subtly and gently embroidered. With Thorpe deeply twanging behind him, Donaldson searches out a chorus that is tender, full of love and connection to the tune's creator. A prime track, this. The latter is a sound-portrait crafted by melody, giving an ethos of age and a life well and fully lived rising from Donaldson's notes.

Angola is a tribute to a sister nation that endured the aggression of the apartheid regime. This tune dances with energy and more joyousness. Price sounds elated and buoyant and Donaldson drums on his keys in celebration of a continent's unity. Perhaps this is the theme too of the poised and aspirational *My Passion*, where Price's floating tones rise from the earth exquisitely and Donaldson explores his friend's dreams and urgent hopes with close and empathetic sounds.

The final, rampaging *Blues For Afrika* will send the listener on a quest for Mseleku's now-deleted albums, certainly not to be found in HMV.

Donaldson's Unity have made a fine and telling album as well as a way of tracing and finding one of Africa's most enduring and singular musicians.

April 14th 2010

Real Sonic Polemics

Christian Scott

Yesterday You Said Tomorrow

(Concord)

When I first heard a prodigious teenage Crescent City-born trumpeter called Christian Scott a decade ago, playing in his alto saxophonist uncle Donald Harrison's band, I had no idea that another ten years on he would create an album like *Yesterday You Said Tomorrow.*

In his sleeve note Scott declares that "the driving force behind this document was to illustrate the fact that the same dilemmas that dominated the social and musical landscape in the 60s have not been eradicated — only refined." And as if to sharpen this parallel, Scott uses in the studio the best of sound engineers Rudy van Gelder, a veteran of many of the most brilliant and pertinent 60s Blue Note sessions.

This is jazz as the true spirit of this era, embracing its central issues and most provocative questions as audacious jazz geniuses like Max Roach, Charles Mingus and Archie Shepp grappled with them in the age that Scott evokes. And straight to its heart Scott goes in the opening track *KKPD* (Ku Klux Police Department), a direct reference to the New Orleans police, whom Scott has has accused of a "phenomenally dark and evil" attitude towards African-Americans.

His four bandmates, particularly drummer Jamire Williams and Kris Funn on bass, lay down a menacing undertow with Matthew Stevens's blues-laden guitar notes. Scott's suspirating horn enters with Milton Fletcher's leaden piano before his harrowing sound rises towards the Mississippi sky, implacable.

The Eraser, composed by Radiohead frontman Thom Yorke, is still melancholic, with Fletcher's dark chords dominant and Scott's virtual whisper of a solo from his custom-made trumpet which he calls Katrina and which breathes sheer tenderness all through the ballad *Isadora.* But something else bursts from his contrary horn in *Angola, LA and The 13th Amendment.* It is explicit narrative from Louisiana's infamous prison work-farm, a slave camp which repudiates Lincoln's 1862 Emancipation Proclamation.

Stevens's delving guitar echoes the notes of hundreds of imprisoned bluesmen over the years and Scott's chorus is quivering, pointed and agonised in its tone over Williams's relentless drums.

Proposition 8 was passed into California state legislation in 2008, eliminating the right of same-sex couples to marry.

Scott's lamentation, as if his very breath and lungs were campaigning against it, becomes almost visible as be blows out his tune *The Last Broken Heart: Prop 8* with Williams's rattling snares close beside him and Stevens's empathetic strings.

Jenacide, Scott's next composition, is subtitled *The Rise and fall of the Bloodless Revolution*, and his horn goes well beyond a whisper, soaring in burnished phrases. But the real sonic polemics are revealed in his tune *American't*, which seems to be an ironic twist on Obama's election cry, "Yes we can."

What is this young US quintet saying in this profound negative? Yes we can continue with the inhumanity of Guantanamo? Yes we can support Israel against Palestinian nationhood and accept Netanyahu's "badge of honour?" Yes we can continue the embargo in Cuba and enhance the war in Afghanistan? Who knows the depth of their indignation? Only they and their music knew.

The final track, written by Scott and Stevens who play as a duo on *The Roe Effect: Refrain in F# Minor*, is a defiant musical reflection on the right to abortion and exposes the reactionary myth that those supporting the pro-choice campaign will shrink as more children are born into families who oppose abortion.

Stevens's heavy chordings contrast starkly with the buoyancy of Scott's clouds of notes which seem to float across the southern Delta skies, touching every woman and man as they pass, with his last, lingering note a sheer exhalation of breath.

A strange and striking subject for a piece of jazz music? Not for Scott and his co-groovers or for the marvellous van Gelder, who assert in their every sound that all the world and its arguments and debates belong to jazz, and its notes will always express its struggles and progress.

December 2nd 2011

Matana the Storyteller

Matana Roberts

Live in London

(Central Control)

As soon as the Chicago-born altosaxophonist Matana Roberts bursts into unaccompanied free sound on her new album *Live in London* — recorded at the Vortex in Dalston, the new jazz hub of the capital, in early 2010 — you know that you are hearing a formidable young reed virtuoso. When I heard her at the same venue at the London Jazz Festival last November I was immediately drawn into both her powerful surge of notes and the explicit narrative themes of her compositions as she spoke between pieces, beyond her twenty-odd years, like one of the true storytellers and griots of jazz.

There, on a wet East London night, she told of growing up in Chicago with music-loving parents, of how her vinyl-head father would take her as a child around a succession of South Side record shops, where she first heard and grooved to the sounds of jazz. "Chicago improvised music was so radical and political," she remembered.

The first and immediate impression of her Vortex album is exactly how attuned to London it is — an unusual truth in itself considering that Matana served a potent apprenticeship with some of the masters of the local jazz scene as an adherent of the Chicago-based Association for the Advancement of Creative Musicians, with her most redoubtable mentor, the late veteran tenor sax player Fred Anderson, who blew with her on her debut album *The Chicago Project*.

She plays as part of a quartet with three equally young British musicians. One is the pianist of Grenadian roots, Robert Mitchell, who is frequently fired into myriad free directions by his Chicago bandmate, the fine plumbline of a bassist Tom Mason and the responsive, multi-inventive drummer Chris Vatalaro.

None of the album's pieces were rehearsed and much of the material the local musicians had not seen before. Yet they play with assurance, fire and such empathy as if the wide Atlantic and their very different cultural histories were sheer irrelevances.

The opener, Frankie Sparo's *My Sister*, is a thirty-seven-minute essay of lyrical climbing and cadence, collective and creative adventure, a US horn moving in errant surprise and discovery, and the realisation of her fellow players that this affirmation of sisterhood moves towards brothers too. Mitchell's runs and flourishes enter the open door of Matana's sounds, Mason's plunging bass ranges through a diversity of patterns and Vatalaro's exploring drums make their own new pathways too.

It is an album in itself, and more so because of its astonishing spirit of oracy, as if Matana's very own voice is telling a story of the woman she has known, loved and spent her young life with, alongside the unabashed support of three men musicians from another country, another history. It is an indelible musical experience.

On to *Pieces of We*, which begins as a duet between Roberts and Mitchell in keyboard excitation and includes a riveting passage where Matana blows a repeated long-wavering note followed by Vatalaro's quivering drum-marks and Mitchell's pointillistic piano.

Glass sounds toughly fragile, beginning with Matana's contrast of deep, then heightening, unaccompanied and lonely notes blown with a tender brilliance, before Vatalaro's drums provoke her horn towards a sudden rapidness of line and high-pitched spikiness. The piece ends with a briefly beautiful exchange between Mason and Mitchell.

The fleeting, buoyant mood of *Turn It Around* is a sudden antithesis with its rhythm changes and Mason's bow humming on his strings. And Matana knows and plays her roots and traditions too in her performance of Ellington's *Oska T*, in which she wraps the theme around some sparkling improvised passages with all three players in full and living radiance, particularly a super-energised Mitchell.

When she played her own composition *Exchange* at the Vortex in November Matana prefaced it by explaining that it was the name of a street she knew as a child, and how much it reminded her of her mother and Anderson, her guru, both of whom had died in recent months. It is the final track of *Live in London* — short, full of feeling of love and luminosity.

Look out for her again in Dalston, and don't miss her.

April 20th 2011

Windy City Shuffle

Ernest Dawkins

The Prairie Prophet

(Delmark)

"It's being relived and replayed over and over again. I lost a gig over that tune, but to lose a gig, what is that? Does that stop me from eating, paying my rent? You have to stand up for what you believe in. No more war. We're saying we're not going to tolerate it." Thus declared the Chicago saxophonist Ernest Dawkins about his tune *Baghdad Boogie*, the final track of his 2010 album *The Prairie Prophet*, a rampaging sound statement about the war in Iraq.

Dawkins was born in the Windy City in 1953 and grew up as a neighbour of another brilliant jazz reedman, Anthony Braxton. As a boy he played bass and drums, but was drawn to the saxophone in his late teens after hearing the irresistible message of Lester Young. He became a member and activist of the union of avant-garde jazz virtuosi, the Association for the Advancement of Creative Musicians (AACM), and is now its chairman.

From 1994 he began recording with a band called the New Horizons Ensemble, featuring an array of pugnacious horns. Their first two albums for the Chicago-based Delmark label, *Jo'burg Jump* and *Cape Town Shuffle*, emphasised their connection with Africa's liberation struggle and the continent's musical heritage. They have performed and toured in South Africa and Mozambique, and Dawkins is adviser to the Jazz Club of Maputo. He also teaches saxophone across the Chicago public school system.

With Dawkins on *The Prairie Prophet* are his long-time ferocious trombonist colleague Steve Berry and slashing guitarist Jeff Parker. Two trumpeters, Marquis Hill and Shaun Johnson, complete the horns, with Junius Paul on bass and drummer Isaiah Spencer.

The opener, *Hymn For a Hip King*, played in quasi-waltz time, recalls Abdullah Ibrahim's 1976 South African classic, *Blues For a Hip King*, although Dawkins asserts that his tune is truly dedicated to his homeland heroes, Martin Luther King and Malcolm X. Both trumpeters in particular are hot and rampant, their horns transcendent and full of potency.

Sketches is twelve minutes of a boiling on-rush of sound, with the horns in blistering mode and Berry taking a near-to-tailgate, street-scorching slide chorus alongside Parker's chiming guitar which returns for a wild and caterwauling solo before Paul's super-twanging bass sends the studio soundwaves vibrating like fury.

The more rhapsoodic dimension of Dawkins' horn is to the fore in the slowly-drawn *Balladesque*. It contrasts starkly with *Mal-Lester*, his tribute to the two departed pioneers of the Art Ensemble of Chicago, bassist Malachi Favors and trumpeter Lester Bowie. It is full of their appetite for surprise and audacity — all the horns present their tribute and Spencer's crashing drums found their notes of fiery and free respect and love.

The repeated ensemble moan that begins and ends *Shades of the Prairie Prophet* precedes an astonishingly rapidfire solo chorus by Dawkins with Spencer rattling beside him. Berry enters, raw and brusque as someone blows a whistle, Parker strums quizzically and Paul delves and bounces. Parker returns with an enigmatic chorus and Dawkins follows him, testifying on his tenor.

Dawkins investigated Iraqi scales before he composed *Mesopotamia*, which begins his focus on invaded lands. Berry plays a bluesy chorus, Parker picks out a creative trail and Dawkins' emotive alto pours its notes over the arid lands. But it is as a haunting prelude to the summative track, *Baghdad Boogie*, superficially playful but spoofed with anti-war parody. The horns and guitar make their messages and the burlesque follows on with snatches from the *Old Grey Bonnet*, *Over There* and *Swanee River*.

Dawkins sings out: "Baghdad Boogie, sure ain't pretty, 19-years-old, 20-years-old, coming home, losing their soul, losing their limbs. Suicide! Homicide! Genocide! All the 'cides, no more war! No more war!"

It's a jazz message for peace and anti-militarism, reinforced by Dawkins' testimony in his sleeve notes: "We as artists need to get funding. Cut some of that funding from the Pentagon and we'll show you how to win hearts and minds."

And it's all in the music of the New Horizons Ensemble — love of peace and unity, hatred of war.

May 24th 2011

From Blue Seas, City Sounds

Denys Baptiste

Identity by Subtraction

(Dune)

I've often thought that the emphatic and unifying cry of the Grenadian revolutionary Maurice Bishop, 'One Caribbean!', had enormous salience to jazz. What a vibrant, groovy and hugely powerful inter-generational big band of jazz musicians of Caribbean provenance could be formed, if only in the imagination. From Jamaica, horn men like trumpeter Dizzy Reece, altoists Joe Harriott and Bertie King, Ellington's great trombonist of muted glory Joe "Tricky Sam" Nanton and pianists Wynton Kelly and Monty Alexander.

And from the eastern Caribbean too, two bristling trumpeters — Vincentian Shake Keane and Barbadian Harry Beckett, or pianist Robert Mitchell, a Londoner with forebears from Grenada. And the impassioned sound of the tenor saxophonist with St Lucian parents, Denys Baptiste, whose fourth album *Identity by Abstraction* is a telling statement indeed.

Baptiste was born in Hounslow in 1959 and his father's record collection, which included albums by Basie and Mingus, propelled him towards jazz. He had his first saxophone lessons as a fourteen-year-old, while hearing the sounds of the West London Caribbean community all around him. He studied music for two years at the West London Institute before signing on for a course in jazz at the Guildhall School of Music. He played with his mentor Gary Crosby and his Nu Troop in the 90s before cutting his first album *Be Where You Are* in 1999, followed by *Alternating Currents* in 2001.

In 2003 *Let Freedom Ring* commemorated the fortieth anniversary of Martin Luther King's Washington speech. It was a contender for Best Album and Best New Work in the BBC Jazz Awards. Baptiste has with him some impressive musical colleagues in *Identity By Subtraction.* Crosby joins him on bass, adding his long-serving Anglo-Caribbean pulse to Baptiste's own diasporan sound.

The pianist is Andrew McCormick, another West London boy and alumnus of Pimlico School, a white Englishman with a deep Caribbean empathy who regularly accompanies other saxophonists of Antillean roots like Jason Yarde and Jean Toussaint. The drummer is Rod Youngs.

Baptiste describes his album as a "collage of thoughts and improvisations" and the title tune includes a rocking chorus by McCormick with Crosby's walking bass and Baptiste pouring out his soundscapes with a weaving beauty. The second track, *Apprehension*, expresses the moments before and during the act of creating music, of pathmaking through notes and Baptiste's solo is ripe with nervous excitation.

Dance of the Maquiritari was born after Baptiste learned from his mother that her grandparents were descendants of Amerindian peoples of the shores of the Orinoco River in Venezuela. It has a south American groove heightened by Youngs' lively and jumping drums, while its successor *Special Times* has another family dedication to Baptiste's wife and children. His soprano radiates intimacy and melodic love.

Evolution from Revolution charts the story of the Caribbean people in Britain since the arrivant experiences of the post-war Windrush generation, through the resistance of the 1970s and the continuing struggles of now-times.

Baptiste plays like a musical griot, each note spilling out the lives of his people, as he compounds a sound-chronicle, with Crosby's ever-present bass marking down the years. Another Caribbean bass doyen, the veteran Coleridge Goode, who played beside fellow-Jamaican Harriott is the hero of *Harriott's Chariot — A Life in the Bass Line.*

Goode recounts his life and musical ideas over Baptiste's swinging horn with a moving eloquence. *Song for You* is a previously unrecorded tune by the late South African pianist Bheki Mseleku, with whom Baptiste toured twenty years ago. Full of life and African free spirit, it uplifts the musicians, has their notes running across the Veldtlands.

And there is more history in *The Long Night*, which marks the bicentenary of the Abolition of the Slave Trade Act of 1807. The horn-chronicler Baptiste tells the story with the sound of truth, passion, the blues and final redemption. And back to this Caribbean orchestra of power and unity. The tremendous Baptiste would be there too with his two great bassmen, Goode and Crosby, alongside now-times altoists Yarde and Soweto Kinch, a part of a tenor saxophone section with Virgin Islands-rooted Sonny Rollins and Jean Toussaint, Jamaica-provenanced Bogey Gaynair and Courtney Pine and Puerto Rican David Sanchez.

What an amalgam of sound that would be.

August 9th 2011

From Beirut to Paris

Ibrahim Maalouf

Diasporas

(Discograph)

As soon as you hear the uniquely singing trumpet voice of Beirut-born and Paris-bred Ibrahim Maalouf on his version of Dizzy Gillespie's *A Night In Tunisia* — which Maalouf renames *Missin' Ya* — you know that you are listening to sounds beyond Lebanese or Parisian streets. You can also hear the people of Tunisia, Egypt, Bahrain, Syria, Yemen and Libya in revolt, of the young and the old marching and shouting in the thoroughfares of their cities, claiming the freedom which is rightfully theirs but which was withheld from them by decades of dictatorship.

And all this from a young man born in 1980 who escaped from his birth nation with his family during civil war, whose mother Nada is a skilled pianist and whose father Nassim is a celebrated trumpeter who invented a trumpet with an extra valve, also played by his son.

This allows the blowing of quarter tones upon which Arabic maqams, or modes, can be essayed.

From the age of seven, Ibrahim learned the trumpet, tutored by his father who taught him classical, baroque, contemporary and Arabic musical techniques which eventually enabled him to win major prizes in world trumpet competitions, playing works by Bach, Vivaldi and Purcell. He is regularly invited to give recitals, teach classes and compose for orchestras across France and the US, where he frequently works with Kansas State University.

In 2007 he began working on a jazz-based album, *Diasporas*, which took him three-and-a-half years to complete. He recorded much of the music with over thirty musicians in Beirut, Montreal and Paris, the album finally being mastered in New York.

There is a strange but dramatic conjunction that this record should emerge as long-oppressed Arabic peoples are making revolution in so many parts of their world. Yet its sounds begin in diasporan Parisian communities, places where, as the sleevenotes describe, "eastern hues naturally mingle with the western urban sounds in which they were created." And out of this sonic cosmos comes Maalouf's horn.

The conception of *Diasporas* reminds me most of the music of another diasporan, the Caribbean-rooted Soweto Kinch, whose evocations of *Birmingham 19* on his albums *A Life in the Day of B19* and *The New Emancipation* generate comparable urban atmospherics —

sounds of traffic, passing voices, the people's circumstances and their music.

The soundscape of a hugely diverse Paris opens into the first track, *Diaspora*, with improvisations of Arab instruments such as the buzuq and stringed kanoun. Violins, cello and bendir drum are introduced in *Hashish*, above radio voices and Maalouf's dancing and soaring trumpet.

The pounding drum, casual street-talk, car hooters and humming strings that accompany Maalouf's flickering horn in *Missin' Ya* are far from the original sky-reaching, late-40s original Gillespie bop performances. The theme subsides under the traffic before Kamel Labbaci's lute-like oud improvises to preface *Shadows*, which begins with the voices of playing children and Antoine Khalifa's worried solo violin. Maalouf's lonely trumpet wails lingeringly and reprovingly like a human voice trapped in sorrow.

The breath of resistance enters with the track *Verdict*, arranged — according to the sleevenotes — with "sounds recorded in Paris during a demonstration for freedom and peace in Lebanon." Maalouf's horn rises and rises as if grasping for liberation like his comrade Arab peoples, and the track climaxes with shouts of defiance. *Last Wishes* expresses the sheer beauty of Maalouf's brass utterance, sounding against choral voices, buzuq and drums.

There is nothing else like it in European or US jazz, a ringing tone of exquisite purity juxtaposed at the end of the track by more random voices and street musicians playing *Que Sera Sera*, showing again how the message of rebellion breaks out of the life of the mundane.

And how can that same golden horn — with the modification of a single added valve — that gave such brilliance to Buddy Bolden in his choruses in Storyville bordellos, or such hope to the young Louis Armstrong at the New Orleans orphans home, blow such fine fanfares to a new life in the tyrannies of Arab lands? Because it is jazz, a music of new sounds, new combinations and new freedoms.

April 28th 2011

Crossing the Gulf

Stefon Harris, David Sánchez and Christian Scott

Ninety Miles
(Concord-Picante)

It is but ninety miles between the Florida and Cuban coasts, yet for the millions of people of both landfalls the shorelines could be in two different hemispheres. But in May 2011 jazz was the unifier, when three of the US's most accomplished jazz musicians defeated the fifty-plus-year-old US embargo to record this album in an unpretentious Havana studio, playing with brilliant young Cuban compadres of sound.

Stefon Harris, born in Albany, New York state in 1973, is a vibist with a clutch of singular Blue Note albums behind him, and he combines leading his band Blackout with his teaching post at New York University. David Sánchez, born in Guaynabo, Puerto Rico in 1969, arrived in New York in 1987 and studied at Rutgers College. As a young contender he played with Dizzy Gillespie's United Nation Orchestra and with other Latin-rooted jazzmen like Brazilian Claudio Roditi and Cuban Paquito D'Rivera. Through the 90s he recorded a succession of powerful albums expressing his proud Puerto Rican heritage like *Travesia*, *Melaza* and *Obsesion*.

Christian Scott, a twenty-seven-year-old trumpeter from New Orleans, first came to prominence as a prodigious teenager playing in the band of his alto saxophonist uncle Donald Harrison. "New Orleans is in many ways an extension of the Caribbean," he said. "There are a lot of Cuban people there. My great-grandmother was born in Cuba and when I was growing up she would sing Cuban songs to me. I grew up around that music."

This potent threesome combined with two groups of outstanding local musicians — pianists Rember Duharte and Harold López-Nussa, bassists Osmar Salazar and Yandy Martinez González, drummers Eduardo Barroetabeña and Ruy Adrian López-Nussa and percussionists Jean Roberto San Miguel and Edgar Martinez Ochoa. Together a true stew of US-Cuban virtuosi that would dismantle any blockade.

The opener is one of the hosts' tunes, Duharte's romping *Nengueleru*. After the opening ensemble Sánchez's wailing tenor hovers over the galloping rhythm and Harris chimes out a final chorus. *E'cha* is a composition by the other pianist López-Nussa, whose thrusting chorus introduces Harris bestriding a stop-time rhythm before Scott's piercing horn peals skyward.

Sánchez is the maker of the next two tunes. The first is *City Sunrise*, provoked by the music of the Cameroons but given a Cuban timbre so that it truly becomes a world groove. Harris' gentle chorus over a shuffle rhythm precedes a tenor/trumpet duet with both horns leaping.

The Forgotten Ones is dedicated to the struggling people of New Orleans after Hurricane Katrina.

Sánchez' solo is part mourning song, part anthem of hope, gliding like a solitary bird over the floodwaters. *Black Action Figure* was the title opus of Harris' 1999 Blue Note album. In that version there was no trumpet but here the track features a burnished Scott and a gyrating Harris swinging sublimely over López-Nussa's rhythmic undertow and the drums of his brothers Ochoa and Ruy.

There is more solidarity with Africa in Duharte's *Congo*, where the pianist solos at length and Scott burns in with some New Orleans horn that could be surging out of a parade in the streets of his city. Harris' composition *This Too Shall Pass* comes from his first album *A Cloud of Red Dust*, cut in 1997.

Barroetabeña's drums pound and crash behind his vibes as if the two men were longtime confreres rather than instant bandmates. Sánchez adds a loping solo before San Miguel's percussion has its day and Duharte creates a chorus full of inchoate melodies. *Brown Belle Blues* is another Harris tune especially composed for the session. Scott's chorus has the power and assurance of youth, and Harris' mallets let fly in a gleeful solo.

The last note is from López-Nussa, whose piece *La Fiesta Va* ends the album, showing again that these young Cubans are anything but simple accompanists or musical underlings of their three prestigious jazz visitors. As Sánchez surges into his wild and wandering solo, the two López-Nussas, González and Ochoa are with him, steaming in their creative Cuban glory all the way to the final note.

Cuba and the black US are one on this record. A universal music is sounding out with empathy and international brilliance across ninety miles or a million, and that is jazz.

And in the end, no reactionary and anti-human embargo or sanction can withstand it.

October 12th 2011

Ants of History

Adam Fairhall and Paul J Rogers

Second-handed Blues

(ASC Roberts)

Steve Plews' expressive and beautiful black and white photograph of a battered upright piano on the sleeve of the Adam Fairhall and Paul J Rogers' audacious album *Second-handed Blues,* was taken in what Fairhall calls a piano graveyard in a storeroom of a second-hand piano shop in Macclesfield. It emblematises the record, with pioneering southern US jazz and blues sounds reanimated by contemporary jazz musicians working in Manchester — an amalgam across time, a syncretism in defiance of time and geography, brilliantly realised by two Englishmen and their "respectful appropriation of the enduring beauty" forged by the elders.

Fairhall was born in Oldham in 1976 but was brought up in the Cornish village of St Neot, where he learned piano and practised blues and boogie in his school lunchtimes before studying music at Manchester Metropolitan University and Leeds College of Music. His keyboard heroes are some of the great eclectics of jazz piano, including Jackie Byard, who would change from free improv to stride and boogie in one flash of notes, Don Pullen's acrobatic and anthemic pianism and the phenomenal jazz wit of the Japanese virtuoso Aki Takase.

For Fairhall these pianists "play all over jazz history," which is his ambition too. "Once you start listening for connections between eras of jazz," he declares, "you find them everywhere. It's like ants."

Fairhall remembers his practising as a young pianist: "Sometimes I'd play along with a John Lee Hooker record and I felt I was there playing with him in reality." It was such empathy and comradeship across decades that was the conception of *Second-handed Blues.* Fairhall speaks of his partner Rogers' skill as a musician, researcher, historian, sound engineer and "sound sculptor" in bringing samples of field blues, railroad songs, work hollers and vaudeville songs from Library of Congress recordings and obscure vinyl — like the creation of Henry Truvillion in *Saw Dog Man* or Margaret Johnson's *The Katy Line* — and fusing them with Fairhall's ever-welcoming now-times piano.

The opening track is *Ivy Smith,* and it is her voice with its bending and sliding pitches — the voice of the early vaudeville blues — which is one third of the cross-generational trio, with Fairhall's aching blues phrases and accompaniment, and Rogers' crackling atmospherics of the original recording. Next up is *Catfish*, featuring Robert Petway's late 1930s guitar and Fairhall's pounding chords bringing the Mississippi Delta to the Manchester canals, the piano sounding as if it were chiming in both places at once.

The same is true for *Stavin' Chain*, where Rogers' soundscapes come to the fore and Fairhall's keys dig into the earth of two continents. *Ballad of a Backslider* radiates churchiness with the quasi-hymnal sounds of Fairhall's notes and the techno-slurred testimony of a fallen worshipper's unchristian foibles.

The words of the bluesman Bukka White recreate a world of the wayward sanctified as Fairhall's rampant improvisations go further and further out to join him. A song of the railroad is *The Katy Line*, with Fairhall's rumbling left hand configurations emulating the sound of a southern train and Rogers' relentless soundscapes describing its motion.

It precedes a swift siderail diversion into Scott Joplin's *Pine Apple Rag*, which Fairhall plays with a relish in Rogers' own echochamber of dreams. The genesis of the track *Okeehumkee on the Oklawaha* is a Fairhall memory he has of a photograph of a steam paddleboat — Rogers manages to create the sound of the paddlewheel while Fairhall explores the sonic currents.

The duo set out to explore something mysterious and evocative in the *Piney Woods Motel*, a paranormal enigma which leaps musical history and place, while the album's last track *Saw Dog Man* unifies vocal growl with stomping piano, as if the Louisiana blues sound comes blasting into the real lives of Mancunians past and present.

As a consequence of its rare artistry and fusion of realities, *Second-handed Blues* would be an invaluable classroom asset, with every track a research challenge and an opportunity for stimulating musical and cultural knowledge and exploration.

A brave and entirely original work, radiating beauty, skill and daring.

November 1st 2011

Another Jazz Journey

Arun Ghosh

Northern Namaste/Primal Odyssey

(Comci)

The first two albums of the young clarinettist Arun Ghosh — seething as they do with the urban joys and tensions of Mancunian life — also inform deeper provenances. As he puts them: "Concieved in Calcutta, bred in Bolton, matured in Manchester and now living in London." Another jazz journey, another telling migration of music.

Ghosh grew up playing recorder and piano at his school in Bury. "When I used to play classical music I was always told to stand still," he quips, but it was hearing Courtney Pine playing at a Free Nelson Mandela concert more than twenty years ago that started him moving towards a clarinet — not a now-times fashionable jazz instrument. When he turned to jazz he explored his heritage of Indian music as "a means to get a different sound for improvisation, a new approach, and it just kind of resonated with me. I found Indian scales and wrote compositions with that. I could always hear the drum parts in it."

And the tabla pulsates in the studio air of *Northern Namaste*, recorded in 2007-08. "Namaste means welcome in Sanskrit, and its sounds — full of optimism, sociability and love — enfold the listener's ears like few other musics," he says. Ghosh's clarinet filigrees like that of the New Orleans pioneer Jimmy Noone in the opener *Aurora*, but it is all Bengal in the sheer riverine beauty of Tagore's tune *O Amar Desher Mati*.

During Ghosh's sublime swirls and cadences of *Uterine* I was also hearing Ellington's great clarinettist Barney Bigard rising from the full orchestral horns, while *Longsight Lagoon*, with Ghosh's lower phrasing, reminded me of a poem called *My Longsight Story* by a thirteen-year-old Ummar Naeem, where he tells of his Manchester neighbourhood: "Turned into the best of places / where people came together / with love and care and a high assertiveness."

Is Ghosh telling a similar Longsight story with its relentless beat, chiming piano and quivering horn over a defiant riff?

The strings-backed tenderness of *Come Closer*, with Corey Mwamba's lyrical vibes summation, contracts with the quizzical *Where Shall I Live Now?* Here, as in many of the themes, Ghosh double tracks himself on a piano. The album concludes with the traditional Bengali tune *Greenhouse*, where Myke Wilson's pounding drums and Idris Rahman's tenor saxophone give extra verve and authority to the surge of the sound.

Whereas *Northern Namaste* used different variations of musicians on each track, Ghosh's second album *Primal Odyssey* is the work of a regular quintet, with bass clarinettist Shabaka Hutchings, drummer Pat Illingworth and bassist Liran Donin. Ghosh called this group the Horn E Bass Quintet, and continued to build his jazz from the melodies of ancient raags and taals while replacing the tabla with bass and drums.

There is immediately a much more powerful harmonic three-horn sound to the album's opening track *Caliban's Revenge*, where Ghosh's clarinet rises transcendentally out of the ensemble. Rahman and Hutchings both have gravelly choruses on *Unravel*, before Ghosh soars away, and the blues-soaked undertow of *Yerma* echoes the world of Lorca's tragic Spanish heroine.

The rebelliousness and love of freedom of Palestinian youth is celebrated in *Intifada*, where Donin's marching bass grounds the theme and the two clarinets whirl high and low, ever-reaching, never silenced. Ghosh's serene notes hover over Illingworth's slow, rhythmic drums all through *Eros*, while in *Damascus* the uplifting, joyous sounds with all horns burning is a message of unleashed hope to those fighting tyranny and nepotism in Syria. All from a recording studio in Worcestershire.

And the horn harmonies of the album's final track *Nocturne* (Chandra Dhun) have an Ellingtonian melodic beauty not easily forgotten.

Hearing Ghosh's Bolton clarinet played through its Bengali currents with British and Caribbean bandmates in *Primal Odyssey* reminds me of the sound of the New Orleans master Louis Cottrell, whom I heard play in an echoey wooden church hall in the Crescent City over forty years ago, in the sweat and humidity of a Delta evening — a naked, pure reed eloquence, close enough to birdsong.

The daring hybridity of jazz's syncretic and internationalist message peals out of his notes and takes the music further down the road of human unity.

January 13th 2012

Trio-X Mark the Spot

Trio-X

Journey / The Sugar Hill Suite / Moods: Playing with the Elements
(CIMP)

The free improvising threesome Trio-X are regular visitors to The Spirit Room, the unique recording studio of CIMP records at Rossie, a rural venue in New York State which records music with its full integrity and honesty — gimmickless, pure and authentic, "capturing the full dynamic range one would experience at a live concert."

There could be no better surroundings to put into perpetuity the drums of Philadelphian Jay Rosen, the bass of New Yorker Dominic Duval and the multiple horns of Joe McPhee, born in Miami in 1939.

Every sound is there, every moment's evidence and beauty, nothing altered, nothing falsified. "Life is our rehearsal and its experiences infuse the stories we tell, colours the sounds we paint and informs the sculptures we construct. Each improvisation takes on its life and persona — if you will — from the very first sounds, without predetermination." Such is the music of Trio-X as defined by its members and co-operators.

February 2003 gave rise to the Trio-X session which produced their first album for CIMP, called *Journey*.

Duval's bass dances and Rosen's drums roll before McPhee's tenor wails in on the opener *That Was / This Is*. The interaction mesmerises the ears, with all the traditional functions of each instrument, rhythm, beat, the horn's leadership and melodic navigation all set aside for new collective discovery.

The album's title improvisation is a search for sonic structure and each musician both leads and is led through sorrow, consciousness and joy in life's holistic trek.

The rhythm of Rosen's drums in *Jaywalking* and McPhee's horn howls are definitely urban and *Blue Moves* with McPhee on alto and its contrasts of volume and quietude sound perfectly poised in The Spirit Room. It is Duval's brilliant, plunging hands that first create the track called *Autograph* and McPhee sounds as if he is confessing.

Not so in the astonishing *Everything in Nothin Flat*, where the trio burst into riotous life and McPhee's caustic tenor lets fly in raging fury. Yet this journey ends in tradition and *Amazing Grace*, played as an anthem for all who have shared love, respect, knowledge and help — the summation of the American odyssey.

Trio-X reassembled in The Spirit Room in October 2004 to record *The Sugar Hill Suite*, a "homage to the history, inspiration and promise of Harlem," and a sense of immense pride and dedication to the achievement of what Harlem means to US life comes bleeding out in the trio's every note.

Harlem up from the South, as in the pain and solitude of *Sometimes I Feel Like a Motherless Child*, which partly evaporated in the brilliant solidarity black Harlemites experienced in the heyday of their culture.

Duval's bass beginning searches for that transformation before McPhee enters with the melody — dirge-like yet beautiful in its transcendence. Or Harlem meaning Ellington and, the Duke's own *Drop Me Off in Harlem*, which the trio make a now-times story, three griots of music, two of whom are white, making a great epoch of black history as if it were today or tomorrow.

The seventeen minutes of the title suite express the trio's unified artistry and that three musicians can become a free orchestra. And then straight on to the jazz genius of succeeding generations to the Harlem flowering — Thelonious Monk, born in Rocky Mount, North Carolina, in 1917 who became a boyhood arrivant to New York, and Indianapolis-born Freddie Hubbard, who came to the Apple in 1958 as a twenty-year-old budding trumpeter.

Monk's pianism is celebrated in McPhee's *Monk's Waltz*, in typical angular Monkish surprise and the trio play Hubbard's *Little Sunflower*, introduced by some sublime solo bass by Duval, as a rhapsody for young Harlemites. The tradition of the early migrants to the black urban village is powerfully evoked in the trio's finale *Goin' Home* — home to a new home, melodised with a moving serenity by McPhee's warming tenor horn.

The next day the trio were back in The Spirit Room to cut another album, *Moods: Playing with the Elements*, and quite a summation it is, until the next time. Mixed into more steps on the journey from *Sienna Sun* with some questing McPhee and *Wegatchie Run* where his tenor gyrates in creative frenzy, are bebop's favourite ballad, *Stella By Starlight*, Ornette Coleman's *Lovely Woman*, and McPhee with pocket trumpet on *In Evidence* and Rosen's crashing drums.

But this is 2004 and US and British armies are in Iraq, marauding in places like Fallujah, Basra and Abu Ghraib. *A Valentine in the Fog of War* is Trio-X's testimony to a Bush and Blair-led war-torn era and rattling percussion, a precious bass bloodline and an insurgent horn with traces of *My Funny Valentine*, leave their evidence in a small country room collecting every sound, every sonic human moment.

January 25 2012

A Penine Horn

Nat Birchall

Sacred Dimension (Godwana)
World Without Form (Sound Soul and Spirit)

The Lancashire-born tenor saxophonist Nat Birchall lives in a Pennine town and the spirit of the peaks and moorlands pours from his horn, a mixture of the sounds of hillside birdsong, of upland winds in the pines, of the rain striking the gritstone, of the streams rushing down the slopes.

It is all there in a powerful amalgam, in the thickness and depth of his sound. Spiritual yes, but solidly elemental too.

Birchall has absorbed the sound of his antecedents, particularly the profound and loving message of Coltrane, but when you hear his sextet on the 2011 album *Sacred Dimension* you realise a special northern England quality to their sound, a timbre which is deeply humane yet bursting with the natural world in the resonance of Rachael Gladwin's ancestral harpsong, in the living current of Corey Mwamba's vibes and in the chiming, quasi-orchestral notes of his long-time piano colleague Adam Fairhall.

The opener is called *Ancient World* and what we hear from Birchall's soprano saxophone is that ancient world around him, of old and deserted quarries, aged pathways, the endless miles of dry stone walls, abandoned piles of millstones, the evidence of a long-historied northern peakside people whose stories teem from his horn, from Mwamba's unrelenting solo strikes, Gladwin and Fairhall in close harmony, bassist Nick Blacka's pulsing beat and Andy Hay's roaring drums, called by Birchall a "force of nature," which is what they certainly are.

The essence of pure melodism is at the centre of the title track, with Birchall's pastoral tenor, Hay's loping percussion and Fairhall's chiming chords, almost continuing into another sphere with Gladwin's more spiky and penetrative harpnotes. In *Dance of the Mystics* the rich, tumbling cadences of Birchall's tenor fall from the tors of his own peaks of sound above Blacka's grounding bass, and through *Peace in Nineveh*, the lyrical simplicity of melody is Birchall's soprano ringing down the Hope Valley and across Edale. Fairhall picks up the air, then Mwamba in a beautifully serene vibes chorus.

Sacred Dimension is an enduring album of mountainous sonic shape, but to me Birchall's new recording, called enigmatically *World Without Form*, is even more wondrous and, as yet, his finest achievement. Perhaps this is so because it is his first album on his own label, but more so because he and his bandmates have never sounded so together, so much in unity. Also, on five tracks there are two drummers, with the Leeds veteran free drummer Paul Hession playing on all tracks and Hay added on five. And Jon Thorne joins Blacka with another bass on three tracks. So the album holds quite an undertow, and the music seethes below the horn, vibes and piano.

The midway track is called *Divine Harmony* and it is eight minutes of astonishing sound. Birchall begins like a Coltrane of the Derbyshire peaks, playing with huge poise and authority, Mwamba's powerful chorus follows, then Fairhall's riveting keyboard runs and beneath them the transpennine drums of Hession and Hay and the dancing basses of Blacka and Thorne create a benevolent thunder, before Birchall's final hymnal chorus completes the miracle and puts into perpetuity a collective sound of rare beauty.

Speak To Us of Love follows, close to a ballad and full of melody, for Birchall is a tunemaker too. Impassioned gentleness comes in succession from Birchall, Fairhall and Mwamba. A classical narrative is evoked in *Return to Ithaca* with the double drums and basses sounding as if he were coming home at last. Birchall's soprano gyrates and sings like a giant bird, and when he reverts to tenor for *Principle of Beauty* it is as if every new note is a fresh discovery, as it is for all his confrères too.

World Without Form is an intriguing album title, for it is the artists of eyes, words, senses and sounds who in their own unique ways seek to render to that world human shape, form and progress. As a listener you hear this happening throughout this record from the title track onwards. *Through the Black Ark* where Birchall's tenor dances over the rhythmic pulse of the two drummers, then gives way to the restless creative power of Mwamba's mallets and Fairhall's intense sonic pictures.

This album is British jazz at its most inventive, surprising and unexpected, a record made in a Salford hall, created by a middle-aged saxophonist born in a village near Blackburn, who with his northern friends has forged a work of exceptional power and beauty which is true art and a better world in formation.

Section 2: Live Reviews

Incendiary Meeting by the Thames

Archie Shepp and Andrew Hill

Queen Elizabeth Hall, London SE1

Here was a stateside union made on the south bank of the Thames. It seemed incredible that Archie Shepp and Andrew Hill, two incendiary jazzmen and post-bop pioneers of the 1960s and beyond, had never met before, let alone played together. Yet here they were, brought together by a Joyful Sound concert in the salubrious surroundings of the Queen Elizabeth Hall.

Shepp, jazz radical and subversive, saxophone comrade of John Coltrane, master of the rasping reed and the breathy, adenoidal fury of his classic Impulse albums of the 1960s, and now the supreme eclectic and interpreter of blues, ballads, spirituals, Ellington, Parker and anything beyond and between.

Hill, Haiti-born and Chicago-bred, with a rhythm and blues apprenticeship overlaid on a Caribbean-grounded jazz vision, collaborator with the great Eric Dolphy on the momentous Blue Note album *Point of Departure* and maker of other hugely influential recordings like *Black Fire* and *Judgement!* during the 60s. He has been underestimated and underexposed, yet, for four decades, has burnt a flame in the all-but-forgotten margins of jazz. It was a meeting fuelled by elegy. Two oldish and brilliant men of huge musical originality, looking back and around together, fusing their disparate imaginations.

Shepp introduced Charlie Parker's *Mohawk*, offering a tribute to the revolution in Parker's sax. "He liberated blacks from rustic values," he declared, before the duo moved into a slow, searing, bluesy version of the tune.

Hill's sombre, chiming piano wept through a moving *Good Morning Heartache*, with Shepp's hoarse, spluttering tenor coughing up strained, terrifying and twistedly joyous tears, like the Billie Holiday voice of her final years. His powerful crying coda concluded a sparking of the memory of an iconic jazz woman.

In *Mama Rose*, Shepp's tribute to his Florida grandmother, he repeats the vocal assertion of the US peoples in all their cities, shouting: "We want a change!" Lines such as "Take this ex-cannibal's kiss and turn it into a revolution," accompanied by Hill's sombre and noble notes, relit an old fire, never doused. Yet, unusually, despite the haunting invocation of memory, loss and pain of the final tune, Billy Strayhorn's *My Little Brown Book*, it was the duo's playing of their very first selection that stayed in the memory.

It was the eponymous *Steam*, named after a young cousin of Shepp, killed in a Philadelphia street fight in the 60s when only a teenager. The waste of youthful life came through Shepp's lamenting soprano and Hill's aching piano sounded like a multivoiced church bell.

I thought of all the young lives lost to futile urban violence — of Stephen Lawrence, Ricky Reel, Maurice Bishop's teenage son Vladimir, stabbed to death in a Toronto gangfight and of the two young men knifed and thrown from Hungerford Bridge into the Thames, just splashing distance behind the riverside venue where Hill and Shepp poured out their sadness and hope in the universal language of jazz.

Well met indeed and an encounter that those there will not easily forget.

April 29th 2000

Mosaic of Sounds

George Coleman and Julian Joseph

Wigmore Hall, London W1

The Memphis tenor saxophone of the veteran George Coleman blew shudders into the placid walls of the Wigmore Hall last week and the blues eased their way between the soft seats and moved below the skins of all who were listening.

Coleman is a giant jazzman — underestimated, under-recorded, but a magnificent musician and collaborator with BB King, Miles Davis and Max Roach. And here was an unusual context too. As pianist Julian Joseph introduced his sidemen, Adam Salkeld clutched his guitar like a nervous sixth former about to play at his first school dance while bassist Orlando le Fleming stood there beaming in neat casual gear as if he were modelling for Top Man.

But they played like the angels in the heavenly mosaic above the Wigmore stage. When Joseph introduced Benny Golson's *Blues March*, a Jazz Messengers standby, famously grounded by Art Blakey's thunderous drums, you wondered how this drummerless group would cope. But with Joseph's percussive chimes and speed-changes, le Fleming's walking bass and Salkeld's bluesy solo, a ripe context was created for Coleman's passionate surges of notes and dazzling runs.

His tender playing on Nat King Cole's *You're Looking at Me* saw the old master and the young black London pianist working within the closest of empathies. Coleman blew a pretty phrase: Joseph emulated it, creating the cue for the next Coleman response. As the saxophonist concluded his final coda, it had all the loving sound and reassurance of a lullaby. Joseph is a hard-striking, highly rhythmic pianist capable of sudden moves into a virtually orchestral sound. On Coleman's *Blondie's Waltz*, dedicated to his wife, Joseph created a complexity of feeling from a simplicity of tightly-struck notes which shadowed the composer's melodic beauty.

His other composition, *Uncle Frank*, shows his listeners that this uncle was definitely from the islands. Its calypso base, close to the echoes of *Brown-skin Gal*, became a saxophone romp with a joy fixed somewhere between Trinidad and Tennessee.

Likewise, there were soundings of *All The Things You Are* in Coleman's fluid playing of *You Mean So Much To Me*, his saxophone so close, so much a part of his voice that the notes were as words themselves, the true poetry of jazz.

Between Coleman and Joseph was a musical union of the black jazz traditions of two arms of the diaspora. As the evening finished with

Joseph's composition, *Ray's Blues*, his own powerful blues piano suddenly became a match for his partner's South-soaked saxophone, and invoked a fusion that had been boiling up all through the performance in this most unlikely, yet curiously sympathetic, of jazz venues.

May 6th 2000

George Coleman

Night of the Foursome

The Bobby Watson Quartet

Ronnie Scott's, London W1

Bobby Watson, the 47-year-old from Charlie Parker's home town of Kansas City, is the prime alto saxophonist of his generation.

He was musical director of Art Blakey's Jazz Messengers of twenty years ago, in that stellar version that included Wynton Marsalis, James Williams and Billy Pierce as well as Blakey and Watson. His later albums for Red Records and Evidence included the gorgeous all-solo effort *This Little Light of Mine* and the epochal *Love Remains*, recorded with two members of his current quartet, pianist John Hicks and bass man Curtis Lundy.

Watson's playing holds within it the whole history of the alto saxophone in jazz. Johnny Hodges's soaring notes and melodic finesse are there, with Parker's blues and instant changes and Ornette Coleman's capriciousness of sound and audacity. Yet he achieves this and more. It is as if, somehow, inside him are twice the body's resources of breath, accumulating tall spirals of notes like great towers of sound, empowering all his invention and daring.

Perhaps it is because Ronnie Scott's is so small that its very intimacy privileges and presses the lucky listener to watch the musicians so closely. You become as a participant, sharing the union fused by these extraordinary musicians. And this was a night not simply of luminous individuals — although each is a leader, composer and virtuoso of their own instrument.

It was, above all, a night of the quartet, the binding together of four — each one playing for the others, inside each other's music as well as their own. Hicks from Atlanta, picking out his musical sentences — jagged, Monk-like, each one as a conscious thought-pattern, as stone by stone, each note attains a shape within a solo. Leaning over his keys, and sideways at acute angles to the stage floor, the most expressive shoulders and forearms in jazz.

Lundy, Watson's old friend and musical partner at the University of Miami, embracing his big-boned bass as if it were another live bandmate and the closest of comrades, plucking its nerve-strings and tendons or using his bow to produce a sombre and grandiose beauty in his own melody *No One Needs to Know*.

The unforced, unsweating, lyrical drumming of Victor Lewis from Arizona, by turns quiescent, modest and supportive in his accompaniments, then pounding into his own *Hey, It's Me You're Talking To*, the engine of his percussive power changing from the delicate to the sublime. And meshed with it all, Watson's saxophone, its bell gleaming like Aztec gold under Scott's pierced spotlights, its sounds as rich and ancestral.

May 13th 2000

In the Heat of the Night

Kenny Garrett Quartet

Pizza Express, London SW1

A sizzling Soho night and you'd think that the temperature was intense enough that you needed no more heat — until you walked down the basement steps of the Pizza Express.

It came in ever more burning licks with Kenny Garrett and his Quartet.

You look at and hear Garrett and his alto and soprano saxophones. He prowls the stage area, bending and curling his body around his instrument while he surges into *Two Down and One Across* or the *Delta Valley Blues*, swaying between bass and drums as if his breath and muscles are keeping a new rendezvous with every note. In a winding, serpentine version of his own *Charlie Brown Goes to South Africa* he finds a fusion of passion and playfulness. The simple, percussive theme gave him the map of a journey of discovery to reach the people of the great continent of music and its many diasporas, quoting Sonny Rollins, edging toward calypso and salsa and coming back to phrases that could have soared from the Cape Town heart of Abdullah Ibrahim.

Garrett is forty now and not such a young lion as he was in the days when he played hot from Detroit in some of the final bands of Miles Davis. Yet his quartet radiated a sense of unquenchable youth. Carlos McKinney, a roaring pianist, softened his touch to interplay some loving phrases with Garrett on the restrained and beautiful *Spanish Go Round* which borrowed quarter and half choruses from *Body and Soul* with no feeling of theft.

McKinney's very own chiming, bell-like chords and furious keyboard intensity, clumping his palms down on the notes to match Garrett's passionate soprano cries on the *Delta Valley Blues*, made a very particular piano sound indeed. But it was a furious rendition of Coltrane's *Giant Steps* which expressed this quartet's sheer physicality of sound. As Garrett pounded into the master's cadences, making every note a step of discovery, he pointed his instrument and fired his phrases toward the young Marcus Baylor on the drums. He responded with a conflagration of sound, his sticks whirling with so much speed that their movement in his hands became fans of light.

And below it all — placidness personified — was the incessant bass of Nat Reeves, every founding note accompanied by a nod of the head, beneath but not submerged, holding the bass-ment with power, modesty and aplomb.

Heat generating heat. And as these four musicians reached for their towels between numbers, you knew that their music, like their sweat, ran deep and real inside them.

May 27th 2000

A Ferocious Beauty

The Mingus Big Band

Ronnie Scott's, London W1

A fusion of disciplined orchestration and ensemble playing, with burning solo work shooting from the musical brilliance of its fourteen-member composition — the Mingus Big Band is in town again.

From the first blasting notes of *Jump Monk* and the searing trumpet work of Philip Harper and Kenny Rampton — with the musicians' occasional frantic jostling to find room to physically co-exist, draw their trombones or find some precious elbow room on Ronnie's tiny stage — the spirit of cramped but bursting freedom roars out of the programme of Charles Mingus creations.

In *Haitian Fight Song*, Russian Boris Kozlov's cavernous bass solo opening recalls Mingus's sublime sound, followed by leader Alex Foster's spiky soprano sax. But suddenly you realise that it is the trombone section that propels this band with its grounding, unremitting foundation. Jamal Haynes's guttural notes, Conrad Herwig's melodic, Jimmy Knepper-like solos and the grounding, elemental depth of Earl McIntyre's bass trombone, shaking the airspace in fusion with Gary Smulyan's baritone sax.

With the energetic Foster jumping in and out of his seat in the saxophone section, signalling solos and numbering choruses, waving his limbs like an impassioned bookie at Kempton Park, Mingus's tribute to Toussaint L'Ouverture and the Haitian people's struggle ends with third trumpeter Alex Sipiagin's lyrical and shapely solo, beautifully crafted and flighted. The band's ensemble beauty, fierce brass and the rolling, mysterious blues piano of David Kikoski fronted by the contrasting tenderness of John Stubblefield's flute, flows from the restrained phrases of *Children's Hour of Dreams.*

Philip Harper takes a self-mocking vocal in *Baby Take a Chance With Me*, followed by a brief gem from altoist Michael Shim, but Mingus's huge power and radicalism are expressed in the full-band eloquence of his cold-war classic, *O Lord, Don't Let Them Drop that Atomic Bomb On Me.*

Beginning with Haynes's vocal chorus and a growling trombone solo, a muted series of choruses on wa-wa mute from Rampton with stirring Ellingtonian overtones of Cootie Wiliams or Rex Stewart to the accompaniment of hoots, laughter, urging and leg-pulling from the other players, then suddenly it is John Stubblefield's moment. Roaring, foaming, screaming, glass-shattering sounds and incandescent notes above a full ensemble — and you wonder if Ronnie's small and shallow chamber can take any more of this ferocious beauty as Soho is set on tenor-saxophone fire by this most accomplished and furious playing.

It is a sound that is essential and glorious — and not often heard. Mingus's revolutionary genius lives, broods and sours again in every note. You'll regret it if you miss it.

Ends tonight.

July 15th 2000

Bringing it All Back Home

David Murray Octet

Queen Elizabeth Hall, London

David Murray, the tenor saxophonist from Berkeley, California, is one of the most complete and extravagant jazz musicians of our age. Now in his mid-forties, he has behind him an astonishing range of achievement and a tree of recordings. From his early years with Sunny Murray, James Blood Ulmer, Jack DeJohnette and the World Saxophone Quartet to leading his own quartet, octet and big band, Murray is usually classified as an avant-gardist, yet his playing reveals a whole life of influences.

His CD *Saxmen* shows him emulating the genius of tenor maestros from Coleman Hawkins to John Coltrane, from Lester Young and Charlie Parker to Sonny Rollins and Sonny Stitt. It is as if he has absorbed them all and plays from their combined brilliance.

At the Queen Elizabeth Hall, he came with his latest octet — seven men and a woman, fusing the decades of experience of altoist James Spaulding, a hero of both the bop and post-bop eras, and the youth of pianist Lafayette Gilchrist and trombonist Sarah Morrow.

The concert was to be a tribute to Coltrane, but, as the night surged into *Lazy Bird*, it seemed to be much more. Coltrane's works they all were, and Murray's introduction to them stressed 'Trane's spirituality, but they were played full pelt, teeming with bop rhythms and pace, with the musicians lining up for their solos, much in the manner of a free-blowing jam session.

Murray set the standard with the awesome energy of his blowing and a fullness of pumping, engine-like sound that reminded you of the great Hawk. His sudden mutations of notes and miraculous instant shifts from low to high register and his deft control that moved his sound from a cavernous boom to a high-pitched squeak in adjacent notes astonished the ears.

In *The Crossing*, Morrow played a long, dexterous trombone solo that held within its shape moments both of gruff drama and poignant sadness. Trumpeter Nathan Greenlove's horn sang and wailed and Murray, now on bass clarinet, spat through his reed to give a sonorous version of the strange, elastic twanging sound that the New Orleans clarinettist Joe Darensbourg made when he played with Kid Ory.

Spaulding climaxed the piece with a spiralling high-note finish. There are few saxophonists who can match Murray's formidable musicianship and Spaulding is certainly one of them. His long life in jazz was told in every note of his soaring alto, lucid and audacious in front of the other riffing horns, which gave the impression of the brass and reed sections of a much larger band.

An uproarious jam (including a truculent solo by bassist Jaribu Shahid) led into Murray playing *Acknowledgement* from Coltrane's *A Love Supreme.*

We'll never see Coltrane again, but Murray has the technique and empathy, perhaps more than any other, to move closest to him. And his screeching, loving, tender, wrathful and ecstatic horn brought back the glory of Coltrane, in itself an achievement quite immeasurable and deeply moving.

December 16th 2000

Healing the Wounds of Empire

Abdullah Ibrahim and Ekaya

Canary Wharf

This is the beautiful and deep music of Africa played with passion, dignity and brilliance on the very landfall where the profits from the African slave trade and the sugar plantations were hauled into London to help to build the industrial revolution. In the basin of the West India Dock now towers Canary Wharf. Below its foundations, there is still the sickly stench of burnt molasses and the black blood that was set aflow to produce it. Below this eastern adjunct of the City of London are the bones of the Middle Passage. Abdullah Ibrahim consecrated them again through the haunting sound of his first melody.

As the growling Stafford Hunter sounded dirge-like notes from his muted trombone, Ibrahim chanted names, places and associations as if he were invoking the identities of every African man or woman who had made that most terrible of voyages. And Jean Toussaint, a Caribbean man of St Thomas in the Virgin Islands, played a triumphant, roaring tenor saxophone solo, as if this venue of such historical meaning was no longer to be accursed, but to be reclaimed.

Ibrahim calls his group of musicians Ekaya — the word means "home." As they moved from one sublime melody to another, with Ibrahim's solo piano forming the transitions, each musician revealed the home of his sound.

There is baritonist James Stewart and his lush notes that made you think of the voice of a Robeson, the soaring solo work of alto-saxophonist Horace Alexander Young, Belden Bullock's grounding and relentless bass and the intermittent light touch of drummer George Johnson — his brushes sound as soft as ripe cashew fruit as he answered Ibrahim's own expressive keyboard phrases.

During the second set, it was as if the pianist was celebrating his own musical heroes — the tribute to Monk, for example, emerged through a finely toned version of *Round Midnight*, featuring Toussaint's profound and lonely tenor notes. But it was toward Duke Ellington that the most respectful nod was made.

When Ibrahim exiled himself from South Africa in 1962 in the dreadful wake of Sharpeville, he travelled with his singer wife Sathima to Switzerland, finding work in a Zurich club. The travelling Ellington went to hear him and offered both husband and wife the opportunity to record their first European albums. And more than a gasp of Ellington's spirit has stayed with Ibrahim.

As Stewart emulated Ellingtonian baritonist Harry Carney's solo flight of *Sophisticated Lady* with a quivering lyricism and Hunter blew a darkly pitched, haunting version of *Mood Indigo*, the greatest jazz orchestra man of them all seemed to be close again. Young pitched in with a lucid solo version of Ibrahim's own elevated melody *The Wedding*, sounding like a doubly rhapsodic Johnny Hodges, his horn bending respectfully over the master's piano.

This is music that is, once heard and internalised, never forgotten, always reprised in the mind and the blood. And the performers taking back the territory of exploitation with the sheer beauty and power of their sound.

Suddenly Canary Wharf belonged to Africa, belonged to the struggling humans of the Americas, belonged to the world.

November 8th 2000

Blowing with the Voice of Millions

Hugh Masekela

Ronnie Scott's, London W1

It is now musical folklore. Father Trevor Huddleston gave the young boy Hugh Masekela his first trumpet in the Johannesburg suburb of Sophiatown, before the apartheid bulldozers crushed it into rubble — destroying a unique culture as well as the life-genius of many. The young trumpeter became a star turn of the legendary Huddleston Jazz Band.

Masekela went on with his trumpet — struggling, achieving, inspiring. At the age of twenty, he played with the luminous Jazz Epistles alongside Abdullah Ibrahim (then, Dollar Brand) and altoist Kippie Moeketsi, before leaving South Africa in 1961 and sending out his brassy notes and dreams of freedom from the US. Musicians from Dizzy Gillespie to Yehudi Menuhin to Thelonious Monk, Johnny Dankworth and Cannonball Adderley combined to secure him a scholarship at the Manhattan School of Music. A string of popular hits followed from 1968, beginning with *Grazing in the Grass.*

Sixty-one now and still blowing with a shattering power and creative force at Ronnie Scott's through the lucid bell of his flugelhorn, he embodies those years of isolation while his music throbs with the revolutionary hopes of a resurgent Africa. He comes on stage singing — gruffly, rawly, with resonance and vibration, ringing with the real earth-bound and city-bound life of his people.

His trumpet sound catches the same phraseology, essentially vocal, unpredictable, storytelling and insistent — with a narrative to unfold that cannot be blocked. Standing with a cowbell, clanging it repeatedly, he tells the story of "all those people of unskilled labour in cheap labour pools all over the world building tunnels, skyscrapers, harbours and highways. All those who work in the mines, who generate the millions which never hover over their dinner tables."

He depicts the *stimela* "coal train" bringing them to South Africa from Namibia, Malawi, Angola, Mozambique, the contract labourers who work sixteen hours a day "deep, deep, deep, digging for that shiny mighty, evasive stone." He pictures them in their forlorn hostels and barracks, cursing the train that ever brought them to Johannesburg. His voice, as brass itself, makes the terrifying sound of this hellish locomotive — screeching, roaring, hissing, chirping, screaming, booming, whistling, yelling.

Then a passionate, breathy, horn solo that is racked with Gillespie-type runs, high notes, bent notes, screeches and moans.

This is an astonishing performance and nothing could illustrate with huger power the roots of his music and the origins of South African jazz.

This is jazz with its own principles, tempos, sounds and realities, that has been created on the margins where the countryman enters the city, where the migrant becomes the urban sojourner, where metropolis pushes out to dustlands and the bush — where the voice becomes brass and brass becomes the voice.

Masekela's sound and passion embody a whole human process. Now leading a quintet, it is his partnership with John Selolwane which earths Masekela's soaring sound.

Playing guitar with the aching testimony of a southern electric bluesman, Selolwane trades musical phrases and sentences with the flugelhorn. It's as if the two musicians were telling their lives to each other in a city-edge shebeen, pouring out their notes as authentic, living experience.

For, in the cave of Masekela's horn are the dreams of Africa as well as its history. His is a horn of empathy as well as aspiration and, from its innards, comes the hopes and struggles too of Chris Hani and Joe Slovo, Ruth First, Steve Biko and Bram Fischer, Kotane, Mandela, Huddleston, Miriam Makeba and a whole seething continent of humans.

His is a music which gives a note to us all. So, don't be waylaid. Get to Ronnie's before December 2.

November 25th 2000

A Remembrance of Things Present

Junior Mance Trio

Blackheath Halls

Imagine a suburban front room in the late 50s. A group of teenage boys are clustered around the host's portable Dansette record player. EP sleeves are scattered over the carpet. But they're not listening to Elvis, Buddy Holly or the Everly Brothers. On the turntable are the jazz sounds of Art Blakey, Miles Davis and Charlie Parker. One of the listeners puts on Lester Young and the tenor saxophone of the "Prez" filters through the room, filling every square inch of stale Romford air.

Was it *Three Little Words*, *Lester Leaps In* or *Let's Fall in Love*? The bluesy, bouncy piano sounds behind the tenor enrich the melody even more sublimely.

"Hey, who's the pianist?" exclaims one of the young groovers, still in his school blazer and grey pullover. His friend grabs hold of one of the strewn sleeves and consults the personnel notes. "It's Junior Mance," he declares. That was this reviewer's introduction to the seventy-two-year-old Chicagoan pianist playing at the Blackheath Halls as if he were still in his starry prime.

Having been tenorist Gene Ammons's accompanist in the mid-1940s, Mance went on to play and record with Young, Gillespie, Dinah Washington, the Cannonball Adderley Quartet and he was always recognised for the way in which he fused bebop rhythms, pace and harmonies with the strongest of blues foundations.

So Junior Mance has quite a lineage, now playing with two young British stalwarts — bassist Andy Cleyndert and drummer Steve Brown — who, both smiling and glowing, radiate a kind of wonder at being there.

Mance invents long, unaccompanied intros to all the tunes that he plays. Starting off with *Falling in Love With Love* and dashing lightning runs all over the keyboard, his blues sound is always discernible, subliminal, even through such velocity of the ivories.

Short, white-bearded, bespectacled with a quiet and modest manner, Mance came to the jazz age in a Chicago teeming with migrated southern bluesmen and it is as if that Delta tradition seeps out of his every note. He plays Benny Golson's *Whisper Not* as a blues, with an indelible sense of sadness and yearning. Yet, when he introduces himself as "the late Junior Mance," you know that you will rarely hear such jazz piano that is so vitally alive.

His versions of Ellington — *In a Sentimental Mood*, for example — sound almost orchestral, but still exude that blues tinge, as if no matter how sophisticated the tune, it still stays as the defining sound of his playing, making every melody cry. The cascades of blue notes were wrung too from the Duke's *Single Petal of a Rose*, full of human tears.

Monk's *Rhythm-A-Ning* is taken at breakneck speed, with some deft drumming for the empathetic and closely listening Brown. And Nat Adderley's *Work Song* has a boogie-woogie uplift which rises from Mance's bluesy notes. Cleyndert adds an intricately booming solo and, with Brown affixing a cymbal to the tip of his hi-hat, the performance suddenly takes on a churchy, revivalist sound.

And for this listener, reveries of the "Prez" come back to play on that stage, gliding his notes even there in the posh, rarefied enclave of Blackheath, somewhere in south-east London.

December 9th 2000

The Dane and the Deltaman

Mulgrew Miller and Niels-Henning Ørsted Pederson

Ronnie Scott's, London W1

A jazz meeting of Greenwood, Mississippi and Ørsted, Denmark in a crepuscular room in Frith Street, Soho. In other words, the duo of pianist Mulgrew Miller and bassist Niels-Henning Pederson at Ronnie Scott's.

Miller is an ex-gospel and rhythm-and-blues man who played with Art Blakey, Woody Shaw and Tony Williams as well as having a spell with the Ellington orchestra. The Delta is never far from his blues-soaked notes, and, from the first phrases of *Whisper Not*, by another ex-Jazz Messenger Benny Golson, you know of Miller's provenance.

Niels-Henning Ørsted Pederson

Pederson is a virtuoso bassist, one of the world leaders on his instrument. Having made his first records in Denmark as a fourteen-year-old prodigy — he was a teenage starter with a sojourning Albert Ayler — and being compelled merely by his age to turn down an offer to join the Count Basie Orchestra, his youth was spent accompanying the great visiting jazzmen who played at Copenhagen's Montmartre Club. Rollins, Lateef, Dexter Gordon, Don Byas, Ben Webster and even the fading Bud Powell all passed through and played with Pederson or NHOP, as he is familiarly known. Since then, years touring with Oscar Peterson and every conceivable jazz horn has made him a legend in Scandinavia of a music born in the Southlands.

As these two men, black and white, played as one, their eyes fastened upon one other, the Dane and the Deltaman made each phrase of melody and riff a jazz discovery, from *Mood Indigo* to *Oleo*.

Playing as much for each other as for their wider listeners, touching each other's musical genius with the most surprising and novel exchanges, the lucid, aching blues themes of Miller moved from *Old Folks* to *Take the "A" Train* as if they were parts of a whole.

The quicksilvered fingers of Pederson, his deeper than deep bass lines cascading into every waiting ear, moved forwards and backwards from Ellington to Bach as if the Americas and Europe were the same great continent and music was music anywhere. How close is Bach to the blues, and the blues to Bach!

This was a presentation of deep musical empathy, rare and blessed. Two men born in such worldspread places combining sounds so different, yet playing as one, while the unflinching contact of the eyes affirmed the fusion of the notes.

If you want an illustration of the one world of jazz and how its disparate energies join in the concentration of musical beauty, go no further tonight than Ronnie Scott's London grotto of sound.

April 1st 2000

Four Feet Away

Geri Allen

Pizza Express, London W1

To sit about four feet away from the miraculous piano hands of Geri Allen while she plays her dazzling keyboard, caressing and discovering improvisations is a musical experience not easily forgotten. With her trio in the homely basement of Soho's Pizza Express, she played an evening of intimate, incisively thought-out jazz that was spellbinding.

Always exploring in a world of sound that's still being charted, every note was taking her closer to a musical newfoundland. Allen is a Motown woman with a different musical history to those who are more well-known.

Born near Detroit in Pontiac, Michigan in 1957, her inspiration came from Monk, Herbie Nichols and Eric Dolphy and, by the 80s, the multiple influences of bop, free jazz, hard bop, funk and rhythm and blues found her as an accompanist on recordings with powerful jazz musicians from Betty Carter to Wallace Roney. In Altman's film *Kansas City*, she played the pioneering woman piano genius Mary Lou Williams.

Accompanied by the solid bass of Billy Johnson and Mark Johnson on drums, they are of a piece, knowing and anticipating each other's phraseology like siblings. Johnson the Drums uses his brushes with a special empathy, turning to tablas on Allen's own *Angels*.

Geri Allen

This is a selection from the pianist's brilliant CD *The Gathering*.

As Allen forges her own full-blooded, yet tender melody, Mark's tablas tap out a compelling, transcontinental rhythm, Billy's growling bowed bass keeps everything terrestrial and solid. It was a loving and powerful performance.

But whether playing her own compositions or standard jazz themes, such as Ellington's *I'm Beginning to See the Light*,

Allen's complex yet vitally accessible musical shapes take fire between themes which sometimes rise to potent, climactic moments of release and then falling away, back to lucid and beautiful lines which were as simple and memorable as a common song.

The long black sleeves of her dress, which cover her wrists, are too slow for the lightning that she makes with her fingers, as she scatters them across the keys, having to use the very occasional pause in her solos to flick them back out of the way of her musical road.

Pizza Express is a marvellous jazz venue, which is made for a musician like Geri Allen, with her rebellious and marooning musical brain and quicksilver piano hands, creating patterns of sound which paint the listener's mind with a unique beauty.

April 21st 2001

Rising from the Ashes

Pat Martino Trio

Pizza Express, London W1

There is a powerful story surrounding the life of virtuoso jazz guitarist Pat Martino. He was born in Philadelphia, in 1944, to Italian-American parents and reached a prodigious level of prominence during the 60s with a series of albums for the Prestige record company.

Strings, East! and *El Hombre* were considered to be inventive and original guitar statements by a young artist who had followed the road of great black guitar innovators, such as Charlie Christian, Grant Green and Wes Montgomery — with whom the young Martino jammed — but who had struck out on his own road of discovery. He played his guitar like a horn, adapting the musical themes of Rollins, Davis and Coltrane. He took off with eastern sounds using a quick-fire, fleet-of-finger technique and superb fluidity that astonished his listeners.

Other memorable albums for the Muse label followed right through to the 70s.

Then, darkness.

In 1980, Martino was attacked by a brain aneurysm, underwent radical brain surgery and was afflicted with a form of amnesia that removed all his musical memory. He completely lost all ability to play his beloved guitar. So, he had to learn his art all over again. He listened intimately to his own recordings, which became his teachers. With a stubborn perseverance and stamina, he gradually recovered his old technique that is now the palimpsest of a new brilliance.

As his new Blue Note CD *Live at Yoshi's* is released, the guitar man Martino plays out of his skin at Soho's Pizza Express. He is accompanied by fellow Italian-American Joey DeFrancesco on Hammond B-3 organ and drummer Byron Landham.

As they career into Sonny Rollin's *Oleo*, which is also the first number on the CD, the electro-magnetism between the trio is almost palpable. The trance-like, head-swaying, rotund DeFrancesco rolls his organ down great slopes of sound, while Landham is alive to every nuance of his confrères' notes as he punches out a sustained, founding drum fury.

And, as for Martino, his lightning plucking makes his fingers a musical blur, with notes so close to each other and played at such speed as to be ever so briefly touching, copulating, procreating and flying away, newly born into the Soho air, never to be reproduced in exactly the same way again — the uniqueness of jazz in perpetual movement.

In Miles Davis's *All Blues*, the sedentary DeFrancesco makes his organ shriek and scream and physically imitates its soundmaking with his wide-open mouth and rolling body gestures. While the pencil-thin and tiny guitarist stands straight in the centre of the low stage, his instrument becomes like another natural limb as he plays his own aching and note-perfect blues.

Martino's dark sound and beautiful ballad touch emerges through his own composition *Welcome to a Prayer*. With Landham's sensitive brushwork and an underlay of sad and mournful chords by DeFrancesco, the guitarist's felicitous phrases, sliding melodic lines and crystalline note definition — each one seeming like a separate, lucid drop of water, sink into the ears.

A team-man too, Martino hardly stops playing all night, providing rhythmic guitar during the organist's pounding solos and his playful, cutting duets with the ever-explosive Landham.

The marvel and achievement of personal struggle over the sudden demons of the body's illness — the plectrum of dreams!

That is all I can hold in my head as I walk up the steps to Dean Street, out into other less melodious sounds of a London night.

July 24th 2001

Birdsong and Streetsong

Regina Carter

Queen Elizabeth Hall, London

In the great wave of Southern black labour that came north to work in the car plants of Detroit, Don Carter was the first of fourteen siblings. He became a car worker for the Ford Motor Company and married a Detroit schoolteacher. One of their children was Regina. She took tap, ballet and piano lessons, but became one of jazz music's great violinists. And much more too.

In 2001, she was invited to Genoa to play a jazz concert commemorating the victims of September 11, using Paganini's violin. "Canon," the familiar name of the Genoan virtuoso's instrument, was never absent from a brace of armed guards, even during Carter's rehearsals and final performance. In November 2002, she returned to Genoa to record *After a Dream* and, after a mountain of bureaucracy and regulations had been climbed, it was worth it.

It is a unique album, the fusion of a legendary instrument and an extraordinary musical technique with a vibrant and vivid jazz imagination. Carter's performance includes works by Ravel and Debussy, as well as the Brazilian *Manha de Carnaval* from the film *Black Orpheus*.

Carter leads a quartet, within a full string orchestra. Her borrowed violin cuts through it all with the most lucid of sounds, pure and immediate, as if its tone carries the incisive insight of history within its every note. I wonder if Guarneri del Gesù, the violin maker who built the instrument in 1743, could have foretold his most precious masterpiece being played by a US artiste, the descendant of slaves, in memory of those killed in such a disaster in a huge city an ocean away The performance of Ástor Piazzolla's *Oblivion* expresses this living nightmare with a terrifying beauty.

Reverie picks up the pace and *Healing in Foreign Lands* adds a degree of tenderness and succour, but throughout this sublimely performed album, itself an offering of musical healing, there remains the gaping contradiction between the delights of the sound and the horror of the event that has caused them to be heard.

Regina Carter comes from a great tradition of jazz violinists stretching right through the music's history — from Stuff Smith, Ray Nance and Stéphane Grappelli to the post-bop sounds of Billy Bang and Leroy Jenkins. Hearing her live at the Queen Elizabeth Hall reinforces that continuity.

A tiny figure on stage, she is all but physically overwhelmed by the solid mass of instruments around her, by David Budway's grand, the tall Chris Lightcap's bass, Alvester Garnette's drums and the percussive orchestra of Cuban Mayra Casales.

Manha de Carnaval begins like a spell, first a compulsive bowed scraping, then a leap to beauteous melody and improvisation, a fall into cadence and a shimmering reprise of the theme. She whistles her way into *The Music Goes Round and Round* and off she goes, swinging pure and hard like a grandniece of Stuff Smith — jivey, scintillating, fast as sound itself with the joyous Budway virtually bouncing off his stall.

Her late fellow Detroiter Milt Jackson's *For Someone I Love* is taken directly to Cuba, a powerhouse feature for these two women of the Americas — Mayra Casales's hands springing off her African drums while Carter rolls up her cuffs to pluck her strings fiercely. But it is in Ravel's *Pavane* and Debussy's *Reverie* that her featherweight melodic touch and lightest of bowed voicings like an awakening birdsong and streetsong achieve a fusion of impressionism with the muscle of the urban jazz life, creating a performance to hold in your senses and remember for always.

November 1st 2003

Fire and Passion

Ryga-Rosnes Quartet

Top of the Senator, Toronto, Canada

Canada has produced at least three geniuses of jazz piano. Two of these were born in Montreal — the great swing-to-bop innovator Oscar Peterson in 1925 and the post-bop adventurer Paul Bley, born in 1932. But the youngest of this luminous trio was born in the prairie city of Regina, Saskatchewan in 1962 and bred in Vancouver — the keyboard mistress with immigrant Norwegian and Indian roots, Renee Rosnes.

Rosnes's move to New York in the mid-1980s prompted an immersion in jazz at the highest level. She became piano partner to some of the music's most powerful horns — JJ Johnson, Wayne Shorter, Joe Henderson included — and established a formidable quartet Native Colours with her husband Billy Drummond.

Then followed a series of powerful and prestigious albums for Blue Note, including *Without Words* (1992), *Ancestors* (1996) and *As We Are Now* (1997) and as a part of Drummond's band on his own Criss Cross sessions.

So, for jazz lovers, to hear her back again in Toronto — where she originally trained as a classical pianist — is an unbridled pleasure, particularly as part of an all-Canadian quartet of musicians all hailing from or around the West Coast city of Vancouver — Campbell Ryga, the alto and soprano saxophonist with a pure tone and prodigious fluency, the booming bassist Neil Swainson and the ever-listening and responsive drums of Rudy Petschauer.

The well-trod melodic pathway of *That Old Devil Moon* begins the session, unleashed by the high-octane energy and vibrancy of Ryga's opening solo. Here is a quartet playing with the unity of a familiar jazz comradeship as Rosnes's quicksilver fingers scour the keyboard with the deeply leaping bass of Swainson pounding behind her and Petschauer's drums adding a surging bounce and time.

Tres Palabras exudes a sweet-toned, Latinate ambience introduced with finesse by Ryga, then followed by Renee's beautifully lucid melodic conception. *Deep Cove* is introduced by the pianist as a descriptive piece recalling a coastal beauty spot in British Columbia near where she grew up. As an evocation of Canada's sublime natural beauty, it brings to mind her predecessor Peterson's *Canadian Suite.*

Ryga's perfectly poised soprano sweeps through, over and all around the melody in some clearly described choruses, preceding Rosnes's lucidly formed solo, each note a droplet amounting to an eventual storm of sound as her solo gains a pelting fire and passion.

While she is forging such keyboard power, her eyes are never on the keys, but always directed towards her creative band members. Swainson's sawing bowed bass and Rosnes's ominous chords open up on *Air Dancing* — composed by Buster Williams, one of her former bass partners — with Ryga still on soprano. Swainson returns with a long sonorous solo of the deepest sound before Rosnes's chiming choruses and Ryga's roving excursion — and, through it all, Petschauer underlines every note with his perfectly compatible cymbal-play and a clipping snare-drum foundation.

Ryga introduces his own composition, *One for Boone*, explaining that it is dedicated to a childhood west-coast friend, a hunters' guide. He suggests listeners might envisage Boone closing in on a grizzly or an elk, but the rapidfire stop-time theme gave me thoughts of Boone running like the wind with the grizzly close on his tail. But the Canadian reedman's performance is staggeringly fluent and controlled on his gushing alto, with some of his phrases purely Parkeresque, others bringing to mind the angular control of Benny Carter.

And Rosnes is running with him, tearing through the BC woods in her breathless solo, sprinting up and down the keys.

Altogether a captivating performance of proud Canadian jazz, which I dearly hope sooner or later will come to Britain to show again how inventively jazz can cross frontiers.

December 15th 2004

The Glassblower

NOJO with Sam Rivers

City of Neighbourhoods

The Rex, Toronto

Queen Street in downtown Toronto. In the Victorian pub The Rex, ungentrified and with the original leaded lights gleaming over the long bar. The main room is full, while the small corner bandstand next to the entrance is crammed with the musicians of a ten-piece band, their saxophones and brass squatting in their stands at the front of the stage.

Customers come in and go out in front of them and there is the sensation of continuous movement. In short, it's an old-time authentic jazz venue, redolent with transient humanity, keen listening and musical hope.

The bustling musicians are young white Canadians, except for one elderly black man who sits at the front centre of the stage, surrounded by his flute, soprano and tenor saxophones. This reedman is the legendary Sam Rivers of Orlando, Florida. The octogenarian is a veteran of many 1960s Blue Note recording sessions like his own *Fuchsia Swing Song* and *Contours*. He is also an ex-Miles Davis sideman and musician of the broad realm of jazz from Dizzy Gillespie to T-Bone Walker, Billie Holiday to Cecil Taylor, JC Higginbotham to Andrew Hill, from blues basement to post-bop loft.

He has always been an adventurer, a risk taker and a saxophone genius always on the edge, always a pioneer. His bandmates are members of the Toronto-based Neufeld-Occhipinti Jazz Orchestra (NOJO) led by pianist Paul Neufield and electric guitarist Michael Occhipinti, who are responsible, too, for all the charts on their latest CD, *City of Neighbourhoods*, featuring the superb Rivers.

The title track evokes the new cosmopolitan Toronto, full of diverse musical rhythms from salsa to reggae, from Indian, African, Asian, European and Native American traditions.

As with all the CD selections, NOJO create a sophisticated but vibrant framework in which Rivers pours out his compelling sound, this time a winding soprano solo, preceded by some lyrical trumpet from Kevin Turcotte.

Rivers switches to tenor on *The Human Blockhead* and his dug-in solo anticipates some twanging Occhipinti choruses and a jazz celebration by the rest of the band, creating carefully orchestrated bedlam. In the effervescent *Spend Every Dime*, the excellent Turcotte introduces Rivers's tremulous soprano choruses, while the brass and reeds riff the theme behind him. In the more funky Ellington tribute, *Duke A-Go-Go*, Rivers, now on flute, and trombonist Scott Suttie share an interwoven duet after Sean O'Connor's Harry Carney-like baritone solo.

Occhipinti wrote *Neurotheologians* as a satire on genetic manipulation. It has a Mingus-like quality to it, with Rivers's soprano sounding as if on a cusp of mysticism.

The Glassblower, Neufeld's aptly conceived homage to Rivers, is the heart of the album and the Rex gig.

First, Suttie's lucid trombone slides pair with Rivers's flute, then some more delicate Turcotte introduces the reedman's jagged soprano with drummer Barry Romberg's empathetic punctuations. Neufeld plays some solo tuba before a stirring ensemble passage introduces Rivers, now on tenor, driving up and down the scales, always probing, endlessly discovering.

I asked him during the interval when he was next going to Britain and he surprised me by saying he was touring there very soon with his trio, visiting a number of cities. So, *Morning Star* jazz lovers, don't miss this precious and unique musical survivor when he comes your way, this glassblower of jazz saxophone with sixty years of sound creation behind him and still blowing with beauty, poise and ceaseless invention.

February 23rd 2005

Pealing Out the Blues

Jay McShann Quartet

Montreal Bistro, Toronto

There is a particular pathos, as well as a distinct sense of glory, in listening to a veteran jazz survivor play live — especially one who personifies a whole era of the music. Jay McShann, nicknamed "Hootie," was born in Muskogee, Oklahoma, in 1916 and, by the time he was twenty-two, was playing piano and leading his own swinging band in Kansas City

Kansas City was the Midwest crucible of the blues that had birthed bands like those of Count Basie and Andy Kirk — and the pantheon of musicians who played in them. Then, in 1939, Hootie hired a teenage alto-saxophonist from KC called Charlie Parker and changed jazz reality forever.

Parker played solos on the McShann band's recorded numbers like *Hootie Blues*, *Swingmatism* and *Confessin' the Blues* and a new voice came out from their grooves, playing in a way that redirected the very mainstream of jazz sound.

After Parker left for New York and bebop fame with Dizzy Gillespie, Miles Davis, Max Roach and a new generation of musical genius, McShann continued for decades after his KC heyday with his blues-based sound, still lives in Kansas City, and ventures out on a regular basis to play in US and Canadian cities, even at the age of 89.

At the Montreal Bistro, one of downtown Toronto's hottest jazz venues, he was still pealing out the blues as pianist and singer, with a quartet composed of some long-time Canadian jazz comrades — Don Vickery on drums, Rosemary Galloway on bass and the veteran reedman Jim Galloway, who has been playing with Hootie on his forays into Toronto for the last three decades, sharing several recording sessions on the local Sackville label with him.

For the beginning to almost every number, McShann keeps his audience and, it seems, even his bandmates guessing, spinning out mazes of improvisation up and down the keys before he finds his theme. And, out of the pattern of notes comes the first familiar tune — the entirely appropriate Parker opus *Yardbird Suite*. Yet it sounds anything but a bop anthem. Hootie's sound now is astonishingly lightweight, quiescent, as if, by simply touching and stroking the notes, he can make them swing.

His effect is magnetic. Jim Galloway on soprano sax sounds buoyant, even airy, hanging in the clouds over Lake Ontario, like the pianist, gentle, inventive but full of swing — held upright by Galloway's resounding bass and Vickery's subliminal brushwork.

This sense of intuitive empathy between the pianist and saxophonist, a black man and a white man, intensifies throughout the ballad, *Cocktails for Two* and the Basie band standby *Moten Swing*. Both musicians play the former with a beautiful quietude and, throughout, the relentless swing of Galloway's tenor filigrees around McShann's bobbling notes and the pianist's friendly comping becomes fused with the tenorist's floating solo.

Hootie's every note suppurates with the blues and, with *Foreday Rider*, they come pouring out of his mouth too as he sings of a young man's rambling and his worldly-wise premonitions that "pretty soon I'm going to be too old" to carry on. You'd never believe it, though, listening to him.

As the quartet moves into *Pennies from Heaven*, their sound is so light it was if the four of them were levitating and this song, sung a billion times, was like a sponge rising.

I watch Hootie's lightning fingers still dancing over the keys as if he were barely touching them and hear Galloway's soprano breathing, light as a feather. Even *Red Sails in the Sunset* loses its mawkishness and sentimentality as McShann makes it into a blues, playing it off-centre on the cusp of despair, yet with notes and words so lucid, keeping tryst with Galloway's soft tenor, that there is a rendezvous with hope and union. The very soul and body of jazz on a damp Toronto night.

June 8th 2005

Summoning Ghosts

Oscar Peterson

Roy Thomson Hall, Toronto

A prevailing sadness underlines every note of eighty-year-old Oscar Peterson's piano performance with his quartet and the huge sound of the Toronto Symphony Orchestra behind him at the annual Sonic Bloom in Toronto. Peterson's performances are rare enough now in his adopted city and this one becomes a long dedication to one of his quartet's great bassmen, the Dane Niels-Henning Ørsted Pederson, who died on April 19.

"You're going to hear another side of Oscar Peterson tonight," he announces. "I'll not be burning up the joint tonight, I've got too much emotion inside me." He reveals that "The Viking" had been a powerful influence in getting him to compose. "Everyone knows you can play," he told him years before, "so show them that you can write too!"

The programme is full of some of Peterson's most telling tunes — many of them complemented by the orchestra's sumptuous strings and burnished horns, such as the opening ballad *If Only You Knew* or *When Summer Comes*, which follows and includes an ascendant, vibrating solo from Ulf Wakenius's guitar. Drummer Alvin Queen is restrained but ever steady and new quartet member, Winnipeg bassist Dave Young is much in the prominence, providing a shimmering throb to the music. He and Wakenius are the featured soloists of *In the Sounds of the Woods*, a Danish folk tune played as a tribute to NHOP, while Oscar sits out, bent over his keyboard, too moved to even touch the keys.

He reminds the listeners that two other of his bassmen contemporaries have died this year — Jimmy Woode, an ex-Ellington rock and the amazing Percy Heath, the last surviving member of the Modern Jazz Quartet. So, he says, he has written an orchestral piece, *Requiem*, to remember them. The TSO, conducted by Peterson's longtime collaborator Michel Legrand, plays it as a jazz veteran's salutation, with reverence and telling musical comradeship.

The same orchestra members stand and applaud at the end of the next selection, a rocking quartet number *Backyard Blues*, in which Oscar's combustive keyboard energy, Wakenius's twanging choruses and Young's mesmerising finger work, with Queen's rhythmic propulsion all belie the leader's age and, in the forest of notes, the imaginative brilliance shines bright.

Peterson, the son of a mother from St Kitts and a father from the Virgin Islands who worked on trans-Canadian trains as a sleeping car porter, was born in Montreal in 1924 and grew up in a music-loving working-class home, encouraged at the piano, in particular by his older sister Daisy.

Canadian audiences salute him with a particular spirit of pride, love and awe and strongly empathise this night with his deep loss and sadness. But they celebrate with him too. He reminisces about how his friend NHOP had persuaded him to write the love tune to his wife Kelly and then caresses it, with Young's thudding bassline giving a special heart-filled sound. The jaunty and playful theme of *Celine's Waltz*, dedicated to his daughter touches many a parental chord.

He confides that the long Canadian winters have their advantages. "I write tunes in them," he says and offers many examples. Not the least, the serene but vulnerable melody of *Night Time*. This and the arrangement of the ballad *My One and Only Love* shows how a jazz pianist and massive symphony orchestra can work together to make a huge and beautiful sound, when a magical leader like Legrand is providing both leadership and unity.

Peterson suffered a stroke in 1993 and the walk across a long stage to his piano seems a difficult one. Yet it has something of the epic about it too when he begins to spin out his notes.

An enormous jazz presence brings back the ghosts of all the legendary figures he has accompanied in a long jazz life. From Gillespie and Parker to Young and Holiday — their lights still beam strong around his own.

July 6th 2005

Mind-storming Notes

Amina Claudine Myers

Pizza Express, London W1

Born in 1942, bred in Arkansas with her roots deep in the Baptist church, Amina Claudine Myers is among the most astonishing of jazz musicians. For within her artistry, she embodies the entire history of the music. Her piano and organ brilliance breathe the earliest blues and gospel influences. Yet, she has recorded with some of the most defiantly avant-garde contenders of the music — from Muhal Richard Abrams to Henry Threadgill, from Frank Lowe and Lester Bowie to James Blood Ulmer.

She has also been a member of the Liberation Music Orchestra. Her 1980 album saluting Bessie Smith is a classic, yet her attachment to Chicago's Association for the Advancement of Creative Musicians (AACM) has put her in the vanguard of free jazz experimentation and innovation. Her musicianship defies genre and categorisation, moving through all the huge diversity of jazz utterance.

At the Pizza Express, the blues-derived power of her notes create such intense sonic ructions that the food almost leaps from the plates of the diners. Such percussive strength, yet her notes still resound with poignancy and human suffering. As she plays *Song for Mother E*, the sound is hymnal and sacred, not unlike an Abdullah Ibrahim theme, with ancestral notes and the vestiges of diasporan history. But it is also a mounting song of celebration, continuance and love, as the atmosphere quivers with an amalgam of stories in one single musical performance.

In her opener, *Boogie Ritual*, there are subliminal drumbeats deep in her notes that sound like an ancient foundation in her sound, covered by complex phraseologies and musical pathways stretching to some future music. As she begins to chant, it is like hearing an uncanny fusion between the African-American voices of two continents and those of Native Americans, a Peyote song by Jim Pepper developed instrumentally through the vocal sound of his tenor saxophone.

Myers's piano stylings are hugely inclusive, for, within her blues and gospel keyboard cries, there are hugely rhapsodic and romantic sections. In *Cairo*, the quality of African glory is welded within a timbre of sadness and displacement that is almost terrifyingly moving.

Do You Wanna Be Saved? is played as if there are dank melodies pushing their way to the surface of the powerful sound, echoes of Southern churches and impassioned oracy, coming from both voice and a preaching piano.

"Hate will bring you misery/Turn you into stone/It will kill your beauty/It will leave you all alone/Love will bring out your lasting joy/Now this principle/Is easy to employ/Do you wanna be saved?/Love will save you."

Myers transforms a religious, sacred concept into a deeply humanistic cry with a mountain of words and notes. Her voice has might. It is a lesser might than that of her great ancestor Bessie Smith, but you can only wonder how Myers would sound accompanying her.

Smith's piano accompanists were all men, some of them were fairly ordinary and the greatest of these, James P Johnson, had a northern stride style, rather than being a pianist nurtured in the blues. As Myers plays and sings Smith's *Wasted Life Blues*, it is easy to wish, quite idealistically of course, that they were contemporaries and Myers's piano and Smith's voice would both have mutual enhancement and borrowed glory from each other. Just another jazz fantasy of duos which defy history and generations, but you can't help imagining as this London basement pulsates with the Arkansas blues.

Myers's albums aren't always easy to find, but they are well worth the search. Get the Smith tribute and also *The Circle of Time* on the Italian Black Saint label. You'll have a storm of sensation and exposure to one of jazz's most under-recorded and neglected artists. You won't forget her — her notes storm your mind.

May 3rd 2006

A Toronto Gift

Joe McPhee and the Association of Improvising Musicians, Toronto

The Array Music Studio, Toronto

A large room in a community arts centre off King Street West in Toronto is transformed into a performing space by the dedicated members of the Association of Improvising Musicians of Toronto. New sounds pound and drift through stacks of improvised and homemade instruments, African percussion and an array of electric music devices. In the middle of it all are the bristling and blues-soaked notes of the US free jazz multi-instrumentalist genius, sixty-seven-year-old Joe McPhee from Poughkeepsie, New York state.

He is playing with two Canadian musicians — drummer and percussionist Joe Sorbara and pianist and vocalist Lee Pui Ming, who says of AIMT music that it "is about going beyond boundaries. It is about transcending the myriad genres, niches and pigeon-holes that trap music, and seek to name it and tame it."

These words eloquently illustrate the entire event. Here are musicians balancing on the very edge of discovery — true adventurers and explorers of jazz who reject all categories and frontiers within the music and, with a daily authenticity, reject the notion that jazz has gone as far as it can go.

Take the Toronto-based trio Odradek, who followed McPhee's first trio set. James Bailey, a local east Toronto musician who makes instruments — or implements, as he prefers to call them — from found objects on construction sites and other places, including plastic pipes, building materials played acoustically or with electronics for sound manipulation.

Or Italian-born Michelangelo Iaffaldano, who likes to draw, play music and build musical instruments out of discarded materials. Or Andy Yue, who plays piano, various electric keyboards and analogue synthesiser.

Together, they play a set of haunting sounds. Iaffaldano with a clarinet and homemade wooden stringed instrument played with a bow, Bailey with what looked like a metal wheel flat on the floor and Yue with a multiwired keyboard sounding like a rumbling storm.

When the US jazz critic Whitney Balliett wrote of the music being defined as the "sound of surprise" he would not have conceived of Odradek, but their spirit and prowess manifest his words, as do the vital democratic credentials of the AIMT, who declare themselves to be "a not-for-profit musicians' collective that promotes the work of local musicians who are committed to creative improvisation." And the pioneer McPhee speaks of the process at work. "Being thrust into situations with unfamiliar collaborators where you haven't got a clue what might happen may be a daunting idea for some musicians, but I find that really exciting. Some people compare performing solo to a high-wire act, but, to me it's more like walking naked on the edge of a razor blade. I try not to do too much advance planning, maybe just have some basic idea of where I want to go in the time allotted. I just try to tell a story without playing too many notes."

Stories — the essence of jazz.

And as Sorbara uses his bow, sawing down the edge of his cymbals, taps a handbell with his sticks, lays a towel on his snare to muffle the impact of their sound, Lee plays striking, transparent piano notes while a statuesque McPhee mournfully blows his pocket trumpet and Sorbara's brushes dance across his cymbals, freeing the trumpeter's breathy notes.

Lee is small in stature and slides up and down a wide piano stall to reach the high keys, making harsh vocal sounds against Sorbara's rocking snares, as a fanfare of life springs out of McPhee's brass. As he switches to tenor saxophone and the blue breath pours from his horn, Sorbara saws the snare's rims and clashes his large cymbal with handheld miniature cymbals.

New versions of the blues — unlikely beauty of the unrehearsed in a Toronto room before fifty or so lucky people. Jazz lives and grows.

October 11th 2006

Enter a Land of New Sound

Liberation Music Orchestra

Royal Festival Hall, London

Ornette Coleman was a jazz outsider. Born in 1930 in Fort Worth, Texas — not known as a jazz town — Coleman migrated to Los Angeles in the early 50s and worked as a lift operator while studying music. He picked up a plastic alto saxophone and played it with such a dissident sound that even many of the rebellious geniuses of jazz turned their backs on him, fearing his iconoclastic notes.

Now, is his eightieth year and curator of the South Bank's 2009 Meltdown festival, he is still at it. At the concert with his two bass-playing confrères Greg Cohen and Tony Falanga, his drummer son Denardo, the flickering Denver guitar of Bill Frisell and the eight members of the Master Musicians of Jajouka from the Moroccan mountains, he steers alternately his swooping alto, a shrieking trumpet and sawing violin into a land of ever-new sounds.

The Jajouka men begin the evening, and in the sound of their rasping African horns Ornette's musical roots become suddenly clearer. Sitting sedately in their green smocks and white cloth hats, blowing fire, rock, earth and sand through their horns, they bring the drum-birthed anthems of the Rif mountains to the banks of the Thames.

I was sitting between two old and engrossed friends, Robert Wyatt and Alfie Benge. "When I hear Ornette," exclaims Wyatt in wonderment with a harvest of prepositions, "he goes further out, yet further into the world."

On the Tube home, I thought about what Robert had said, knowing that the following night I was going to hear him singing as a guest of Charlie Haden's Liberation Music Orchestra.

This ensemble was first formed in 1968 during the final stages of the Civil Rights campaign and the depth of the war in Vietnam by Haden, the bassist of Ornette's apostate quartet, and the pianist, arranger and bandleader Carla Bley. Both are still here, in London this time, with a union of visiting US musicians and some marvellous British talent of another generation — the full-blooded altoist from

Jazz Jamaica, Jason Yarde and the gurgling tenor of Shabaka Hutchings.

John Parricelli's strident guitar notes dropped like miracles through all the familiar tunes, from Bley's *Blue Anthem* to *We Shall Overcome*, and Hutchings' belching solo on *This Is Not America*, ending with a soaring, guttural coda told a whole story in itself. Trombonist Fayyaz Virji's slide narrative in *Amazing Grace* mixed the dust of the earth with the transcendent sounds of the stratosphere.

When Wyatt sings his two songs in Spanish with a touching delicacy, Silvio Rodríguez's *The Tail of the Tornado* from Cuba and Haden's own anthemic *Song for Che* written shortly after the Argentinian's death in Bolivia in October 1967, with the composer's pulsating bass and Parricelli's chiming notes, it was both stirring and poignant in a powerful amalgam of music and struggle.

Yarde blows black diasporan history from African and Caribbean roots over three continents into London's cosmopolis, in his blues-laden but joyous choruses from Dvořák's adaptation from the *New World Suite* of the spiritual, *Going Home*.

I doubt whether the Royal Festival Hall had ever known the like.

Before the concert a large group of singers — men, women, young, old, black, white and brown, some in wheelchairs — toured its lobbies, bars and entrance halls singing *The Internationale*, *Nkosi Sikelel iAfrica* and *The Solidarity Song*. And Haden and Bley with new comrades still blow out revolution into their jazz through the storming transatlantic notes of justice, internationalism, peace and freedom, echoing and rededicating Ornette's brave and prophetic sounds of fifty years ago.

June 29 2009

Carter's Glory

James Carter Quintet

Ronnie Scott's, London W1

To hear James Carter in live horn glory is to experience a sound so huge and unremitting that all the spaces between ears, brain and consciousness are filled with outrageous and joyous sensation.

At Ronnie Scott's he was blowing soprano, tenor and flute alongside the searing trumpet of Corey Wilkes and a trio of pounding veterans. Pianist Gerard Gibbs approached his piano on metal crutches, then sat down and blew the keys away. Nigh-spherical bassist Ralph Armstrong thanked London "for getting my career started!" as he shuffled off the stage and grey-locked drummer Leonard King gave life to every split second of the quintet's performance on relentless snares and bass drum.

Motown man Carter was in prime blasting mood. Brimming with good humour, mischief and unvanquished artistry he radiated sheer excitement as he burst into *Going Home* on soprano sax. He confessed to being "fired up," having spent the day in Jimi Hendrix's London flat and he played as if he shared the late guitarist's spirit with that of Sidney Bechet. Free and audacious, his fingers flashed up and down his golden horn above the enormous twang and bounce of Armstrong's bass.

Gibbs's potent sonic muscles sublimated the Carter tenor on a familiar Clifford Brown theme which ended with an astonishing final colloquy between some screeching declamations from Wilkes and Carter's horn-sucking responses. As the quintet sallied into Fats Navarro's melodic *Nostalgia*, buttressed by Armstrong's bowed bass, Wilkes's piercingly beautiful harmony-muted solo balanced the bird-song sweeping from Carter's flute.

The two horns found a living amalgam too on Rahsaan Roland Kirk's *Many Blessings*, with Wilkes's scintillating notes provoking throwaway blusters as his tenor frequently disappeared with a leonine roar over his left shoulder.

It was an evening of inspiring, ferociously tender inter-generational performance of empowering sound — two younger yet mature horns blowing the breath of freedom, coupled with three older rhythm men setting them up and testifying to their own jazz message.

Together, the whole story of jazz and its artistry was in their sound, roaring through Soho.

May 3rd 2010

A Big Noise in the City
The London Jazz Festival, 2011

The festival started for me at the Barbican with the Pole Marcin Wasilewski, plunging bassist Slawomir Kurkiewicz and clipping drummer Michał Miśkiewicz. Here they played with a moving panache and crystal clarity of timbre, particularly on their trio version of *Ballad of the Sad Young Men* and other tunes from their ECM album *Faithful.*

Once again they made me realise just how much Poland is a land of jazz and groove.

On the same night the twenty-eight-year-old Italian Stefano Bollani from Milan and octogenarian Algiers-born Frenchman Martial Solal locked keyboards and generations in a duo of tumbling piano brilliance. Their combination of dazzling notes on standards like *Body And Soul* and *What is this Thing Called Love?* stick with me all the way home on the tube.

The next night on the South Bank, veteran German piano maestro Joachim Kühn from Leipzig teamed up with with another veteran, the "Lion of Florida" Archie Shepp. Kühn's hailstorms of notes made a contrary narrative with Shepp's tenor saxophone gargles, sighs, howls, hushabye breaths and running streams of melody, especially during their sublime duet choruses of Ornette Coleman's *Lonely Woman* and Shepp's suspirating tribute to Nina Simone. The sonic rebelliousness of his sound mellowed to a timbre of deep, deep pride and beauty.

Back to the Barbican to hear the thirty-plus members of Jerry Dammers' Spatial AKA Orchestra. Such an insurgency of huge, blasting ensemble sound also featured some of Britain's most powerful horn soloists — Larry Stabbins and Denys Baptiste on tenor, Shabaka Hutchings on bass clarinet and Nicholas Facey and Jason Yarde on alto. The most potent and memorable moments were Francine Luce's Martiniquan French vocal version of Coltrane's *Naima*, her voice followed by a shimmering Yarde chorus.

Harry Brown's massive trombone roared with fury out of the volcanic orchestral underbelly, particularly on Ellington's *Blue Pepper* from *The Far East Suite* and the dynamic stew of jazz, reggae, Sun

Ra's interplanetary harmonies, two-tone delights and the sheer cacophony of marvellously original sound nearly blew open the enveloping Barbican concrete.

Saturday night on the South Bank sees a very rare visitor to these jazz shores. Henry Threadgill is a pioneer of Chicago's Association for the Advancement of Creative Musicians, whose free and often surrealist sound has inspired generations of experimental grooves.

His band Zooid is a rare conjunction of instrumentalists, with London-born guitarist Liberty Ellman, cellist Christopher Hoffman, trombone and tuba virtuoso Jose Dávila, drummer Elliot Kavee and Stomu Takeishi — with the bulkiest and boomiest acoustic bass guitar imaginable — and Threadgill himself on alto sax and bass flute. Together they burn the Waterloo air with their searing notes.

Notwithstanding all this immense US and European jazz eminence and talent, the band which fires me most — with its three vibrant horns, bass and drums just two yards away from my earlobes — is at Ray's Jazz Cafe.

Led by Bolton-born Arun Ghosh, they start with their throbbing verve and attack on *Caliban's Revenge*, segued by Ghosh's own tribute to his Mancunian neighbours in *Longsight Lagoon* with his gyrating clarinet curlicues and the quietude and serene evocation of a Bengal waterscape in *River Song*.

You know that there's something akin to a unique musical experience afoot, and the young African-Caribbean saxophonists, altoist Chris Williams and tenorist Wayne Francis blow up a storm too on *Damascus* and the rousing *Intifada* — dedicated by Ghosh to "uprisings across the world."

Here is the true spirit of jazz, blowing all the way down Charing Cross Road and transmigrating down the Thames towards anyone with rebellion in their ears and in their blood — and a little bit of groove boiling in their soul.

November 22nd 2011